W9-APM-488

THE MEANING OF
HUMAN EXISTENCE

THE MEANING
OF HUMAN EXISTENCE

by

LESLIE PAUL

GREENWOOD PRESS, PUBLISHERS
WESTPORT, CONNECTICUT

CONTENTS

1

THE MEANING OF NATURE

2

THE NATURE OF SUBJECTIVITY

3

THE MEANING OF REVELATION

'God is the meaning of human existence'—N. BERDYAEV

'Une grande philosophie n'est pas celle qui prononce des jugements définitifs, qui installe une vérité définitive. C'est celle qui introduit une inquiétude, qui ouvre un ébranlement.

'Une grande philosophie n'est pas celle qui n'est jamais battue. Mais une petite philosophie est toujours celle qui ne se bat pas.—Une grande philosophie n'est pas une philosophie sans reproche, c'est une philosophie sans peur'—CHARLES PÉGUY

ACKNOWLEDGEMENTS

The author begs to make acknowledgement to Doubleday & Company for permission to quote from *Bases of Modern Science* by J. W. N. Sullivan. Harcourt, Brace & Co. for permission to quote from *Speculations* by T. E. Hulme: *Modern Man in Search of a Soul* by C. G. Jung: *Historical Introduction to Modern Psychology* by Murphy and Kluver: *Gestalt Theory, The Problem of Configuration* by Bruno Petermann. Harper & Brothers for permission to quote from *Science and Human Life* by Professor J. B. S. Haldane: *Religion Without Revelation* by Dr. Julian Huxley: *New Translation of the Bible* by Dr. James Moffat. Henry Holt & Co., Inc. for permission to quote from *Time Machine* by H. G. Wells. Longmans, Green & Co., Inc. for permission to quote from *Peguy and Les Cahiers de la Quinzaine* by Elie Halévy. Messrs. Sheed & Ward, Ltd. for permission to quote from *St. Thomas Aquinas* by Jacques Maritain. The Macmillan Company for permission to quote from *Science and the Modern World* by A. N. Whitehead. Messrs. Routledge & Kegan Paul Ltd. for permission to quote from *Between Man and Man* by Martin Buber. Messrs. Macmillan & Co. Ltd. for permission to quote from *The Problem of Individuality* by Hans Driesch. The Syndics of the Cambridge University Press for permission to quote from *New Pathways in Science* by A. S. Eddington and *What is Life?* by Professor E. Schrodinger. W. W. Norton & Co., Inc. for permission to quote from *Deep Analysis* by Dr. Charles Berg. Hogarth Press Ltd. for permission to quote from *Autobiographical Study* by Sigmund Freud. The Oxford University Press, Inc. for permission to quote from *Autobiography* by R. G. Collingwood: *Soren Kierkegaard* by Theodor Haecker: *Philosophy of a Biologist* by Professor J. S. Haldane: *Wilhelm Dilthey* by Professor H. A. Hodges: *Kierkegaard* by Dr. Walter Lowrie. Pantheon Books, Inc. for permission to quote from *Poems* by Stefan George, *Basic Verities*

ACKNOWLEDGEMENTS

by Charles Péguy. The Princeton University Press for permission to quote from *Either/Or* by Soren Kierkegaard, *Training in Christianity* by Soren Kierkegaard (both translated by Dr. Lowrie). Charles Scribner's Sons for permission to quote from *The Destiny of Man* and *Slavery and Freedom* by Nicholas Berdyaev: *I and Thou* by Martin Buber: *Outlines of Psychology* by Professor William McDougall: *Types of Modern Theology* by Dr. Hugh Ross Mackintosh: *True Humanism* by Jacques Maritain. Sheed and Ward for permission to quote from St. Augustine, *Confessions* (translated by F. J. Sheed). Simon and Schuster, Inc. for permission to quote from *History of Western Philosophy*, copyright, 1945, by Bertrand Russell. D. Van Nostrand Company, Inc. for permission to quote from *Modern Materialism and Emergent Evolution* by Professor William McDougall. Messrs. Chatto & Windus for permission to quote from *Poems* by Wilfred Owen.

The author also expresses his personal thanks for secretarial help, and assistance with proof-reading and indexing to Hilda Blake and Joan Stephenson, and finally wishes to thank Dr. J. H. Oldham and Professor Donald Mackinnon for reading the first draft and for their generous encouragement.

INTRODUCTION

We know quite well that there is a crisis in Western civilization. The most difficult thing to decide is what kind of a crisis it is. One has only to look at present events to see that something unusual, and in a special sense unexpected, has descended upon the world. Indeed, the word unexpected contains the key to the crisis—for there were great expectations and they have been disappointed. There were Victorian expectations and Edwardian expectations and post-1918 expectations. What was characteristic of them all was the vision of a comprehensible future opening out to man in which would flower those contemporary institutions, such as schools and parliaments, regarded as most flattering to man; and in which would be realized those concepts, such as peace and liberty, which aroused the greatest idealism and sacrifice.

The common denominator was belief in progress. Progress was the *mystique* upon which all Western political doctrines were founded. The *fact* of modern history, Lord Acton explained in a lecture delivered at Cambridge in the nineties, was just 'this constancy of progress, of progress in the direction of organized and assured freedom'. And Herschel wrote, with an optimism with which it would be difficult to find a parallel to-day, that 'in whatever state of knowledge we may conceive man to be placed, his progress towards a yet higher state need never fear a check, but must continue till the last existence of society'. The same optimism led John Stuart Mill to argue that 'all the grand sources . . . of human suffering are in great degree, many of them almost entirely, conquerable by human care and effort' —as if human effort and care were not of themselves sources of suffering!

Lord Acton spoke of progress as a tribute to the theory of Providence, and we may accept that, at its simplest, progress is the Christian idea of redemption in secular dress. The basic

13

Christian doctrine is, however, personal and moral rather than social or material. But personal redemption does not rule out social redemption—the effort to secure a social redemption would seem to be a necessary part of it. To redeem others is part of the task of redeeming oneself. It is the attack on the wordliness of the world one is commanded by God to undertake.

It would be wrong to assume that the Victorian *mystique* of progress is to be dismissed as nothing but a renegade Christianity. It has other elements. It contains also that lyric note of Renaissance thought which was the enthusiastic and enterprising acceptance of the world so typical of Renaissance man. The world was a knowable world to him. He could shape that world. He was under no obligation to despair of it, or to reject it. His restless worldly inventiveness has borne fruit in an ant-like accumulation of human knowledge and in triumphant contemporary technical progress—and by these it justified itself. But to these *motifs* must be added the mighty organ profondo of the second half of the nineteenth century—the evolutionary thunder, the intoxicating theme of which was that progress was inevitable, for the universe was travelling in a direction which man could morally approve, and carrying him joyfully along with it.

There is just no fulfilment of the progressive hopes with which our century, now half-spent, began. Everywhere social and political ideals have been perversely thwarted. Instead of peace, the bloodiest of world and civil wars, instead of freedom, the most implacable tyrannies, instead of increasing rationality, the hysteria of Fascism, instead of the liberation of man by science, the atom bomb. Contemporary disorder has grown *in the face of* what is known, what is planned, what is understood to be rational and desirable and even 'practicable' by thoughtful persons everywhere. In place of the orderly articulation of events, of the grandeur of human betterment under natural law, of an irresistible and God-given progress, there is nothing. Nothing is certainly known. The future cannot be conceived. It is the moment of the death of past hopes. It is the era of the death of the future.

It was the special task of Marxism to narrow down the notion of an ascending and progressing cosmos to sensible and manageable limits. Marxism shuts out the cosmos. It is not bothered by the effort to relate man to the universe. In Marxism man has only a social, not a cosmic significance. His home is the planet, not eternity. The 'world' of man is the very world of social and economic circumstances which he himself has created and might therefore change. Yet despite the narrowing down of the problem of man's progress to that sphere of which he appears indubitably the master, the idea of progress is nevertheless not saved. The disaster to the theory is all the greater in the light of the limitation of it by Marxism to 'the possible'. For it is above all in the realm of 'the possible'—in human social, political, and economic affairs—that the future is most terrifyingly dark.

During my military service I was compelled to try and elucidate these mysteries because I was daily lecturing my fellow-soldiers about their consequences. I was drawn particularly to the attempt to explain the eruption of a movement so irrational and nihilist as Fascism into the 'progressive' modern world. And that brought me up against the fundamental crisis in the Western world. My published study, *The Annihilation of Man*, sought reasons for current disorder not (simply) in social or economic injustice and disorganization but in the collapse of the image man had been forming of himself since Renaissance times. The real crisis, then, is to be found, I argued, *in the failure of man's idea of himself*. My argument led me, almost against my will, to a Christian conclusion. *Against my will* because when I began I had the feeling that 'it would not be propitious', or 'it might be misunderstood' if I declared my Christian convictions. I had originally intended therefore no more than 'not too compromising' murmurs of approval in the direction of theism and the theistic view of man. Yet I was driven beyond that point by the argument which seems to me still quite irresistible, that it is precisely the humanistic and pantheistic idea of man which has most disastrously failed, that it is Goethe and Rousseau and Hegel and Spencer who are really on trial to-day. The glorious humanism to which the Renaissance gave birth no longer succeeds in defending man.

I became quite certain that the idea of a self-sustaining culture or civilization of the West, which would go on whether the beliefs which gave it birth survived or not, was an illusion. The notion of a 'progress' from belief to unbelief, as one might speak of progress from superstition to enlightenment, seemed to me stuff and nonsense. Even less tenable was the argument that belief and unbelief were unimportant—because there was something over and above both of them one 'believed' in (honour, good sense, decency, honesty, etc.). It did not seem intellectually justifiable to place belief at the periphery of human activities, an unimportant by-product of society. On the contrary it appeared to me then (and even more now) that society is the product of belief. The bedrock of any human society is the image of himself that man has created. What is dying in our times is not so much the idea of Christian man, but the confident atheistic and humanistic ideas of man which nearly everyone once argued had replaced the Christian image.

And this is made more plain to see when we realize that to-day humanists seek alliance with Christians, in order to defend the human person, and that atheism itself talks in religious terms. The atheistic man to-day is the existential man—it is the haunted, anguished creature of Jean-Paul Sartre, a wraith surrounded by the void and 'forsaken by God', and who is robbed not only of God, but of the world too. It is man absolutely alone and free, creating for himself a personal way of life out of the chaos of an uncreated future. Atheism does not speak to-day of the emancipated, brawny materialist man hewing a future of happiness for himself out of the material of social relations as he might hew a railway track through a mountain. This mythical being has disappeared like the sunburnt proletarian of the posters of the first Russian Five-year Plans. No, atheism speaks of the dread and despair of man in a world in which God is dead. In this sense, existential atheism sounds often a more truly religious note than conventional Christian phrases of consolation, for it asks over and over again, as if it really meant to extract the answer—What is man? what is the meaning of human existence? what is to be done?

So much then for the background of the present work. This book is not an evaluation of 'progress' and it does not enter into political and historical problems, except by the way. It is concerned only with the *What is man?* because no idea of progress or of human good has any meaning until one has decided *what man is for. The Annihilation of Man* led, as I have said, to a Christian conclusion. It came to such a briefly defended conviction out of a study of contemporary history. It was plain to me at the time that I had not said enough, that I had left an argument undeveloped, and that I should have to go on. The present work is the consequence. I shall not seek to anticipate its arguments further save to say only that it confronts the confused mass of modern thought almost peremptorily with the central Christian question which can no longer be burked, and which gives the book its title—What is the meaning of human existence?

I

THE MEANING OF NATURE

Chapter One

NATURE AND TIME

I

The most profound problem of our age concerns the reality of God. We live in an age which cannot accept the traditions of men and inclines to the view that if a certain thing was believed in the past there could not be a better warrant for its present falsity, and therefore the more readily takes the view that God is dead because our fathers believed in Him. If it is really and finally so that 'God is dead', it is necessary to know it quite certainly. But if it is not so, if there is doubt, then it is possible that God lives, and that His world may reveal how He lives. The questions about this matter thrust themselves imperiously at one and clamour to be answered. For upon the answer to the question of the reality of God all other things in life must turn. Nothing is answered unless this is answered. So we must ask—Is God real? Is there really God? And if He is real, can He be experienced? And if He is real and can be experienced, can His purposes be understood and His intervention sought in human affairs?

And by reality one means *existence*. Does God exist? Does He exist in an immanent or in an absolutely transcendent sense, or in both modes of being? When one has assembled a picture of the universe as rational as science can make it, and one has assumed, as one is bound to assume at the scientific level, that events move according to natural law, there is, of course, always something left over. However detailed and logical the whole analysis proves to be, and however hard to shake by examination, yet there is still, standing above it, the mystery of the totality, the mystery at the very heart of existence. What is the nature of the totality? By what fiat is it a totality? Why is there a universe at all? Why do *I* exist? What is the *meaning* of my existence?

One can say of the problems left over, like totality and existence, that through them we can find God. God is a term as convenient as any other for the final mystery, though in the context no more than a grudging recognition of an inexplicable something, or a makeweight in an argument, like the nineteenth-century 'ether'. Or one can say that since something calls the universe into existence, then that which affects its concretion, that is God. 'God is not concrete, but He is the ground for concrete actuality.'[1] Or that, with Whitehead again, He is the ultimate limitation or irrationality against which one butts one's head in vain in search of the final truth. But it is not, or not only, of God in these senses that I am speaking. No, it is not of God as an irreducible minimum, or as a label pasted over a question mark that I am thinking. Nor yet God as a concession wrung from our agnosticism—as one might say patronizingly, 'I do not know that God does *not* exist, and as there is a mystery here I cannot probe I might reasonably credit the possibility of His existence'. No, the search is for none of these things. It is a search for God as a Presence in the world, as a Power in the world. The search for Him is a search for Someone hard and real enough to knock up against—'Hard as the world God nailed with stars'—and whose Presence makes the universe more, not less, intelligible. And yet not that alone: it makes no sense for God to be in the universe but not possessed of a nature with which relation is possible. It makes no sense *to me*, for it is in *my person* that I must apprehend both the universe and God. Therefore it is God the Person, indeed God the Saviour, that I must struggle to meet.

Yet in a way all this is to anticipate. At this point one cannot do more than essay to state the questions which the rest of the book will seek to answer. One can indicate only the approach one has in mind. And as to this—there are, of course, three ways in which one might seek to approach God. The first involves the effort to discover Him in nature or creation. The second is the way of inwardness or subjectivity—one may look within and ask

---

[1] The whole passage reads: 'God is the ultimate limitation, and His existence is the ultimate irrationality. For no reason can be given for just that limitation which it stands in His Nature to impose. God is not concrete, but He is the ground for concrete actuality. No reason can be given for the nature of God, because that nature is the ground of rationality.' A. N. Whitehead, *Science and the Modern World* (1928).

what is to be discovered there about oneself, one's fellow-men, and God. The third is the discovery of God through His own acts of revelation. These are the familiar ways of approach, and I shall follow them, yet without any intention to be schematic or doctrinaire. One has to give an argument its head. One has to clear the springs and then the water will find the brooks and the brooks will run to the river and the river will surge to the sea. There is no intention therefore of forcing 'evidence' to arrange itself in support of a conclusion constructed in advance, but rather of illuminating a central conviction by a variety of approaches.

With this proviso in mind one can speak again of the first approach—of the discovery of God through His creation, which belongs essentially to natural theology. An easy way to illustrate what is implied in this approach is by reference to the Old Testament.

The tribes of Israel and Judah were conscious of a bond or a compact between them and their Creator which endowed them with their special historical role. But over and above this relationship to the Godhead, essentially an inward one, they were constantly exhorting each other to consider God at work in the world and manifesting Himself in His Creation. It was here that they felt Him to be most surely and gloriously revealed. God in creation, the God of natural theology, is the summit of man's rational investigation of the world in which he dwells. It is found in Thomism, the greatest Christian theological system, in the *creation* of God ascending to meet God in His *revelation*. But it is to be found outside Christianity too. It leads easily to pantheism, to the 'life-force' religions or creeds of Bernard Shaw, Julian Huxley, and a score of others for whom the natural world is the sum total of the revelation of God.

The second approach, to God in subjectivity, is very often a mystical view and Christianity has no particular monopoly of it. Indeed, the belief that man in his own subjectivity holds the key to the knowledge of God, and that by mystical practices he can obtain power to approach 'the Divine Ground' which is 'susceptible of being directly experienced and realized by the human being'[1] is the view of another modern, Aldous Huxley, who though he finds this direct experience of the Godhead the

[1] Cf. Aldous Huxley's *The Perennial Philosophy* (1946.)

23

ultimate reason for human existence is nevertheless impatient of the Christian view. It is the argument of a kind of human power of divination made by Rudolf Otto,[1] who even seeks to trace an evolution of man's sense of the awful and holy through many religions until it finds its peak in the Christian faith— and so makes subjective experience the basis of a natural theology. It is Schleiermacher's concept of the faculty of divination or intuition to be found at the core of man's being, so that there is a natural, but still subjective, experience of God. It is demonstrably present in the philosophies of Kierkegaard, Berdyaev, and Buber, in the far deeper sense of the meeting with God in inwardness, as between persons. Prayer is a subjective approach to God.

As a matter of historical fact Christianity has contained both these approaches but has subordinated them to the supreme act of Revelation contained in the Life and Passion of Jesus Christ. But Christianity does not have to depend on the support of natural theology. It can rest all upon the subjective experience of revelation, and the battle of those titans of Calvinistic theology, Brunner and Barth, rages round just this point, as to whether there is one revelation of God or two revelations— a general as well as a special revelation. Brunner leans to natural theology but Barth sees only the revelation made in Christ.[2] Our awareness of God is the pure gift of the Holy Spirit, an act of grace. We cannot find God by our own efforts but must await, in the Pauline word, 'the love of God . . . poured abroad in our hearts through the Holy Ghost that was given us' (Rom. v, 5). Far from evidence of a continuity of being and experience between man and God, which would permit, say, the subjective identity or union with God, in the words of Luther which Karl Barth quotes, *man has a passion against Deity, he cannot abide Deity.*

The obstacles, then, to a view of God which would embrace all three approaches are great. It would seem most necessary if we are to embark upon that search for God which the times thrust upon us to begin first with the idea of God in nature, and then to examine the notion of God in subjectivity and come

[1] *Das Heilige* (The Idea of the Holy).
[2] Karl Barth, *The Holy Ghost and the Christian Life* (1938), and Emil Brunner and Karl Barth, *Natural Theology* (1946).

finally to the experience of revelation. This indeed I shall seek to do and by a logical movement from left to right to arrive at an understanding of the *idea* of God. One hesitates, I repeat, to speak of more, of 'amassing proofs' for example, for right at the beginning one is brought to a most salutary full stop by the ironical voice of Kierkegaard, that God-tormented man, exclaiming that 'to prove the existence of a person who is actually in existence is the most shameless affront one can offer him, being an attempt to make him ridiculous; but the misfortune is that people have no inkling of this, that they seriously regard this as a pious undertaking'.[1] It is an absolute check, for if one accepts it, one can move no farther along the first road; for an objective way to God makes no sense if God is only Subject, and 'subjectivity is inwardness' and man comes at God only because of the 'endless passion of his inwardness'[2] and if to seek to do otherwise is insulting. To Kierkegaard, the inconspicuousness of God, His invisibility in His creation, is the first and most necessary mark of His omnipresence. The inward, the purely spiritual relationship which is the meaning of Kierkegaard's creed demands that he shall not be externally perceptible like an idol or a hill or a tree. Just that mystery of His invisible, intangible nature *constitutes the revelation* of Him. And faith has to do with just this—with the hardness, the impossibility, even absurdity of belief in the absence of objective evidence. If one has established 'proof' then there is no longer anything to believe, no longer any occasion for faith.

Yet when Kierkegaard says, as he does in his *Journal*, that in contrast to all the learned proofs of God or the immortality of the soul, the best proof is that 'It is perfectly certain, for my father told me', he draws a line between the activities of the intellect and the activities of faith which makes passage from one to the other impossible. Perhaps one must proceed with caution about Kierkegaard even so, and confront him if necessary with the irony which was his own weapon against bourgeois and philistine conceptions of Christianity. Somewhere in his massive works he speaks, for example, of his own father in terms readily turned against himself, saying of him that he was able to prove that the most insignificant man in the world was a

---

[1] *Concluding Unscientific Postscript*, by 'Johannes Climacus' (S. Kierkegaard), from Walter Lowrie's *Kierkegaard* (1938).   [2] Ibid.

genius compared with him, and one was so dazzled by his
dialectical proof that one overlooked what was before one's very
nose—that his very dialectical skill denied the thesis.

What is true of Kierkegaard *père* is true of Kierkegaard *fils*.
The dialectical power with which he defends and explains his
faith is intellectual power and—oh irony!—it is in a way an
amassing of proofs.

Of course one cannot treat the reality of God like a bourgeois
in his counting house adding up two opposite columns and
striking a balance—sixty 'proofs' that God exists, and fifty that
He does not!—and so permitting Him to exist by a small margin,
a balance in hand. Perhaps presently the balance is expended,
then renewed again, so that then one would wink Him in and
out of existence like an electric sky-sign. No, this cannot be done.
In all reverence it cannot. Once and for all Kierkegaard has the
last word on this point. Either God exists or He does not and
proofs and disproofs do no more than point to the necessity to
make a personal decision about belief in place of which proofs
cannot stand. To hold belief politely suspended until there is a
sufficient ballot of 'evidences' to elect Him God is to disbelieve.

Yet if this is no way to come at Him, there is equally no reason
for dismissing God from His natural creation and saying that He
and I belong together in private inwardness and isolation from
which the world is excluded. That also is a kind of bourgeois
attitude, from which Kierkegaard is not altogether free. It
threatens to establish some sort of possession of God, always the
bane of Protestantism carried to great personal lengths; to make
one say, Here He is, at home with me in my soul while the wind
and the rain beat at the windows. The most genuine humility
of Kierkegaard does not altogether free him from the charge
that this was a part of his attitude.

It is necessary to introduce this argument of Kierkegaard's
concerning the unknowability of God at this stage in order to
show, on the one hand, that here is a protest which must be
known in advance by anyone setting himself the tasks I have
outlined, and on the other hand to make good a claim, a
Christian claim, for the use of the *intelligence* in the examination
of nature in relation to God. Not indeed to follow in the footsteps of Paley and construct God from natural evidences of
design—one remembers that it was the bloodless construction

of a Hegelian Absolute which aroused in Kierkegaard an anti-intellectual, or anti-speculative ire—but to affirm that reason enters into man, is a most conspicuous property of man, and must be exercised upon the problems and environment of man. Moreover, it occupies a special place in Western civilization, and not by accident, but because that civilization is unconsciously Christian in its thinking and draws from Christianity ideas of the rationality both of God and His creation. We may find indeed that Christianity has, at least from the days of scholasticism, thrown so much weight upon the purely rational elements of religion as to narrow the region of, and diminish the need for faith—and so founder for lack of faith. But we have not yet arrived at that stage—the point is the very present one, Is one to seek for signs of God in nature? The deep inwardness of Kierkegaard contains after all a view of 'outwardness': the reduplication of thought in existence implies a 'real' existence in a 'real' world. What is that world? It is necessary at least to ask questions about it.

Believing in God, one may in all honesty approach His creation and ask in what ways He is manifested within it. Indeed, it is imperative that one should do so, for the obligation is laid upon men to seek to understand His ways. The idea that with nature God has nothing to do enforces a new dichotomy—that on the one side there is the objective world which only science and metaphysics make plain, and on the other there is God which I discover in my inwardness. To shut out that other light is not to serve God. One is not under any obligation to quench that light. E. L. Allen has written[1] upon this very point of Kierkegaard's: 'Few men have offered to God such a sacrifice as he did, yet surely what he gave was that one sacrifice which God does not ask of His children, for it was the quenching of the Inner Light.' And Maritain salutarily reminds us in the preface to his study of the angelic doctor[2] that there is a special task 'to disengage from the enormous contribution which the experimental sciences have accumulated in the past four centuries, a genuine philosophy of nature—as, in quite another sphere, to integrate the artistic treasure of modern times in a philosophy

---

[1] E. L. Allen, *Kierkegaard: His Life and Thought* (1935).
[2] *St. Thomas Aquinas, Angel of the Schools*, transl. J. F. Scanlan (1931), cf. Maritain's *Art and Scholasticism* for a discussion of Christian aesthetics.

of art and beauty which shall be truly universal and at the same time comprehend the efforts being made at the present moment'.

We need not let the best reasons, like the best tunes, go to the devil.

Belief in an intelligible universe appears fundamental to Western man, and one begins by asking, What is known of the universe, and in what sense is it intelligible? In the modern age which began with the Renaissance the universe has been the subject of the most exhaustive speculation and examination, initially in the certainty that it was God and His will which were thus made clear beyond a peradventure. It is an event unparalleled in history. Knowledge about the world has been sought with passion, and exploitation of this knowledge in the manipulation of matter has reached in our own days a frenzied and destructive momentum. So much, indeed, has the pursuit absorbed the energies and established the intellectual disciplines of our times that the exercise of the disciplines has come to stand for the one fruitful way to truth. The end of human efforts has been conceived to be to get to know the external world. This is a point then at which one is not merely permitted, but compelled by intellectual necessity to begin.

The African tribe may find nature full of hostile and irrational forces to be placated by fetiches and ritual magic; the Greeks found an order of Gods who differed from men only in their ability to satisfy their appetites everlastingly; the Buddhists in their agnosticism find no individuals and no meaning and the final reality—if one may use this term—in annihilation from experience. But Western man has been nurtured in the school of thought which finds nature explained by God, who is at once personal, all-powerful, and providential. He is an ordering God. And Western man is forced constantly to act and to think as if the universe had meaning, even when the evidence seems to him to point the other way. Nothing causes him more anguish than the feeling that all is chaos and anarchy, that life is without meaning and the universe a 'fortuitous concourse of atoms'. Even the sense of the transience of the planet, though it will well last out his life, is hard to bear. That his own unique personality should be simply an illusion, without significance, cannot be borne. So that even when meaning slips from his grasp of things at one point he must import it at another. If he does not find meaning for his individual life in itself, then he justifies it vicariously in group life, or mass life, or the nation.

Nor is this in any sense a passive belief. He believes not only that the universe is intelligible, but that he has a number of obligations towards it. Not the least that there is laid upon him the necessity of discovering what the meaning, the order of the universe is, and of profiting by it, as Moses sought once to discover the will of God by his ascent of Sinai. Without this acceptance of an intelligible and rational role within a rational universe it is impossible to imagine the growth of Western civilization. 'The enterprises produced by the individualistic energy of the European peoples presuppose physical activities directed to final causes.'[1]

And Western man is constantly finding that the universe is intelligible, if only in parts. It can be understood. The behaviour of its stubborn material can be controlled. The laws—even though they may be in the last resort only statistical laws, only average ways of working—yet *are* average ways of working, and subject to his examination and even his operation. It is the initial assumption of science that the universe is intelligibly ordered and that by proper and patient investigation one is able to comprehend that order. And the very triumph of science is that the assumption appears to work out. The order is comprehended so exactly (in increasing degree) that it may be repeated artificially by man to produce the results required by him. In this sense the universe partakes of the things Western man discovers in his own mind—pattern, law, logic, order, significance, value.

Yet this assumption is, on its own, irrational. One has no right purely and simply as scientist to say that the universe is going to be rational and explicable. As a prior assumption it can *only* be regarded as a faith, 'an inheritance from a

1 '. . . the enterprises produced by the individualistic energy of the European peoples presuppose physical actions directed to final causes. But the science which is employed in their development is based on a philosophy which asserts that physical causation is supreme, and which disjoins the physical cause from the final end. It is not popular to dwell on the absolute contradiction here involved.' A. N. Whitehead, *Science and the Modern World* (1928).

system of thought of which the other terms have been discarded'.[1]

II

We discover that a logic of things persists. If a stone is moved uphill, energy sufficient to overcome the force of gravity must be exerted upon it. To compensate me for the loss of energy involved in moving the stone, should I undertake to do so, I must eat. To neutralize an acid one adds to it a substance containing a sufficient amount of the opposing alkaline property. The law of conservation of energy expresses the view that you do not strictly *lose* anything in the universe. What leaves one point must turn up at another. A process of addition and subtraction appears to persist throughout inanimate and animate nature and one can express it in formulae and equations in a manner aesthetically satisfying.

Yet an illogic of things persists too. When one gets down to the individual atom, there are only indeterminacy and disorder. It is impossible to predict anything. The radioactive atom may explode to-day or it may last a thousand years. No one can say why it should do one or the other, and the chances of it doing one or the other remain always the same. One gets order out of all this disorder of the basic material of the universe only by taking up masses of atoms and drawing up declarations concerning them based purely on averages. The resultant law is an abstraction, an inference about things based on the probability that 'on the whole' they will behave in such and such a way, and not an iron determination that each thing *must* behave in such and such a way.

The old logic of the universe is in other ways shaken. The safe Euclidean and Newtonian universe, the parts of which were

[1] 'The scientific belief in the rationality of Nature is seen to be, historically, an inheritance from a system of thought of which the other terms have been discarded.

'Nevertheless, the rational character of Nature as assumed in science is quite different from the character assumed in medieval thought. According to the medievalist nature is teleological; according to science it is mathematical. The two statements are not incompatible with one another. They do not conflict, but they testify to entirely different attitudes towards phenomena.' J. W. N. Sullivan, *The Bases of Modern Science* (1938 edition).

bound to each other as rigidly and inescapably as if they were fastened by bolts and bars, was a convenient scientific fiction which is no longer upheld, though for more than two centuries Newton's *Principia* was the basis of all scientific thought and could no more be upset than Euclid's geometry. Now the three-dimensional world of Newton gives place to the four-dimensional world of Minkowski. One has no longer a physically discrete world occupying the three dimensions of space against the background of absolute time. No, time is dethroned. 'Time is robbed of its independence.'[1] Instead of disparate space and time we have a space-time continuum by which we describe events in terms of four co-ordinates, not three. The fourth co-ordinate is the time co-ordinate added to those which measure space. And nothing is accurately described or finally measured until its time co-ordinate is added to the space co-ordinate. Indeed, it turns out by the theory of relativity that we are unable to measure things one against another purely in terms of space, or purely in terms of time, and that it is only when we describe them in terms of the space-time continuum that they become commensurable—that we are using a measure which is the same for all events or things.

The great mystery of time is thus harnessed by mathematical science. Yet it remains true that time is not an objectively experienced or measurable continuum like space. It is not something which exists outside us, as space appears to do. And when we measure it we can only do so by using, not strictly a time device, but a space device. We picture it *spatially*, that is to say, and know no other way of picturing it. Time is experienced subjectively, it is an inward sense of duration. Relativity even implies this. For it says that there is not one generalized time for everything, but different times, or different speeds of times for different objects. And so accurately to measure events one must have a measure superior to the accidents of time and space, and that happens to be space-time. It is another way of saying that one cannot separate space and time from the events or objects to which they belong. They take part in some way quite inexplicable as yet in the very nature of existence.

One conclusion of the mathematical physicists has been that

---

[1] Albert Einstein, *Relativity, the Special and the General Theory* (1920), transl. R. W. Lawson.

there is no reason why one should not conjecture a reality existing in more dimensions than four. Einstein once wrote[1] of the peculiar properties of a two-dimensional universe on a spherical surface in order to explain the paradox of a universe which is finite and yet has no limits. And though, indeed, the six-or seven-dimensional universe is as imaginatively and experientially beyond us as our universe would be to those living in a two-dimensional one, yet it is mathematically arguable and can be formulated. If one speaks of the possibility of a reality based upon other dimensions than those known to us (recalling in this connection that time is also a dimension) this is surely a way of saying that the ultimate reality may have qualities or a nature we are incapable of apprehending, though we may express mathematically some of its formal attributes. Side by side, therefore, with an atomic disorder we have to admit the proposition, uncongenial to science, of limits to human knowledge.

Already one is compelled to accept the uniqueness of the universe. Its space is finite. Its matter is embraced or enclosed by this finiteness. One might even say that space is created by matter, is an attribute of it, since it is a principle of relativity that space is deformed by matter. It is a short step to similar arguments about time. Within the universe things return upon themselves: space is curved. One cannot conceive of the universe any longer as Newton did—as an island of matter in an ocean of space. No, there is *the universe*. One cannot talk of it 'being in something'. One cannot even express a 'beyond'. There is a finite universe with no beyond. Perhaps there are other universes. One cannot conceivably know since one's own is finite, and to postulate the existence of others means to postulate a relation between them. There is the universe and 'the rest is cinders'.[2]

We find that space is finite. Other attributes are finite. There is an absolute velocity, which is the velocity of light. The law of the increase of the mass of a body demonstrates this. For if a body moving with half the speed of light increases its mass by one-seventh, a body moving at nine-tenths the velocity of light

[1] Albert Einstein, *Relativity, the Special and the General Theory* (1920), transl. R. W. Lawson.

[2] 'There is difficulty in finding a comprehensive scheme of the cosmos, because there is none. The cosmos is only *organized* in parts; the rest is cinders.' T. E. Hulme, *Speculations* (1936).

increases its mass by two and a half times. *At the velocity of light its mass becomes infinite.* The finite universe has an absolute speed which is the speed of light. If space and velocity are subject to these limitations, what then of time, the independence of which we are told has vanished? Is there a limited space, a limited speed but an unlimited duration of time? Can we logically suppose an infinity belonging to only one of the properties of the universe? It seems on the face of it improbable. We may have to accept a universe which possesses only so much time, which has therefore a beginning and an end, which comes into existence for its purposes and works through its time—*spends* its time—and ends. It is a conclusion incompatible neither with relativity nor atomic theory, and if accepted poses acutely the question of the purpose of time.

A time which has no ending, operating in a universe otherwise materially limited, is in a strict sense a reversible time, for having no end to its endurance there can be no end mathematically to the possibilities of repetition of events. Statistically, therefore, there could be no irreversible phenomena, for in time all phenomena would be reversed. On the other hand a time which is finite becomes creative. It is endowed with a role. It is no longer the passive street along which the procession marches. The street is moving with the procession, and both street and procession come to an end. There is an end to all things, even to time, and to comprehend the tremendous significance of this one must leave the spatial approach to time which is so habitual with us that we are unable to think of it easily in any other way and look within ourselves where we experience this property of duration and ask again its meaning. It would seem, as J. W. N. Sullivan has said, that the adventures of science have brought us near to a tremendous revelation about the nature of the cosmos.

III

The mystery which lies at the root of things is not elucidated by atomic physics. In the structure of the atom one comes up against something infinitely attenuated and extraordinarily powerful, the ultimate nature of which the physicists find it hard to determine. It is not matter in the solid experience of the sense, and nothing like the minute indestructible particles of nineteenth-century physics. The *particle of matter* has vanished in favour of an arrangement of energy and motion. The atom has a nucleus, the electrical charges of which are balanced by the charges of the electrons which circulate round it. There is considerable mystery associated with their orbits. Why do they not obey the laws of dynamics and collapse into the nucleus? Perhaps because there are rigid orbits and the electron can move only in one of the many orbits and cannot pass through any intermediary positions. When it jumps from one orbit to another it must do so without touching the intervening space. That makes it discontinuous and rather of the nature of a whirl-pool or vortex which may disappear at one point in the water and reappear in another without passing through the interven-ing space simply because it is not a 'thing', but an arrangement of forces. There is yet another theory, that associated with Schrödinger, that the atom consists of waves and not of moving units or masses. Either theory tends to make the field of more importance than the sub-atomic entities which move about in it. And if we ask what the *field* is, if we want to know what it consists of, there is no present answer. One can say that it is a field which behaves as an electromagnetic field does—that it possesses the same properties. That leaves one with the dilemma of explaining what an electromagnetic field is.[1] No, the answer is that 'modern physics does not deal with the nature and struc-ture of atoms, but with the processes which we perceive when we observe atoms'.[2]

Ernst Zimmer writes, in his thoroughgoing analysis of this situation in *The Revolution of Physics:*

'In this stage of science, the mathematical symbol, such as the wave equation of Schrödinger, ceases to be a tool and be-comes an end in itself. These waves are almost more than

---

[1] There is of course (May 1947) the new Law, announced by Professor Blackett to the Royal Society, which declares that rotating bodies produce their magnetic fields by their spin, and the rate of spin has direct relation to the strength of the field. This important and fascinating hypothesis sheds no light, however, on the question we are faced with—what *is* a magnetic field!

[2] The statement is by Heisenberg. I borrow it from Ernst Zimmer, *The Revolu-tion in Physics* (1936).

form. They are a form to which we can ascribe no substantial content, or at least only one of a psychical nature. For one cannot find this something that undulates. We can only interpret them as *waves of probability*. The fac' 'hat Schrödinger's equation has quite a special mathematical form, the same as that which describes the wave processes of classical physics, is the sole link between quantum processes and classical waves. This is the reason why we are able to interpret natural phenomena up to a certain point in terms of waves; but the waves are only a picture. *What really exists is the mathematical foundation.*'[1]

We observe then that in atomic physics the realities elude definition save by a mathematical symbol. We must be quite clear as to what this implies for knowledge. It is almost as if all that we know is something we have invented to know. Suppose men were invisible, yet able to go about their normal tasks. Then suppose that an observer arrived from Neptune on this planet. He would witness everywhere certain activities—the growth of crops, the movement of ships, the erection of buildings—which might lead him to suppose the existence of certain agencies, or because of the interlocking of all human activities, of many agencies all similarly constructed. He might by many devious routes eventually award this unknown agency a symbol to illustrate the size of it and the energy at its disposal. But that symbol would not be a man, it would simply stand in the place of an unknown. It would help the Neptunian to make certain calculations, but it would not reveal the unknown man to him.

Much the same is occurring in atomic physics. We can award the forces we encounter a mathematical value and that is all. Beyond that we know nothing about them. As a matter of fact, we discover that to describe the complexities of the physics of relativity the geometrical axioms with which schoolboys are familiar are not essential. We can dispense with Euclid. Indeed 'We can invent what geometrical axioms we like, provided that they are consistent with one another, and the logical consequences of these axioms form a system of geometry'.[2] And so we arrive at the structureless, characterless continuum from which Eddington deduces the 'quantities of our physical perceptions' and arrives at his immaterialist conclusions.

[1] Italics mine.
[2] J. W. N. Sullivan, *The Bases of Modern Science.*

With other physicists he is driven into something like idealism. In the fantastic world of physics one gets beyond pain and personality and death into a reality formal and mathematical. The universe is a mathematical idea. It exists as a thought in the mind of God. Or there is no longer matter, only spirit, or only the mind of God or man working upon some immaterial stuff. The physicists have driven right through matter and out again on the other side. And what they begin to postulate is not God as the remote Prime Mover in the Aristotelian sense, but a universe in constant creation by the thought or will of God, a conclusion not inconsistent with the idea of finite time. Yet these conclusions about the subjectivity of scientific knowledge are most remarkable, emerging as they do from modern physics, and ultimately they will have their effect upon the whole of science.

The God of the physicists turns out to be curious and unreal. But this, as Eddington points out,[1] is only to be expected for if we proceed to analyse religious experiences by scientific methods then we get the only kind of God that science can think of— a personification of abstract principles. And so the God which results is unreal in the sense that one is compelled to think of Him as having affinity to the nature and organization of an atom—that is, of pure mathematics—rather than to the nature and organization of a man. It is a Pythagorean God which the physicists have conjured up. But this is far from the annihilation of God which was at one time the confident expectation of those who felt that the more we knew scientifically of the universe the less room or necessity there would be for any power standing beyond it, for anything 'supernatural'. One is compelled to take note that the scientific observer no longer occupies

[1] The full argument of Eddington is: 'The fear is that when we come to analyse by scientific methods that which we call religious experience, we shall find that the God whom we seem to meet in it is a personification of certain abstract principles. I admit that the application of any method which would ordinarily be called scientific is likely to lead to this result. But what else could we expect? If we confine ourselves to the methods of physical science we shall necessarily obtain the *group-structure* of the religious experience—if it has any. If we follow the less exact sciences they involve the same kind of abstraction and codifying. If our method consists of codifying, what can we possibly obtain but a code? If scientific method is found to reduce God to something like an ethical code, this is a sidelight on the nature of scientific method; I doubt if it throws any light on the nature of God.' *New Pathways in Science* (1935).

36

the safe anonymity which belonged to the Newtonian observer, who was quite certain that he was observing something quite outside himself. The modern scientist finds it hard to continue to claim that neutrality. He is no longer peering through the window, but walking about the room. He cannot dissociate his mathematical formulation from the reality it formulates. The latter might originate with the former. He cannot be certain that he is not fixing upon a formless, disordered 'reality', an order existing only in his own mind. One might argue that it is quite catastrophic for science that there should be any kind of doubt about external reality, let alone a doubt as to whether it possesses a discoverable objective order.

One must note also that the physicist's universe has become an expression of 'something else'—the clothing of a thought, or an equation, or the incarnation of an idea. Sir Arthur Eddington asserts 'that the nature of all reality is spiritual, not material, nor a dualism of matter and spirit. The hypothesis that its nature can be to any degree material does not enter into my reckoning, because as we now understand matter, the putting together of the adjective "material" and the noun "nature" does not make any sense.'[1]

That is the extent of the revolution of thought we owe to Einstein, Eddington, Jeans, Planck, Lorentz, Minkowski, Schrödinger, Riemann, and the rest of the brilliant team which upset traditional physics.

Classic physics were not inconsistent with the notion of a transcendent God or Prime Mover. Something or someone, it might be argued, had brought the whole scheme into existence and set it in motion. The *Evidences* of Paley, and Kant's awe before the heavens, were tributes as sincere as the psalmist's to the majestic certainties of the laws of such a God-given system. But classic physics left no room for other aspects of divinity, certainly not for the intervention of God. The idea of interference of a Divine nature in the working of those harmonious laws of nature in order to produce results not predetermined by chains of causality was somehow more impious, more blasphemous than disbelief in God. And so the rigidly closed Newtonian system produced the mechanistic materialism of the last century, the scientific determinism of which became a genera-

[1] Ibid.

lized mode of thought which still underlies and paralyses the contemporary will.

Organisms, in the classic argument, were material aggregates subject to the laws which governed the separate, non-organic components which made up the totality. It was hardly likely therefore that organic 'events' could occur except in obedience to physical laws, such as the conservation of energy, governing all matter—indeed they were expected to reveal themselves as more complicated physical processes. The classic system of physics made God unnecessary and free man absurd. It made *man* absurd. It would have been more convenient if he had not existed, or if all materialists had become Buddhists.

By contrast the new physics almost permits the reading of organism and freedom into the atom and its parts. From notions of organism some atomic processes might be explained. Certainly the conclusions so many physicists derive from the new physics entreat a transcendent God to reoccupy the throne which so very recently He was supposed to have abdicated.

IV

In the light of the immaterialist conclusions of modern physics it would not be strange if we were to discover that the theoretical disorder produced a practical disorder, even a breakdown of the science. Yet this is far from being the case. Indeed, the power of the physicist over his mysterious material grows continually greater. The formulations of the physicists *do* produce results, as the world discovered at Hiroshima; and we may suppose therefore that they deal with some order of reality. This is not a reassuring situation, for the incoherence of thought about physics suggests that it is quite possible to touch accidentally upon something terrifying in its consequences, but there are no signs that the physicists are deterred. On the contrary the tremendous mystery at their disposal spurs their curiosity.

Let us accept then the hypothesis of a real if unknown foundation to physics and look once again upon some of the problems that this poses, but from another angle. We have already noted that in the individual atom there is only indeterminacy or disorder. If one is to make reliable calculations about the behaviour of atoms one must produce really vast aggregates of them—thousands of millions of trillions of them. The larger the aggregate, the less the statistical error. According to Schrödinger there is one strange exception to this, and it is to be found within the living cell. More accurately, it is the gene of the living cell.[1] This consists of *comparatively few atoms.*

'Not more than about a million or a few million atoms. That number is much too small (from the $\sqrt{n}$ point of view) to entail an orderly and lawful behaviour according to statistical physics —and that means according to physics.'[2] 'A single group of atoms existing only in one copy produces orderly events, marvellously tuned in with each other and with the environment according to most subtle laws.'[3]

And these events are no less remarkable than the transmission of the nature (phenotype) and vital energies of the organism without appreciable basic change through tens of thousands of years. Here we have, from a physicist looking at biology, a strange somersault of theory indeed—in physics, indeterminacy; in biology, the strictest of determinism controlled by a group of atoms 'much too small to entail an orderly or lawful behaviour' anyway! It is a situation which cries out for investigation. The world of physics and the world of organisms are so completely separated that the tracing of a determinant influence of one upon the other is of tremendous importance—this is a matter which goes without saying. The discovery of atomic determination of cellular structure would, without doubt, deeply affect the biological sciences. That too must be granted. But what, perhaps, is of fundamental importance is that a group of atoms which, apart from the cell, could not be relied upon for orderly or lawful behaviour become possessed of this power in the gene of the living cell.

The gene of the living cell endures tenaciously. It offers extraordinary resistance to change or to instability. To what end does the enduring molecular formation of the gene lead? To the

---

[1] In the nucleus of the cell is a protein-network. It is this which breaks into rod-like bodies which we call chromosomes (from their capacity to accept staining) during cell-division. It is believed that every inherited characteristic has a particular location in a chromosome rod—this locus is called the gene.

[2] Erwin Schrödinger, *What is Life? The Physical Aspects of the Living Cell* (1944).

[3] Ibid.

maintenance of the living being in face of all the physical laws which seek to break it up. For Schrödinger speaks of all this in relation to, especially, entropy, which is the universal tendency of all things to chaos and disorder, the famous Second Law of Thermo-dynamics.[1] The matter and energy of the universe are tending to become universally dispersed and equalized by the laws of physical behaviour. Heat goes one way only, from the hot to the cold body. All motion or action must *ultimately* cease. A state of inertia, or thermo-dynamical equilibrium called 'maximum entropy', so soon reached in any closed system, is the fate of the entire universe ultimately. Organisms are expressly not exempted.

We may describe it in another way by saying that the universe we live in is running down. We are inclined to think, of course, of the universe in terms of an evolutionary winding-up because we have been taught to contemplate the awe-inspiring ascending scale from amoeba to man. The increase in the complexity and diversity of the forms of living things, the fruit of evolution, consoles us with a vision most flattering to humanity of a benevolent building-up process at work, of which man is the peak. Yet this is merely one aspect, and a very small one too, of the cosmic process, and one which has been accomplished

---

[1] Here are two descriptions of the famous Second Law:

1. Schrödinger (*What is Life?*): 'When a system that is not alive is isolated or placed in a uniform environment, all motion usually comes to a standstill very soon as a result of various kinds of friction; differences of electric or chemical potential are equalized, substances which tend to form a chemical compound do so, temperature becomes uniform by heat conduction. After that the whole system fades away into a dead, inert lump of matter. A permanent state is reached, in which no observable events occur.'

2. Eddington (*New Pathways in Science*): 'Ahead there is ever-increasing disorganization in the universe. Although the sum total or organization is diminishing, certain local structures exhibit a more and more highly specialized organization at the expense of the rest; that is the phenomenon of evolution. But ultimately these must be swallowed up by the advancing tide of chance and chaos, and the whole universe will reach the final state in which there is no more organization to lose.'

Here are two definitions:

1. Clausius: 'It is impossible for a self-acting machine, unaided by any external agency, to convey heat from one body to another at a higher temperature, or heat cannot of itself (that is, without compensation) pass from a colder to a warmer body.'

2. Kelvin: 'It is impossible by means of inanimate agency to derive mechanical effect from any portion of matter by cooling it below the temperature of the coldest of surrounding objects.'

40

only against the grain of the pure processes of the physical world, only against the tide of entropy. By its very nature and setting it is a battle lost before it began, for if the evolution of organisms is just part of the larger physical motions of matter, then the only observable end to the evolution of organisms is the chaos of dispersed fields of inorganic matter and energy in which all movement and action have ceased. Long before this final stage is reached all life will have been rendered insupportable by interstellar cold.

This is no more congenial a conclusion for scientists than for anyone else and it leads (among others) J. B. S. Haldane, a biologist looking at physics, to question, indeed, whether this *is* the observable end of the universe and to speculate whether it might not after all be a cyclic universe, capable therefore of building-up once again the peculiar constitutions of matter with which it seems so irrationally endowed at this present moment. In *Science and Human Life* he asks us to imagine the universe to have run down into uniform temperature, with most of the existing matter 'blazed away into radiation'. In such a field, without appreciable temperature differences and no movement, nothing could ever happen but a 'blind jostling of radiation and the surviving atoms'. Nevertheless, on the analogy that one does observe in a resting liquid at uniform temperature fluctuations in which microscopical particles jostled by their neighbours pick up 'unusually large' amounts of energy and dart across the field—on that analogy he argues that there might turn out to be a restoration of heat and motion after the universe has run down. 'Hence, if the universe is finite spatially and contains a finite amount of matter and energy, then in the course of eternity fluctuations of every possible magnitude will occur. I have made a rough calculation from data put forward by Jeans of the time which would be needed before a run-down universe got back to a distribution as improbable as the present.'[1]

Though there is just *no evidence* that this can occur, some logical support can be afforded J. B. S. Haldane. If all physical laws are statistical, then there is no more a *must* about entropy than about anything else. It happens that entropy is what we

[1] J. B. S. Haldane, *Science and Human Life.*

statistically determine, but logically it does not follow that all atoms will obey its laws. If indeed this law is only capable of determination statistically some atoms *must* be exempted. From the exceptions to the law the new cycle of cosmic activity might presumably be born. Indeed, in the Brownian movement we seem to witness an interesting exception in the transmission of heat (energy) from the colder body to the warmer body without compensation.

However, the fundamental postulate of this hypothesis of J. B. S. Haldane's is *time*. It is necessary to have unlimited time. For a run-down, absolutely inert universe has no use for time. One day or a million years is exactly the same. In a constantly changing universe time does appear to play a role. For the cyclic universe events must have the possibility of going on to infinity—there must be enough time. Then, in a universe finite in all things except its allowance of time, as J. B. S. Haldane says, 'every configuration [of matter and energy] will occur and has occurred an infinite number of times'.[1] What is more, this promises to each and every one of us a materialist eternal life for 'if the nature of the mind is determined by that of the body . . . it follows that every type of human mind has existed an infinite number of times, and will do so. If, then, the mind is determined by the body, Materialism promises something hardly to be distinguished from eternal life.'[2]

Professor Haldane finds this more satisfactory than the thought of annihilation, even though it is impossible to see how there could be any memory in the Haldane of some millions of years to come of the Haldane of to-day. The possibility of repetition of atomic aggregates presents him with other puzzles for he also writes 'if a super-biochemist made a working model of me, atom for atom, this robot would, on a Materialistic view, have all my memories. This may be the case, but if so I do not see how knowledge is possible.'[3] Yet this is precisely what he is postulating *time* may do. In time a working model *will* be made of him, atom for atom, which will—or will not?—have his memories. Is it then him, or is it not him? To recreate him and

---

[1] J. B. S. Haldane, *Science and Human Life*. 'If the number of possible configurations of matter and energy is finite, however large, then every configuration will occur and has occurred an infinite number of times.'
[2] Ibid.   [3] Ibid.

his memories it is necessary to recreate *in toto* the situation that exists at this moment. He would then return to this present moment, in infinite recurrence. Or is it him, without his memories? If so this is a poor watered-down sort of immortality.

Now all this may be more worthy of the pulp magazines than of a great biologist, but it focuses our attention on what, indeed, is the key to the whole mystery of time in this problem. For memory is associated with time. Memory is the recollection of past time. Time enters into the nature of an organism in a way which we cannot overlook. The peculiar quality of the endurance of an organism through time is made the root of Schrödinger's essay on the nature of life, to which we thus return, and when he works as a biologist J. B. S. Haldane automatically concedes, I assume, the irreversibility of time, which means that he concedes that time plays a creative role. For birth, growth, reproduction, decay, and death are events in time of a nature strictly irreversible in so far as any known organic entity is concerned. It does not enter into the biologist's calculation that we can reassemble in their present form in some future utterly remote the atoms which at present constitute an organism. There would be no organic continuity which would make this life *that* life. The new assembly would not possess the memories of the present one, and therefore would not *be* the present one, it would not possess its identity. Such a future re-creation, even if it were more than a hypothesis, would have no bearing on the complete life observed in an organism living at this moment of time.

Organisms exhibit two kinds of behaviour, instinctive and acquired. For both of these memory is essential, for acquired behaviour is behaviour which is *individually learnt,* and something learnt is something remembered. Instinctive behaviour is something *racially* learnt and remembered. The inheritance of the racial pattern of behaviour absolves the individual organism from the individual act of learning and remembering, but it does not absolve it from the individual act of *repeating* and *transmitting.* For both kinds of behaviour irreversible time is necessary. It is not any time which is important, but this particular track of it along which it has passed, just as it is not any assortment of memories which is useful, but just this particular group which belong to this particular individual or racial track through time. Neither time nor memories are neutral.

A reversible time in which there was no more distinction between past events and future events than between events on my left side and events on my right side could play no creative role. The meaning of time for the organism is that it cannot enjoy the same piece of time twice running. Time is history. When we say that organisms endure, we mean that organisms have histories: it is quite beside the point as to whether that history is individual or racial or both. Without the history they could not endure as organisms, and we shall see presently that no small role of organisms is the extension by all means of what we might describe as their historicity—the exploitation of time and space for their organic ends. Speech and written language have just such significance. It is interesting to note that Schrödinger, faced with the discovery of the absolute determination of organisms through the dictatorial operation of the gene, makes precisely the same mistake as Haldane over memory. For him, too, loss of memory is preferable to death. 'And even if a skilled hypnotist succeeded in blotting out entirely all your earlier reminiscences, you would not find that he had killed *you*',[1] he writes.

This is naïve. A simple loss of memory of earlier experiences is no fatal accident. Some loss, or obliteration of memory constantly occurs within us, perhaps mercifully, for it would be unendurable to have to remember all that is past. But in the kind of amnesia of which Schrödinger is thinking the catastrophe is limited by the fact that one falls back instinctively upon one's biological (or racial) memory, that is to say, on one's natural equipment of instinct and impulses. And not merely upon them, but upon all one's learnt behaviour, all one's acquired modes of response which have become part of habit—how to button one's trousers, how to eat one's soup, how to know when water is boiling, how to read and how to speak! What it really means when loss of memory is total, when aphasia follows amnesia, and in the end all associations and nearly all motor controls are lost, may be observed in certain mental diseases like cerebral arteriosclerosis which brings its victims in the end to a purely vegetative existence.

Besides, Schrödinger is thinking, as Haldane does, of one individual memory. The loss of the memory in one person of

[1] *What is Life?*

44

certain events is no disaster, for the sick person, like one who has lost the use of his limbs, is sustained by those in society who are whole. The amnesia case continues to live upon the accumulated memories of society and of the supplements to his personal memory provided by those nearest to him: for they will remember, if he does not, where he lives, and whether he has to have a ration book, or a visa or an identity card, and what to do about them if he has lost them along with his memory. Though he loses all memory others will continue to remember how to grow food and work machines and speak words and write books. To understand the consequences of the loss of memory upon individual life one must ask that it shall be absolute. When it is absolute for the individual it produces his annihilation as a social being. It brings death to the world, to be followed immediately by physical death. When it is absolute for society—the loss of memory of all peoples within that society —what consequence is possible but its utter disappearance? We have witnesses constantly around us as to what it means: the cemeteries are full of nations of people to whom this has occurred. They are dead. Death occurs when the material aggregate which is an organism is unable to endure in the patterns it has inherited or acquired—when it is unable to maintain that form which Carus taught was the specific evidence of its soul, and succumbs to entropy. To understand memory in its relation to time is to understand the role of time in organisms. The organism is nothing less than the incarnation of a stretch of time individually lived through, and a summary of the time racially lived through.

And, after all, Schrödinger himself has simply put this point another way when he says that to the organism, as to the universe, maximum entropy is death. The first principle of living things is self-preservation—the preservation of their historic forms. Their most notable characteristic is just this prolonged endurance, this maintenance of form and identity against the forces which would break them down. The living thing must seek to maintain the order with which it is endowed by the genes (through the instrumentality of which it is created) and it does this by a process, in Schrödinger's vivid phrase, of 'sucking orderliness' from its environment. For this is what the intake of food amounts to—it is an exchange of atoms. Schrödinger argues that there is no point in a mere exchange of atoms, it achieves nothing. The significance is not in the exchange of atoms, but in the acquisition of ordered groups of them to replace the groups which have become disordered by the activities of the organism. 'It is by avoiding the rapid decay into the inert state of "equilibrium" that an organism appears so enigmatic.'[1]

The organism opposes its own peculiar pattern of behaviour to the pattern which exists in inorganic nature. It displays integrity to type, endurance of form, and, Schrödinger argues, is subject to the strictest determination of its nature (phenotype) through the unexpectedly orderly behaviour of quite a small group of dominating atoms which, in the physical world, would be too small for reliability. It is no wonder that Schrödinger is compelled to point out that there must be new, undiscovered physical laws to account for this apparent exception to the general rule. These laws must, he believes, conform to existing laws, or at least embrace or explain them. They will not be physically unlawful laws. It will not be necessary to introduce some *non*-physical explanation of their contrariness, but it is not on that account any the less remarkable or significant that organic forms seek to defy—moreover succeed in defying—the universal katabolism.

V

I have spoken of how the organism appears to be based on the strictest determination of its parts and how this contrasts oddly with the actual indeterminacy which is now the accepted (if temporary) basis of physics. If the principle of indeterminacy is maintained it is problematic whether biologists can continue to uphold a strictly deterministic view of the nature of organisms (and many do not, of course) for the accepted scientific principle is that there must be a logical consistency of behaviour between the parts and the whole—that you cannot have the parts subject to one set of natural laws and the whole obeying a contradictory set, or none at all. It is indeed this principle, which means

1 *What is Life?*

that life must be ultimately comprehensible in terms of physical laws, which is behind the effort of Schrödinger to show precisely how the behaviour of the gene can be accounted for in atomic terms. And it is the discovery of the atomic determination of organisms which he makes which leads him to the concept of the living thing as pure mechanism.

Yet the principle of strict determination is made only to be lost again. For the theory of the atomic mechanism of the gene must account not merely for the endurance of organisms but for mutations also. The phenotype of organisms is not only subject to endurance without change, but occasionally to change also. The Darwinian theory of natural selection presupposes variations in organisms of the same species. Not all will be born alike, and of the variations, however slight, between organisms of the same species some will be more favourable to survival than others. Hence over a long period of time organisms 'evolve' in the sense that they adapt themselves with increasing success to their environment by the accumulation of useful variations on the original type. This is the Darwinian hypothesis which explains the origin of species. For long, however, the accepted theory has been of quantitative jumps, or mutations. There is, on the one hand, a process determined on strict Mendelian lines, of ringing the changes on given inherited qualities and on the other the appearance of quite new qualities. A new type is born as a freak is born, by some accident, rather than evolved through the accumulation of small, almost unnoticeable variations. How can one account, therefore, for the fact that the gene not only demonstrates extraordinary resistance to interference or change, but may also suddenly and unpredictably change?

Schrödinger founds his theory of the gene upon quantum mechanics. The mutation of the gene is related to the quantum-jump familiar to physics—'we conclude that the dislocation of just a few atoms within the group of "governing atoms" of the germ cell suffices to bring about a well-defined change in the large-scale hereditary characteristics of the organism'.[1] On the other hand the stability of the gene is related to molecular stability. It is necessary to try to make this abstruse relation rather more clear.

The accretion or expenditure of energy on a large scale is

[1] Ibid.

47

properly regarded as a continuous process. The dying fire loses its heat gradually, the motor-car increases its speed at a continuous acceleration. There is in each case an insensible passage from one stage to another. Indeed 'stages' are themselves arbitrary assumptions. On the atomic scale the business is differently arranged. Energy is discontinuous. Instead of a gradual movement from one stage to another, there are simply energy levels. There are discrete amounts of energy, distinct quantities of energy, and the only means by which a body or a system can move from one energy level to another is by a jump—the quantum-jump. It is the difference between sliding down the banisters and jumping down a series of flights of stairs. An atomic system can reduce itself to another on a lower level at the price of radiating away its surplus energy. This is a process taking place in radio-activity. Radium is blazing away its energy and reducing itself to lead. But the *reverse* activity cannot take place spontaneously, but only by the introduction of energy from the outside, and the least amount of energy that is required is the difference between the two energy levels.

This is not the whole story. Atoms close to a common lowest energy level may form a molecule, a stable and enduring arrangement of atoms. This arrangement will only change to a possible higher level if the necessary gap of energy is made good by another agency. Now there are molecules which consist of identical parts (atoms) but which yet produce different substances. These are called isomeric. What is interesting about them is that their differences derive not from the constitution of the molecules but from the *arrangement* of atoms within the molecule. Professor Schrödinger gives the example of two kinds of propyl-alcohol of which 'all their physical and chemical constants are distinctly different although the molecules in each case are of identical size and composition'. A similar situation exists in the case of dextro-tartaric acid, laevo-tartaric acid, and mesotartaric acid. This is ground very familiar to modern chemists. These atomic configurations are stable. The passage from one to another cannot easily take place. In order for the necessary rearrangement of atoms to take place to permit one configuration to change into another molecule of the same size and composition but of a different structure, *energy sufficient to pass through configuration of still higher energy must be received from*

48

outside. There is so to speak a threshold between one molecule and another of the isomeric class: the energy required is not simply the difference between the two, but that necessary to jump the threshold. One may picture it as a series of steps each of which is protected by a gate. In order to go from step A to step B one must climb *over* a gate. In order to reach a level higher only by one foot one must produce the energy to climb two feet, as this diagram shows:

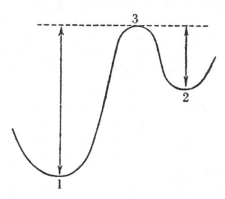

A diagrammatic description of the energy threshold (3) between the isomeric levels (1) and (2). The arrows indicate the minimum energies required for transition. (From Professor Schrödinger's What is Life?*)*

If it is now assumed that the gene of the living cell is a huge molecule, which to change needs a bombardment of energy from the outside, moreover probably a bombardment demanded by an isomeric transition, which means strong enough to enable it to leap a threshold, we have a clue to Schrödinger's arguments about the durability of the small group of governing atoms in the face of the evidence of physics of their unreliability.[1]

Simply then, a bombardment of the gene by some powerful force outside it is the unpredictable element bringing about the quantum-jump which produces the well-defined organic change

[1] This summary is necessarily a simplification and omits many considerations of importance, for example the Heitler-London theory of bondage. The reader is referred to Professor Schrödinger's own books, to Max Planck's *The Universe in the Light of Modern Physics*, to Hans Reichenbach's *Atoms and Cosmos*, and to Ernst Zimmer's *The Revolution in Physics*.

which we speak of as a mutation. In physical terms, only a comparatively rare and unpredictable event such as ionization can produce this. Cosmic rays and X-rays can also produce an 'explosion' within the gene.

We are back here, it is important to notice, to the principle of indeterminacy. The genes strictly determine the phenotype of the organism: each gene is a strict reproduction of that which derives from the union of male and female chromosomes within the zygote, or marriage cell. In that union nothing is produced which was not present before. No procedure of inheritance or of obedience to natural law could be clearer. But nothing determines the introduction of new qualities except the quite random bombardment of the living thing by cosmic rays or X-rays producing (rarely) an explosion within the gene compelling a rearrangement of the atoms within the molecules. By this means some accidental new qualities are produced which have survival value. But if one continues to fire accurately at a target one produces as many shots to left of centre as to right. And by the same means that qualities of survival value are produced, freaks, monsters, sterile forms, Calibans must also be conjured up. A devolution of species would be just as proper a result as an evolution. There is in this no observable principle or law at work producing evolution, unless we assume that someone or something is directing the bombardment. It is extraordinarily difficult to reconcile this chance activity with the aesthetically satisfying picture which Schrödinger gives of the nature of inheritance. It is even more difficult to reconcile it with the sense of adaptation which one cannot help deriving from a study of the stages in the development of bodily organs, for example, the eye. The eye does not arrive, a fully blown mutation to be accepted ever after. Nor do we witness the arrival of several mutations which have a hit-and-miss relation to the eye. We witness a succession of small, but well-defined changes which have the result of improving the structure and functioning of the embryonic eye in the very field for which it is necessary. For such a result not *any* rearrangement of the atoms of a gene is necessary but only *one* particular rearrangement. I leave teleological considerations out of account, for the moment, and remark only that evolution does not seem consistent with random bombardment, chance mutation, but more with the arrival of acceptable and necessary variations which logically derive from the nature and limitations of the earlier form.

Of course we are back again, with this assumption of random bombardment, into that irrational and horrifying universe pictured by J. B. S. Haldane where 'given time' and the limitations of matter and energy all possible configurations of matter have occurred and will recur endlessly. In such a universe, as a matter of pure accident, one might get an evolution which started with man and ended with amoeba. One might? One *must*. Now it seems absurd to me to call such a universe determined. It is strictly indeterminate, in the sense that any and every combination of its material components must occur. Like shaking tennis balls in a bag it is all a matter of the law of permutations. But the law of chance is not the law of nature, which demands a logical and inevitable connection. Biologists looking at evolution discover a *direction*, and when they talk of the determination of events they are thinking of the supersession of the law of chance by the law of direction. And one cannot have a direction if it does not matter if the direction goes into reverse at any moment. The idea of direction assumes an irreversibility, which is another way of saying that it *does* matter that a man 'evolved' *later* than a monkey or a mouse.

Of course this makes the mere existence of time creative. The assumption of random change, like the assumption of a cyclic universe endlessly repeating all possible permutations of matter, rests solely upon the idea that time is infinite while all else is not. If one starts, however, with the assumption that time and space are in some way the properties of what we call matter, or of matter and spirit, then random changes, endless cycles, are as naïve a conception as batteries of monkeys banging at typewriters and ultimately by the pure laws of chance producing Shakespeare's sonnets. If space-time is the unity which embraces both space and time, can space be finite and dependent on matter, and the time that is related to it infinite and independent of matter? Both must belong to the finitude to which it is not improbable that matter also belongs.

In the opening pages of *The Time Machine*, H. G. Wells's mysterious Time Traveller, who fascinated our boyhoods, says:

51

THE MEANING OF NATURE

' "Nor, having only length, breadth, and thickness, can a cube have a real existence."

' "There I object," said Filby. "Of course a solid body may exist. All real things——"

' "So most people think. But wait a moment. Can an *instantaneous* cube exist?"

' "Don't follow you," said Filby.

' "Can a cube that does not last for any time at all, have a real existence? . . . any real body must have extension in *four* directions: it must have Length, Breadth, Thickness and—Duration." '[1]

Though that was a passage one tended to skip as a boy, it is fundamental. It transcends the fiction for which it was written. No duration, no existence. Time, and not the spatial extensions normally the properties of solidity or reality, is the basic condition of all existence at present known to us.

We are compelled to acknowledge the irreversibility, or creativity (it comes to the same thing) of time in our own lives. It is pivotal in a way that space is not. Space is reversible, and to some degree neutral. We may occupy one of many optional parts of space without any essential damage or change, and return to a space once occupied before. Not so with time. And much nostalgia in human life blossoms from the deep sadness associated with a relatively unchanging space—i.e. place—through which we ourselves pass constantly changing, and in the end leave altogether because we are at the mercy of time. Time is not simply creative, *but tragic for us too*, for it fastens upon our existence an absoluteness which it could not otherwise possess. Far from making all things fluid, in the sense that there is a washing back and forth of events, it fixes events as a developer fixes a negative.

We are unable to unpick our lives as we can unpick a thread. The past is congealed, unchangeable, terrifyingly immovable. And the belief that this is so, save by the grace of the forgiveness of God (that God also forgets, in the sense of which Kierkegaard speaks of this act), is at the very heart of Christianity. In the absoluteness of our lived lives within time is the clearest assertion of human responsibility that could be made. If time

[1] *The Time Machine. Collected Short Stories* (1927).

52

could be reversed, events rubbed out, why then nothing would seriously matter for in the end all would be made over again somehow. But because this alone of all things is inconceivable, everything matters, every deed, every act, every life has significance. Indeed the Christian view advances from this acceptance of responsibility to the conviction that *therefore* the track of a person's life through time cannot be an episode without meaning beyond time, unconnected with the ultimate significance of the universe, that it is not wiped out and all done with, and the person's responsibility along with it, by the circumstance of death, but is carried forward into what is beyond time, eternity. To this belongs faith in judgement and in eternal life. 'Every day I grow older', wrote Kierkegaard, 'I feel happier, and yet only truly blessed in the thought of eternity, for the temporal is not and never was the spirit's element, but rather in a certain sense its affliction.'[1]

---

[1] *The Point of View*, transl. Walter Lowrie (1939).

Chapter Two

THE SELF-GOVERNING ORGANISM

I

Schrödinger does not conclude from his analysis of the mechanism of inheritance that he himself is a mechanism. Like Haldane he falls back upon the subjective conviction of his freedom. Only the body is mechanical. In face of 'incontrovertible direct experience' that he is the controller of his own atoms he is forced into the most complete duality. There is a plurality of bodies, but a singularity of mind. Nature shows us a multitude of physical things, but only one Consciousness.[1] And so the organism becomes purely the instrument upon which some Universal Mind or Consciousness plays, as the pianist plays upon a piano to produce something neither pianist nor piano. The *person* or *consciousness* would then, it might be presumed, control the atomic explosions which produce mutations. Evolution possesses a directing consciousness, or an entelechy as Hans Driesch would call it: this seems to be one conclusion which can be read into Schrödinger's arguments.

It is an idea not easily dismissed. Whatever the ultimate truth of the physical human body may be it certainly is an instrument devised or calculated or evolved to experience only selected ranges of events and to eliminate others. As the view-finder of a camera isolates a field of vision, as the tuned-in wireless set picks up certain electronic impulses and rejects others, so the human body isolates, selects or registers certain events, and rejects all others. The ear is sensitive to certain wavelengths of

[1] *What is Life?*: 'Consciousness is never experienced in the plural, only in the singular.' 'The only possible inference from these two facts [i.e. bodily mechanism and subjective experience of free will] is, I think, that I—I in the widest meaning of the word, that is to say, every conscious mind that has ever said or felt "I"—am the person, if any, who controls the "motion of the atoms" according to the Laws of Nature.'

sound only; waves beyond these lengths, which may be sounds to other organisms, are not 'heard' by us. An example is the squeak of the bat. The eye can accept the rays of the spectrum within the familiar range from violet to red: but infra-red and ultra-violet rays are not 'seen' though they are not without their effect on the body in other ways. Through instruments we can measure many of the forces which the body does not 'observe' or 'experience', understand their behaviour, and even reproduce them at will. All apparently solid substances are composed of molecules in constant agitation. Sir Arthur Eddington speaks somewhere of his desk having the property of a swarm of gnats rather than the solidity he is able to observe. The molecular movements of the substances which make the table are neither visible nor tangible. When, on the other hand, he looks at water boiling and generating steam he is witnessing, not the individual molecules it is true, but an actual molecular turbulence. The human body, one must conclude, is not tuned-in to experience all events and vibrations, and an organic system which could not cut out unwanted experiences would be one so subject to the incessant bombardment of sensation as to be destroyed instantly. It is a familiar biological argument that the need for protection from this bombardment is one of the determinants of the size of organisms.

It follows, of course, that the perception of reality that I make through my senses (I am assuming that there is a real world apart from me of which I can have perceptual experience) is incomplete. Even, indeed, that it is important that it should be incomplete, that I should receive only that special range of sensations relevant to me and no others. Therefore I do not from my senses know the whole truth about the nature of the events occurring outside me; I know only such events as my senses preselect for the percipient being which registers them. And though with tools and instruments I can extend the range of my sensual perception and by analogy construct a picture of the events which are beyond my direct experience and after thought allot meaning to these events, I have to accept from the revelations and constructions of science that much of what occurs in the universe is beyond, and even foreign to my direct experience.

This follows for all other organisms too. All, conceived as

55

instruments, function to accept certain impulses or sensations and to reject others. All are limited spatially, are finite, and are confined with strict ranges of experience. In the selective and limited and instrumental nature of the organism, in which Schrödinger finds the very reason for its being, if I understand him correctly, lie implications of the highest order. Certainly we have to realize that the two orders of reality, the organism and the physical world, are not co-extensive, that just as the organism is incapable of the experience of all physical events, so on the other hand the totality of physical events does not embrace the experienced reality of the organism. We are dealing with disparate worlds of events. Perhaps presently we shall be able to understand what this means.

We may well ask what is the meaning of the aggregation of atoms which constitutes a living organism. What is the meaning, that is to say, in an atomic sense of the aggregate *qua* aggregate? And to this there is no possible answer, for it cannot be conceived how it serves any atomic end. It is true that it is a most impressive aggregate and that it stands in relation to any one individual atom which goes to its composition much as the planet must stand to the brick of a house built upon it, but mere aggregation is neither here nor there. If on the other hand you compare the organism to the universe, in relation to its immense space and aeons of time it is the merest of ephemeral specks. Someone—I forget whom—found life so unimportant when measured against the macrocosm that he felt compelled to describe it as an ephemeral planetary scum. Though the scum does happen to endure as complicated organisms in defiance of the known processes of physical bodies, yet this endurance is relatively unimportant. The specks of scum soon die and only overcome this individual death by the propagation of new specks. Nor is it to be imagined that, in relation to the hypothetical time-endurance of the universe, they can keep this process going for very long. From the point of view of the atomic, or sub-atomic universe, the universe of pure pattern, motion, and equation—which it would seem could best fulfil itself in an eternal and non-living vibration—the intrusion of *life* seems an impertinence. In that sphere life plays a role as tortuous as it is unnecessary.

Once one begins to think of organisms, and especially man,

56

as possible vehicles of the Universal Mind or Consciousness which Schrödinger postulates, and in which creative powers reside, then instantly the atomic world begins to recede in importance. In man we have an aggregate of atoms one of whose peculiar properties is this apparent ability to understand the nature of the most infinitesimal part of the universe and of himself, or at least to seek to do so. This is a capacity which Schrödinger thinks 'may well be beyond human understanding'. Man understands not by virtue of properties we can read into the atom or observe in the gene, but by powers of perception, cognition, conation, and feeling which are certainly not the given properties of the atom, and which appear inexplicable altogether in terms of atomic material. That the motion of one thing should generate the motion of another is not strange, that the motion of one thing should be experienced as a sensation in another is strange. To make sense of the role of instrumentality one must argue in terms of complete duality—that side by side with the material world lies the mental world. One must introduce something not given in the beginning, a new concept altogether, one must say that man and the universe are inexplicable in terms of their material and that understanding of them must be sought in terms of the spirit.

What emerges from these speculations is an opposition between the world of physics and the world of organisms. There appears to be a most decisive break between the two worlds, even a defiance of the first by the second. For this reason it is essential to be quite certain as to what we mean by evolution— whether that is to say it is a process belonging to the whole cosmos or only to organisms. Now evolutionary theory arises in the field of biology and only by analogy can it be applied to the social life of man or to events occurring in the cosmos. As a biological theory it serves to account for phylogenesis; it is a theory to explain the increasing complexity and specialization of living forms and their parts. It must above all explain development, and as limited to the biological field it makes good sense, for there is evidence which cannot be ignored of the changes in living forms on the planet. Even the theory of the struggle for existence, though it may not be the whole answer, fits planetary circumstances admirably, for if the earth is anything, it is a life-producing planet. Though there are stretches of the earth without life, and though it cannot be maintained with equal facility in all its hospitable areas, if one sought to describe that which gives, as far as we can tell, uniqueness to the planet, that which certainly in our eyes 'justifies' it, we have to say that it is a life-producer. It generates and sustains living things in such abundance that there is not room for them all to grow.

Now there is absolutely no evidence that in the rest of the cosmos you have any kind of process at work of a like character. There is change, but not development. But by a conjuring trick of popular thought, by an acceptance of an idiom of evolution in thinking, as if this theory had forthwith unlocked all doors, we are inclined to accept a main road of evolution which starts with the nebula, or earlier, and proceeds by way of the creation of suns, formation of planetary systems, the cooling of the earth, the birth of organisms and through the long history of their development to *man*. And even beyond *man*—mind, conscious-ness, social history, and so forth are also argued to be products of the same process. By this convenient argument it becomes, so to speak, the *purpose* of the universe to produce man and mind, as it appears to be the purpose of the planet to produce life. Now when one speaks of the planet having the 'purpose' of producing life one is using the word most loosely. Yet there it is, the planet *does* produce life, it is an important characteristic of it. But to track the purpose farther back, so to speak, one would have to say much more than that 'somehow' the cosmos produced the planet, one would have to argue that the cosmos is the producer of life-producing planets in exactly the same way that the planets themselves are producers of life. Only on this hypothesis can one establish any kind of cosmic main road from nebula to man.

One has only to establish the necessity for this proof to demon-strate how absurd the thesis is. There is no continuous cosmic process. We do not know of other planets which produce life: we are quite in the dark. Even where conditions are similar to those of our planet, we do not know for certain that life will be produced. The peculiar constitution of our own planet—its size, temperatures, atmospheric conditions, and so forth—makes it unlikely that the cosmos is a producer of many similar planets.

If it is possible to make any valid assumption about the cosmos one is compelled to say that either it has no direction, or its direction is altogether away from the production of life-producing planets. The earth is a curious accident which will, life or no life, eventually be sucked into the main cosmic 'stream' again. By an eddy, a powerful stream can create a current which flows in the opposite direction to the main bore. No one argues that the eddy is the direction of the stream. In the same unimportant way the life of the planet moves against the main cosmic stream, it would appear.

Now it is not a flattering conclusion for man that the main cosmic stream does not lead to his front door. He is unwilling to make this conclusion, and well for him that he does not take the cosmos too seriously. But the resultant of his thinking, a Hegelian smuggling-in of the cosmos 'on to his side', disguises the tremendous affirmation that man is making when he seeks to interpret the cosmic process as ending with him, or argues for a universe either organic or spiritual at bottom. *The hidden declaration of this thought is faith.* The immensity and indifference of the cosmos are twisted to mean something special to man, or it is roundly asserted that they have no meaning in themselves, but need to be interpreted in the light of higher human experience. Value becomes superior to immensity: that the cosmic stream is not going man's way is, as it turns out, held to be of less importance than the quality of human life.[1] But, in face of

[1] There is a fascinating parallel between the movement of the centre of the universe farther and farther away from the earth and the rise of the point of view 'All hail to man in the highest/For man is the master of things.' It is usefully put by Michael Roberts in his valuable biography, *T. E. Hulme* (1938): 'No sooner had Copernicus shown that man was not the centre of the universe than philosophers like Pico della Mirandola began to assume that he was. The justification of man's existence was placed in this world—at a great distance in time perhaps, but not altogether outside of time. In these writers the idea of the sufficiency of the natural man appeared for the first time, and this idea has been assumed by nearly all philosophers since. It may be expressed in very different languages and with very different degrees of profundity, but Hulme says that even Hegel and Condorcet are one, from this point of view. Humanism thus contains the germs of the disease that came to its full development in the romantic deification of Progress and the Natural Man.'

Speaking of the dialectical theory of the movements of world history Bertrand Russell makes this comment (*The History of Western Philosophy* (1946)): 'Like other historical theories, it required, if it was to be made plausible, some distortion of facts and considerable ignorance. Hegel, like Marx and Spengler after him, possessed both these qualifications. It is odd that a process which is represented as cosmic should all have taken place on our planet, and most of it near the Mediterranean'. Or, one might add, that it should have terminated in the Prussian state of Bismarck.

the apparently valid cosmic evidence which witnesses to the hostility of the cosmos to life, one must repeat that belief in evolution and man is an act of faith. It is nothing less than the assertion that there is an organic, or perhaps personal, principle not hostile to man at work in the universe and of greater importance than the cosmos. Theoretically, the proposition that man is unimportant and the cosmos hostile to him may be held. But in life it is not held, in living it melts away, and presently, despite one, the opposite proposition is being held, that it is the cosmos which is unimportant. And never more so than in the griefs, the loves and despairs which crowd the soul of man. Even when the proposition of man's cosmic insignificance is being advanced intellectually, in the process the opposite proposition is being demonstrated for the cosmos makes absolutely no comment. The cosmos is quite silent, with the eternal silences which struck terror into the heart of Pascal—'le silence éternel de ces espaces infinis m'effraie'. It is man alone who is counsel for the defence and attorney for the prosecution. And for modern man, 'L'angoisse des espaces infinis est en train de s'évanouir', Emmanuel Mounier has remarked. In *Letter* William Empson describes

> The eternal silence of the infinite spaces,

derogatorily as—

> That net-work without fish, that mere
> Extended idleness, those pointless places

and a contemporary genius of the spiritual life, T. S. Eliot, remarks that 'the effect of popular astronomy books (like Sir James Jeans's) upon me is only of the insignificance of vast spaces'.[1]

The final point which needs to be made here as we leave the extended idleness of the net-work without fish is that if there is no main cosmic road from the nebula to man then there is discontinuity in the universe. Life is not 'simply' a more elaborate organization of matter: mind is not 'simply' a product of higher material organization. Both are new principles in the universe, putting the cosmic process into reverse, or moving off

[1] *The Use of Poetry and the Use of Criticism* (1933).

at a tangent from the main line. There is discontinuity between the cosmos and life, between physical entropy and organic anabolism, and there is discontinuity in the relationship between matter and mind.

II

This conclusion leaves us free to approach the organism as organism, as something existing in its own right and explicable only in its totality. The most characteristic thing about the organism is that it is an enduring, autonomous whole entity which is not to be arrived at by dividing it up into parts and adding them up again. And this view leads, of course, to the theory of emergence—that the whole has qualities or characteristics not to be observed by investigation of its parts, and that life is characterized by the emergence of new qualities belonging to new wholes. In a strictly naturalistic spirit, in his Gifford lectures for 1923, Professor C. Lloyd Morgan argued his theory out and came to the conclusion that:

'The molecular stage is super-atomic; the crystal or colloidal stage is super-molecular; and so on throughout the whole gamut till we reach the aesthetic or ethical stage as super-cosmic (in Huxley's sense) and the stage of spiritual outlook as super-aesthetic and super-ethical. But all stages fall within the rational order of the cosmos in our comprehensive sense; and for us this rational order is, in spiritual regard, not other than Divine Purpose.'[1]

He takes 'quite literally the statement that from the first to the last there is in bird, beast, or man, one life and one mind, developing on one plan'.[2] This effort to explain evolution in some sense on non-teleological lines meets with the disapproval of both Haldanes. The one (J. S.) describes it as hiding away 'in the gap which exists between mechanical and biological interpretation'[3] and the other (J. B. S.) speaks of it as strictly unscientific, as 'radically opposed to the spirit of science, which

[1] *Life, Mind, and Spirit* (1926). It is necessary to point out that 'in Huxley's sense' the ethical stage was not super-cosmic, but anti-cosmic.

[2] Ibid. (1926).

[3] J. S. Haldane, *The Philosophy of a Biologist* (1936).

has always attempted to explain the complex in terms of the simple, and has on the whole succeeded'.[1] Yet even though the biologist rejects the theory of emergence, he finds himself compelled to act as if it were true. Though he may believe in, and wish to demonstrate the essential identity of physical and biological processes, arguing that the observable differences between them are quantitative, or differences of complexity, and not of nature, yet he is compelled, in default of actual proof that this is so, to introduce new non-physical concepts to handle and describe the properties he registers as native to the whole organization of matter which is called an organism. And he cannot, usefully, apply these concepts to its basic physical elements. He may describe some of the behaviour of organisms in physical terms—the measurement of the intake and output of energy for example—but he is lost when he gets beyond these seemingly simple phenomena.

'Life must thus be regarded as something which from the standpoint of biology is objectively real,' J. S. Haldane has written. 'We cannot describe it in terms of ordinary physical and chemical conceptions because these conceptions apply only to what we regard as isolable phenomena in both space and time, whereas the phenomena which we perceive as life are not isolable from one another, and can only be described as manifestations of the unity which we call life. The real basis of biology as a science is the conception of life, and apart from this conception biology would only be a chaotic collection of imperfectly defined physical and chemical observations—imperfectly defined because they do not express the co-ordinated maintenance.'[2]

The biologist is forced to concede that a living thing is generated, and in turn generates its kind, that it has a hereditary structure after its kind, that it is possessed of instincts, that it has percipience and sentience, and that it has the separateness and autonomy[3] which is meant when we speak of its being an individual. It has, if an animal, power of movement from place to place which is under some kind of inner control if

---

[1] *Science and Human Life.*   [2] *The Philosophy of a Biologist.*
[3] In primitive cell colonies in which the individual is the cell rather than the colony it is difficult to speak of separateness and autonomy in the same sense that a bird or a cat possesses them.

external forces are not too strong—it can swim against a tide, it can walk up a hill, it can fly in the air, it does not have to take the path of least resistance. One has got to describe it not merely in terms of its history and structure, but in terms of its functions, for it is not solely passive, a thing to which events happen. It initiates events. It exists for action. It has the *appearance* of being dynamic, and it possesses powers and properties which are only to be interpreted in terms of the things it proposes to do. Its hereditary structure anticipates its subsequent actions—the human baby possesses lungs before it breathes, legs before it walks and a blood circulatory system of its own before it becomes independent of its mother's. When we dissect an organism we do so in terms of independent *functional* systems—circulatory, digestive, sensory-motor, and so on.

Species do not simply survive, as a stone survives if nothing is done to it, they struggle to survive. They do not merely exist, they 'come into existence' out of non-existence by an effort which belongs to them, and they organize other substances, organic and inorganic, to aid them in that effort—'sucking orderliness' out of their environment in order to overcome their own disorder.

'The biologist thinks in terms of the struggle for existence, competition for food-supplies or territory, sexual rivalry, the functions of parts and processes of the organism in its total economy, how they subserve the great ends of survival of the individual and propagation of the species. The question he constantly asks and seeks to answer is: What is this for? How does this tissue, organ or process contribute to these great ends? And if he finds no answer to this question in respect of any part or process of the organism, he calls it a "vestigial remnant"; i.e. he assumes that at some time in the past history of the species it did have a function.'[1]

III

The capacity for autonomy seems to be shown as low down in the biological scale as the unicellular animal. The protozoan

[1] William McDougall, *Modern Materialism and Emergent Evolution* (1934).

Stentor described by Professor Jennings appears to possess it. The Stentor is a minute, trumpet-shaped animal which fixes itself to some object and with rotating cilia circulates water into its system and from it extracts food. When carmine particles were introduced into the water there was at first no reaction on its part. Then it began to turn, first one way, then another. Then it reversed the rotation of its cilia. Next, it withdrew into its sheath and finally, after a while, broke off from its support and swam away. If this is to be described as autonomy it is because it indicates something more than a 'reaction' in a passive sense, an automatic response. There is action at different levels, abandoned when without result, and all in a persistent and total effort of the whole organism to avoid something unfamiliar or unpleasant. This organic persistence continues in the Stentor even if you cut it into little pieces. Each piece containing a small part of the nucleus develops after dismemberment into a small Stentor.

It is when we come to action which can be described as anticipatory, as undertaken in preparation for events as yet in the womb of time, that we face the most baffling of the characteristics of organisms. So baffling indeed that it is difficult not to describe anticipatory action as purposive, or if one is unwilling to accept that it can be individually purposive, then to postulate instead some mysterious force or substance which carries the purposiveness along with it into the organism. By instinct—if we accept that there is such a thing—we mean an inherited predisposition to follow certain intricate patterns of behaviour without foresight necessarily of their end and in the face of situations not previously encountered, or we mean no more than certain inherited or constitutional urges to secure certain satisfactions, as for example sexual urges, in which the end may or may not be foreseen but in which the existence of the urge cannot be abolished even though its manifestations may be controlled. Or we mean both these things, either simultaneously present and interlocked, or alternating with each other, despite their contradictoriness. An example of the first type of instinctive action—the intricate chain—is the nest-building habits of birds, which do not have to be taught, and are not developed by any process of learning, and operate solely upon the inanimate material of nature. Another example of the urge which cannot be banished but can be controlled is the impulse to flight in the presence of danger. In animals, curiosity can often overcome the desire to flee, in human beings reason as well.

In whichever sense instinct is accepted, it remains an anticipatory type of action. It is action which proceeds to a given end or result, whether the end is apparent to the participant or not. Indeed when we speak of definite instincts like self-preservation or reproduction we are speaking of chains of behaviour which lead to ends we, as observers, are able to specify in advance. It is action therefore which is determined by a future which has not yet arrived. Birds mate, nest, bring off young, feed them, and teach them to fly. That they do not perceive individually what is to come out of their mating is neither here nor there compared with the fact that their behaviour predictably arrives at an end we call the perpetuation of the species. There is this discoverable *direction* in their behaviour, and that we call it instinct solves nothing, for it is not enough to admit that they have inherited predispositions without saying what we really mean by a 'predisposition'.

There are times when these inherited patterns have a prophetic character about them, and it is difficult to see how they have been 'learnt' by some past or more primitive organism and 'embodied' in the compulsory behaviour pattern of subsequent ones. I mean for example the behaviour of the larva of the Ibalia which is deposited by its parent inside the body of the larva of the woodwasp. Without this parasite inside it the woodwasp larva, tunnelling through timber, maintains a course which keeps it parallel with the bark. The presence of the parasite *deflects* it from its course, towards the bark, and finally it dies—killed by its parasite—near enough to the open air to permit the weak Ibalia insect, which presently emerges from the pupa stage after the death of its host, to bore its way to freedom. Everything depends on this deflection. Without it the Ibalia insect will die too. It is the constant, the given of the whole proceeding. Everything depends then upon an act which cannot in its nature be foreseen or controlled by the Ibalia insect laying the egg. It is in that sense prophetic. Not merely can the insect at this moment not foresee the deflection, but it is inconceivable that any previous insect ever stayed to watch what happened after laying the egg and so 'learnt' what was

THE MEANING OF NATURE

the best kind of host, or what happened to the host. Once the egg is laid the Ibalia insect flies off to lay more eggs in other hosts. How did this particular behaviour pattern come into existence?

The adult liver-fluke, living in the bile-duct of its host, lays eggs which pass out with the faeces of the host. *If* the egg arrives in suitable conditions of temperature and moisture, a ciliated organism, gifted with eye-spots and organs for boring, emerges from the egg and swims about until it meets a suitable snail. *If* it finds the snail, it bores its way into this host where it grows an irregular sac-like body or cyst containing organisms known as rediae—each one a parasitic mouth and intestine. These rediae in their turn can develop into larvae of a different type, the cercariae. The cercaria is like a tadpole. It escapes from the snail and wriggles in water until it comes to rest on plant life. Then it loses its tail, secretes a cyst round itself, and waits to be swallowed by a suitable animal in the intestine of which it is liberated; there it penetrates the liver and becomes an adult fluke. There is even a most uncanny variation of this—one genus, in sporocyst form inside the snail, sends brightly coloured and pulsating stems into the head and tentacles of the snail which ensure that it shall be conspicuous to the bird which, eating it, will provide a suitable final host to the fluke. One might say about these cycles that they involve a more careful calculation of odds than even a bookmaker is capable of.

Now of course the behaviour of the Ibalia insect or the liver-fluke may be conceived mechanically. One may assume a clockwork set going and working itself out to the bitter end. In the same way it is possible to imagine a mechanism of the atomic type described by Schrödinger set going to determine the 'phenotype' of the organism. But we should be perfectly clear that there are two types of mechanism involved here. It is one thing to conceive of a mechanism which, when once set in motion, determines the whole form of the organism. One might even suspect some such mechanism at work in the formation of crystals. There is an inward process of determining the complete whole. But with the mechanisms of instinctive behaviour we are on a different level. The form is decided: it has been built up step by step from the moment of the union of its primary gametes. There is no break. But now the completed

66

organism is hatched into its environment *another* set of mechanisms comes into play which has nothing to do with the determination of its form, only with the determination of its *actions* in response to stimuli which lie for the most part entirely outside and in general beyond the control of the organism. It is one thing for an internal mechanism to determine that the baby has blue eyes; the mechanism controls everything which goes to produce them; it is co-extensive, we must assume, with the whole body. Like a closed economy, it really can control the import, export, and manufacture of material according to a prearranged and entirely acceptable plan. It is another thing altogether for the mechanism to control, so to speak, 'foreign affairs'—to determine that the Ibalia insect shall lay its eggs in the woodwasp larva *because* that host will behave in such a manner as to permit the survival of the egg. The 'because'—though it lies completely beyond the control of the organic mechanism of behaviour—is nevertheless there. It has to be there. The only point of the behaviour of the Ibalia insect is that something organically outside it and out of its control will act in a predictable manner in a future not yet arrived.

And even the notion of an organic mechanism which determines the form is full of difficulties. If that cannot be finally admitted it is hard to see how one can decide that there is a *mechanism* which is instinct. For in truth, in the mechanical determination of form, one has not got a simple machine manufacturing all the body cells. There is a union of sperm and ovum, which, after union of the chromosomes, divides into two cells. The two cells divide into four, the four into eight. But it is not the subdivision of a previously determined whole. The eight cells are not of the same total bulk as the original two: there is total growth with each new division. The mechanical process, if such it is, is a chain process. We do not discover one machine producing all the body cells, but one machine producing two machines, two machines producing four machines, and so on by geometrical progression. Each newly created cell has the power to create another like it. But each newly created cell is also fitted into its place in a structural unity. It is as if, first, each manufactured can of soup had the power to manufacture another can of soup. The original egg cannot distribute its original powers in infinitesimal parts—the sheer bulk of the completed body in contrast to the original zygote makes such a proposition absurd. In order to make the continual re-division possible, materials are drawn from the environment and arranged in the order required. *Finally* the internal cellular order can only be arranged by the cell itself. The can of soup must therefore have the power to create itself and another like it from raw materials supplied to it. But that is not the whole picture. The body of the organism, as finally constructed, con-sists of cells adapted to all sorts of purposes—nerve, bone, hair, fat, brain cells. It is therefore more like a building in the variegation and complexity of its form than a collection of homogeneous cans of soup. In addition to the mechanism trans-mitting power to the cell to reproduce itself by fission, a mechan-ism must also be transmitted determining the final place and function of each cell in the completed structure. And, as place and function are different for each cell, this means as many different mechanisms as there are cells! And this arrangement and order, it seems, only persists if the original impetus or in-struction remains unchanged. But biological research indicates that it is possible for the transmitted instructions to be changed to meet accidents or developments arising from the organism's contact with its environment. In which case the whole machine changes, even though the original process has already begun.

In a classic experiment in the last century the biologist Roux killed one of the first two cleavage cells of a frog's embryo im-mediately after the first act of cleavage and then from a survi-vor he reared only half an embryo, a confirmation apparently of a mechanistic process. But Hans Driesch[1] relates that he repeated Roux's experiment on the egg of a common sea-urchin. 'And my result was just the reverse of what Roux's had been: not one half of an embryo was reared out of the surviving cell, but a *complete* embryo of *half-size*. And I also observed the development of *complete* embryos of smaller size when I made my experiments with the four-cell-stage instead of the two-cell-stage. I might destroy one or two or even three of the first four cleavage cells; in the latter case I got a *very* small embryo— but it was *complete* in its organization.'

He describes a series of such embryological experiments. As for example with the Ascidian *Clavellina*. 'In *Clavellina* the

---

[1] *The Problem of Individuality* (1914). Author's italics in the passage quoted.

branchial apparatus is quite separated from the rest of the body. If you isolate it by a cut, it either regenerates the body in the usual way by budding processes, or it behaves very differently: it undergoes a complete reduction of form, until it is but a minute sphere, and then, after a few days of rest, transforms itself as it is into a *complete* little Ascidian.'[1]

Again, much as with the dismembered Stentor described by Professor Jennings, if, at that stage of embryonic development which ends with the formation of the *blastula* (a hollow sphere built up by about a thousand cells) the sea-urchin's embryo is cut into parts not smaller than a quarter, in the end complete larvae of small size develop from each of the parts.

This, as Hans Driesch points out, is an odd sort of mechanical principle, in which the total mechanism is contained in any part of the total mechanism. To put it in terms of the metaphor of the can of soup which produces another can of soup—it is as if, it being designed that enough cans of soup should be made to be arranged in a special pattern on two shelves, upon some accident occurring in the process the cans of soup set themselves (by multiplication) the task of completing the pattern upon a smaller scale on one shelf. As though a deficiency of quantity is more readily acceptable than a deficiency of *form*.

Hans Driesch gives a brief and forcible diagrammatic argument which is here reproduced:

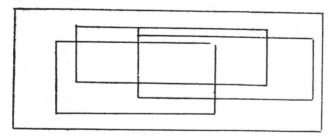

Hans Driesch, in the description appended to the diagram, speaks of it as an illustration of what he calls 'The Harmonious Equipotential System (H.E.S.)' in which all parts have equal potentialities. He says: 'The large rectangle represents an H.E.S. in its normal undisturbed state. It might *a priori* contain a very complicated kind of "machine" as the foundation of develop-

[1] Ibid.

ment. But any fragment of the system (the small rectangles and innumerable others), contingent as to its size and position in the original H.E.S., is equally able to produce *a small* but complete organism. On the basis of the mechanistic theory, then, any fragment of the H.E.S. would contain the same "machine" as the original system. This is absurd.'

From this and similar evidence Hans Driesch argues that *an agent* which arranges the material units, or forms 'the whole' the units exist to create, is required if we are to make sense of it all. In logic and in fact, he argues, this agent cannot be a physico-chemical mechanism. He adduces the necessity for an entelechy, a regulatory agent of a non-mechanical and non-substantial character. He is a vitalist and concerned to prove that there is something in organisms which makes them behave in a manner which transcends the causal chains of mechanisms.[1]

Let it be said again, then, that if in the actual building-up of the form which proceeds from the moment of the creation of the marriage cell or zygote it is difficult enough to discover any real mechanism, how much more improbable it is that the organism will yield a mechanical explanation of instinct. For with instinct one is not concerned with a substantial process quite unbroken in character, but with discontinuous actions occurring in response to two pressures, one internal and the other environmental.

To recount such problems and theories as these unlooses the whole controversy which surrounds teleology. The formal Darwinian hypothesis does not assume the existence of purpose. The infinite variety and subtlety of living things is held to be sufficiently explained by the endless process of adaptation to environment which has demonstrably taken place in the past and presumably is still taking place to-day among living things. Indeed, it was Darwin's purpose to lift the theory of evolution out of the realm of speculation about purpose by showing the natural causes which brought evolution about. For him these were sufficiently revealed in these observable facts (i) the existence of wide variations from the standard or norm in all species, (ii) the struggle for existence (he was thinking of the Malthusian ratio between population and food supply), (iii) the

---

[1] Cf. his Gifford Lectures, *The Science and Philosophy of Organism*, in which his vitalist philosophy is expounded in great detail.

inevitability of survival of those most adapted to their environment. It is true that this left unsolved the difficult problem of the inheritance of variations and Schrödinger's work is one of the latest efforts to determine the mechanism of inheritance and the origin of variations. If various schools of orthogenesis have sought to fill the gap left by the failure of the Lamarckian[1] view (that acquired characteristics are inherited) to meet all objections, yet we must still admit that it is not generally held by biologists that an inherited variation springs from some interior act of a creature. The most that is admitted is the responsibility of a life force.

But without one quality of organisms there would neither be evolution nor theory about it. And that is capacity for struggle. It is taken as axiomatic that organisms *will* struggle for survival both of themselves and of the species to which they belong, and not to define the meaning of struggle begs the whole evolutionary question. In the degree that organisms are considered capable of struggling, they are admitted to be dynamic, to be moving with all their energies in a special *direction*. And it is conceded that by struggling and in struggling they learn, they adapt themselves. They can make mistakes and learn by mistakes and adjust themselves to injury. I mean they learn individually—and this is what we mean by acquired characteristics. And this reveals a paradox—the organism is complete and whole: that is its very nature. But it is also in an important sense incomplete and unfinished, or it could not learn, for learning is the addition of new patterns of behaviour. An organism is a paradoxical thing.

If the door is open to a dynamic, or vital conception of life —that is to say, if the primary quality of organisms from an evolutionary point of view is *struggle*, then the door is wide open for every other purposive kind of idea. For the struggle is just this effort of the living organism to endure through constant change in a hostile physical world which we have already recognized as its peculiar quality. It is this which distinguishes it from the objects of inanimate nature, and it stems from some

---

[1] 'The efforts of some short-necked bird', Lamarck once wrote, 'to catch fish without getting wet himself have, with time and perseverance, given rise to all our herons and long-necked waders.' In other words, a succession of acts of interior will gave the heron its long neck.

will or other, for it cannot be dissociated from the effort to stretch resistance or endurance beyond the limits physically imposed. I do not know whether in this I make my meaning clear: but it seems to me unreasonable to expect life to be dynamic, to struggle for survival on the one hand and then go on to argue that this purposive quality cannot possibly exist, and cannot affect the course of evolution, which is no more than a mechanical sorting out of those fit to survive. It is of the same order of logic which makes Julian Huxley write that the 'latest triumph of mechanistic thought—the Darwinian theory of evolution—has at last given man the assurance that there exists outside himself a "power that makes for righteousness"' and at the same time to identify this power which is striving in the same direction as man with 'blind evolutionary forces'. If it is a power striving for righteousness it is in that degree not blind. In the same way, if an organism is striving and struggling, it is, in the degree that it does these things, not a mechanism. If, however, a dynamic and purposive nature is constantly denied to the individual organism, or to the species, then it comes to rest in the process of evolution itself, the residual legatee.

IV

The arguments concerning the dynamic and purposive nature of living things show up the folly of seeking to resolve the problems of organisms by any save the concepts proper to biology. We may profitably move a stage farther and examine the findings of psychology, not only in relation to the behaviour of living things and to the manifestations of the human spirit, but also in relation to its own problems as a science—to the effort which psychology, like biology, must make to find a secure resting-place for its theories. We shall see how it must oppose itself to the effort to reduce all the phenomena of behaviour to terms acceptable to chemistry and physics. In the degree that biology and psychology are successful in this effort they support the hypothesis of the discontinuity of the universe, they lend credence to the view that we are face to face with a creation organized at different levels.

Before we pass then to an examination of theories of psychology a note on Darwinism needs to be added to the arguments above which seek to establish the special nature of the struggle of living things in relation to a hostile cosmos. So much has been said of the nature of the struggle for existence that the matter cannot be left without further brief exploration. It might otherwise be suspected that less than justice has been done to Darwin.

Now Darwin naturally devotes much space in *The Origin of Species* to a consideration of the struggle for existence. But, strange to relate, it is not the *capacity* for struggle which interests him primarily, but the simple *fact* of struggle. He does not seek to explain the nature of *striving* in living things—he takes it as self-evident that they do possess this capacity. But he takes great pains to bring home to his readers that a fierce and deadly struggle *does* take place for he suspects that they will not relish the notion of a bloody and unending battle between living things.

'Nothing is easier to admit in words than the truth of the universal struggle for life, or more difficult—at least I have found it so—than constantly to bear this conclusion in mind,' he writes. 'Yet unless it be thoroughly engrained in the mind, I am convinced that the whole economy of nature, with every fact on distribution, rarity, abundances, extinction, and variation, will be dimly seen or quite misunderstood.' For him, 'a struggle for existence inevitably follows from the high rate at which all organic beings tend to increase'.

Without being conscious of it he tends to narrow down *struggle* to a Victorian sense of competition between living things. He is by no means unaware of the other side of the picture—the interdependence of living things—and devotes much thought to it, but he never shows any feeling that this interdependence in any way vitiates his argument concerning struggle, not even though in some cases the interdependence of plants and insects constitutes a complex of organic co-operation through which all equally contrive to live.

T. H. Huxley supports Darwin with great eloquence, and in the passage which follows he shows how he, like so many other Victorians, was completely mesmerized by the drama of Darwin's romantic conceptions of a struggle for survival:

'Who, for instance, has duly reflected upon all the consequences of the marvellous struggle for existence which is daily and hourly going on among living beings? Not only does every animal live at the expense of some other animal or plant, but the very plants are at war. The ground is full of seeds that cannot rise into seedlings; the seedlings rob one another of air and light and water, the strongest robber winning the day, and extinguishing his competitors. Year after year, the wild animals with which man never interferes are, on the average, neither more nor less numerous than they were; and yet we know that the annual produce of every pair is from one to perhaps a million young . . . as many are killed by natural causes as are born every year, and those only escape which happen to be a little better fitted to resist destruction than those which die.'[1]

Despite the martial eloquence—or perhaps because of it—the real significance of the struggle is obscured. And we can perhaps deepen and broaden the idea of 'struggle' from the light which Schrödinger has cast upon the subject.

There is not simply a struggle with other organisms; there is, *first of all*, the internal struggle to maintain the organic form against the universal tendency to entropy or disorder. The dynamic impulse *to come alive and to maintain a living form* is the first struggle. Perhaps an essential and inseparable part of that impulse is *to transmit* the living form. From the moment that birth is achieved the most continual and exhausting struggle is not against other organisms but against heat, cold, wet, fatigue, gravity, and so on and so on. Only in the degree that this struggle is victorious can the second phase commence—the struggle with other organisms.

The voluntary and involuntary co-operation of other organisms is essential for victory in the first struggle. There is a widespread interdependence of organisms, even of organisms which also struggle against each other. They prepare the soil for each other, they provide the food, they collect the water, they change the composition of air and water and soil. They give birth to organisms which will presently compete with them for identical sources of food and water! They do that! For reasons like these, the newly-born organism is ushered into a world already made congenial to it. The newly-born squirrel is born into a world

[1] *The Times*, 26 December 1859, 'The Darwinian Hypothesis'.

which already contains nuts for its teeth to crack, and trees to climb. It is nested and suckled and defended by its parents: at a crucial stage they love it more than life itself. Yes, it is true—parent animals will sometimes die for their young! The young squirrel would be most certain not to survive in a world which contained no competing organisms.

The struggle against entropy is primary, and the commonly accepted picture of a war to the death between organisms is secondary, is perhaps only marginal. It is a balance of power relationship rather than a war of extinction. The struggle between organisms is a war of limited objectives.

As to the first point—Darwin's uncritical acceptance of the *fact* of struggle—we can understand how easily this arose out of his natural acceptance of the uniqueness of living things. He accepted without argument that there was a real difference between living and non-living things. The nature of living things was 'given' in his studies. He did not feel that it needed justification, only explanation. He was not concerned to disprove the *created* nature of life, only the supposition of the instant creation of all species. 'I should infer from analogy', he writes, 'that probably all organic beings which have ever lived on this earth have descended from some one primordial form, into which life was first breathed by the Creator.'

For him, therefore, 'evolution' or 'nature' appeared as an anthropomorphic power working among species as man works among domestic forms—'Why, if man can by patience select variations most useful to himself, should nature fail in selecting variations most useful, under changing conditions of life, to her living products? What limit can be put to this power, acting during long ages and rigidly scrutinizing the whole constitution, structure, and habits of each creature—favouring the good and rejecting the bad?'

Of course, we can quite understand his indifference to some of the problems which have bothered his successors. After all, it only becomes necessary to defend the vital qualities of organisms when science argues that they are nothing more than chemical or atomic elaborations. That was an argument Darwin did not have to face.

Chapter Three

THE CRISIS FOR PSYCHOLOGY

I

The argument of discontinuity drives home a notion similar to that of emergence—that living things must be explained in concepts which involve the recognition of their uniqueness, that is in concepts peculiar to biology. One cannot discuss atomic or molecular events in terms of propagation, heredity, self-preservation, instinct, and teleology. Nor on the other hand can one discuss the dynamic qualities of the organism in terms of its atomic or molecular structure. There is even some doubt, I would suggest, as to whether one can discuss all purely chemical processes in atomic terms, but that is another question. That organisms cannot be explained solely by their physical and chemical constitutions explains the existence of the science of biology. And so one might ascend the scale. And sterility descends upon science if one debases the field one is observing in order to compel the evidence to arrange itself in an obviously alien order.

I am thinking for example of behaviourist psychology in which this forcible reduction of phenomena to the order discovered in another field so demonstrably takes place. Biology is the science of organism, and if one denies the distinction between the organic and inorganic one creates a crisis for biology. If one says that all organic phenomena are simply and at basis elaborate inorganic phenomena one is really saying that there is no justification for a science of biology. Or else one is saying, what amounts to the same thing, that the biological phenomena one observes are illusory phenomena. The science of psychology is concerned with the phenomena of mind, consciousness, person, and so forth. Immediately one denies the reality of these phenomena one creates a crisis for psychology. The unique

76

phenomenon of biology is organism: the unique phenomenon of human psychology is person. Crisis is associated with every attempt to evaluate either of them in alien terms.

Biology is determinist—in intention rather than in practice however—and the behaviourists begin where the biologists leave off. If to some biologists the ideal process is to explain the behaviour of living things in terms of the physical laws governing matter, to the behaviourist the ideal process is to explain all mental phenomena in terms of the behaviour of the material body—or to put it more accurately along physico-chemical and/or neuro-physiological lines.

This means the abandonment of subjective evidence. Because one thinks one has a mind, that is no evidence that it exists. And since indeed all that the psychologist can find on the physiological plane is a neuro-cerebral organization of the most remarkable elaboration, then he feels compelled to conceive that this *is* all, and to deny to mind any reality independent of it. Conciousness and self-consciousness are the 'aura' of a physical totality. Behaviourism cannot admit any purely mental qualities, like imagery and will, and it is reluctant to assume th⌐t instinct is as important as it is argued to be. What then does it find? It is compelled to make a new and complicated explanation of why human beings behave as if they possessed minds rather than as if they did not, and it does this by explaining mind as a phenomenon of physiological or nervous elaboration. There are two observable types of behaviour, learnt and unlearnt. In human beings the unlearnt behaviour is quite rudimentary—secondary or learnt behaviour accounts for the greater part of our behaviour chains. But it is not learnt in the sense of using reason or intelligence about it—these are faculties which do not exist for behaviourists—but by an elaborate nervous conditioning beginning at the moment of birth and similar in nature to, but infinitely more complicated in practice than, the 'conditioning' of Pavlov's unlucky dogs. The real basis of behaviour is a nervous system which is organized to receive stimuli and to respond to them and in ever greater complexity to respond to stimuli which stand in place of the original generators of behaviour. The formula is stimulus into response (S→R). Enough of the right kinds of stimuli and the plastic nervous system can be arranged in any particular possible behaviour pattern which an illusory 'mental' power would be helpless to alter. 'Thinking' is no more than a muscular activity or reflex, a silent form of talking.

Now not only does behaviourism, like natural science, seek to break down the time-continuum into a series of *events* (of separate occurrences, as for example the stimulus to a nerve-ending, an impulse to a synapse, a terminal event in the cortex, an efferent impulse to a muscle, a bodily movement, and so forth) but it seeks to break down spatial wholes in the same way that it breaks down temporal wholes. A body must be analysed and one must find out of what 'parts' it consists in the same way that one analyses the constituents of a material substance. The body is discovered to consist of body cells built into systems—skeletal, digestive, the epidermis, blood circulatory system, nervous system, respiratory system, and sense organs. Now if one has, in the somewhat arbitrary manner of natural science, broken down the temporal continuum into a series of events, it is inconceivable how, into this series of events arranged end-to-end like the carriages of a railway train, one can admit any intrusion such as the act of a man's will. Similarly, it is difficult to introduce into the spatial assembly something which cannot be discovered in the parts of which it consists. And so conscious-ness, will, and all those higher processes of the psyche which are indubitably matters of experience (or indeed there would be no such intellectual formulations as behaviourism to discuss) be-haviourism nevertheless cannot recognize.

There is no limit to the ingenuity of man, and this particular ingenuity solves the problems of the human psyche by getting rid of it, a simplification naturally popular in an age which does not know what to do with the psyche anyway, but it is in the end unsatisfactory, for the man who emerges is quite gutless, a mere wraith, the quite illusory product of a nervous and physical system which 'somehow' leads to hallucinations of freedom, conscience, and will. Yet if, after the intellectual analysis has abolished them, one really continues to experience these hallucinations—how far forward has one got? No farther than a crisis for psychology, and one moreover which has lasted for nearly half a century and which looks as though it is in-capable of scientific resolution.

78

II

The crisis in psychology begins in philosophy. It begins with the effort to break away from empiricism. The breakaway seeks to save value, order, and reason from relativism and irrationality. It is grounded in the effort to refute the sensationalism of Hume—that all reasoning is nothing but a species of sensation, and that there is no ground for the preferring of one view to another. It derives from Kantian and neo-Kantian schools but it is not to be assumed that it is hostile to science, for indeed it sought to save science, and especially psychology and human studies, from scepticism. For, of course, there is no ground for science if there is no ground for reason. Science depends upon the belief that there is a truth, and that it can be ascertained through reason and experiment, and when ascertained exists independently of the caprices of the observer—which is nearly as much as to say that it is absolute.

In philosophy and in psychology the movement away from the positivism of Comte and the scepticism of Hume unfolded itself around the idea of the *person*. It was seen that the human person was not only the immediate fact of our experience, but that the idea of the person was central to any theory of knowledge. If there is no valid person then there is no valid knowledge. Behaviourism is fundamentally anti-intellectual, as indeed also are the pragmatic philosophies of James and Dewey, for all are grounded in scepticism about the human person.

In the eighteen-nineties the German philosopher-historian Dilthey[1] (to whose theories I shall return in a later chapter), embarked upon a controversy with the psychologist Ebbinghaus. Dilthey attacked psychology based upon the principles of physics, and all psychology which sought to 'atomize' mental events and explain them in terms which behaviourism has since made familiar. In the place of the accepted 'explanatory' psychology he demanded a 'descriptive' psychology—one which would take human beings as the given units of behaviour and would really and conscientiously describe their behaviour instead of seeking to reduce it to concepts suitable only for the physical sciences. This controversy was a critical one for Ger-

[1] See footnote to p. 131.

79

man psychology and it gave rise to that 'south-west' German school of psychology which sought to shelter psychological truth from the bleak nor'-nor'-west wind of positivism.

Only the expert can unravel all the threads of German psychological theorizing since that time, but it is instructive to consider one or two aspects of this revolt from the atomistic and sensationalist schools. The reality and unity of the whole is forcefully demonstrated by a school of psychology (*Gestalt*), which starts with assumptions quite hostile to the behaviourist point of view. Wertheimer, in 1912, sought to show how inexplicable certain phenomenal experiences were in the light of the atomistic analyses usually made of them. When, for example, movement is perceived, the sense-stimuli must be a series of static images (a series of separate impulses) but these are experienced at the phenomenal level as a continual unbroken flow. It is a matter easily susceptible of proof, for a cinematograph film does actually consist of a series of separate pictures, each of which must be received as a separate image, but nevertheless the film is *experienced* as an unbroken flow. Without abandoning the common analytical approach Wertheimer put forward the hypothesis which might be briefly (if a little inaccurately) described as the presence of short circuits in the nervous system, and of overflows of excitation which would account for the experience of continuity.

Shortly afterwards Köhler attacked the use of the analysing method made familiar by physics as a 'refuted way of thinking' and strictly denied the 'rigorous determination of our sensations by the stimulus'. He was thinking in terms of the intervention of the perception, or of some power prior to the perception in the handling of sense-stimuli. What psychologists had been in the habit of describing as a sensation was more usually the judgement of a sensation, perhaps even a false judgement, an illusion. He argues for the existence of a process which results in unconscious judgements or with judgements which stand in the place of sensations unconsciously received. What does the judging? He calls into existence by this hypothesis an additional set of factors inserted between the process of receiving a stimulus and the registration of it at the higher phenomenal level, a set of central factors which are capable of manipulating the received stimulus and interpreting it. With this we return to the idea of the human body/mind as a selective instrument fashioned to interpret outer reality, or articulated or configured in such a way that it can grasp outer reality, as the hand is articulated and configured to enable it to pick up objects.

Yet even this does injustice to the theory. It assumes that the process of building-up separate stimuli into a whole continues to take place. But does such a building-up really take place? If one assumes it, one must imagine (a) a real, whole tree, (b) a stream of separate stimuli—bullets of stimuli—or of molecules of sensation fired off at the eye, and finally, (c) the building-up of these separate stimuli into the perception of a whole tree. Such a hypothesis seems unnecessary when all indeed that is experienced is *the real, whole tree*. Indeed, it compels a further hypothesis, that there is in the mind to begin with, before the stimuli are received, an *idea* of a whole tree into which the stream of sensations can be built. *Gestalt* theory, as its name implies, considers that this does not occur. There is a real objective configuration *tree*, there is a neuro-physiological configuration which corresponds to *tree*, or which grasps *tree* whole, there is a psychical configuration *tree* corresponding exactly in its own sphere with the previous configurations. Each configuration calls up the other—the house does not have to be taken to pieces each time and re-erected upon its new site. The given unities with which we have to deal, Köhler has said, 'are more or less wholly configured, more or less defined wholes or whole processes, with multifarious very concrete whole properties with *inner conformance to laws*, characteristic *whole-tendencies*, with *whole-conditionalities* for its parts'. And he goes on to speak of 'the primacy of the whole over the part'.[1]

How is it, he asks, that the visual field articulates itself so that the phenomenal result of the reception of a multitude of visual images is the vision of *separated objects*, defined from one another in tonal, coloured, and spatial arrangements? What is the relation for example between the unilateral nerve excitation which is, so to speak, the method of communication and what we *see*, spatially arranged? When the psychologist speaks of the inkpot imaged in the eye—what does this mean? How does the inkpot become separated in the visual field from the other

[1] *Gestalt Psychology* (1932).

objects contained in the field? Or if it is not in fact really so separated that one *perceives* it as an object in itself, what process at a higher level determines that it is to be conceived as one? And, on the other hand, if the vision of a homogeneous plane is constituted of a thousand separate visual units—how is the idea of the plane itself arrived at?[1]

In 'An Aspect of *Gestalt* Psychology'[2] Köhler also wrote: 'I look up to the homogeneous blue sky of to-day, and find it continuous. Not the slightest indication of its being composed of real units, nothing of limits or of any discontinuities. One may answer that my simple observation is not the method to decide this point, but I cannot agree with this argument, since we need, first of all, concepts for the description and understanding of our immediate experience; and the sensation loses a considerable share of its importance as a fundamental concept if, taking it as something of the molecule type, we find nothing to substantiate this idea in direct observation. The continuity of that region of the sky or of any homogeneous field is a positive property of it. And we see that our fundamental theoretical concept in this form does nothing to make this property understood. On the contrary, a special hypothesis would be needed in order to explain how in spite of the existence of sensation molecules the homogeneous field becomes a continuum. Therefore the only thing produced by this useless assumption is a complication of theory.'

And in a comment upon this passage Heinrich Kluver writes[3] that 'seeing a house and a tree does not give us x sensations corresponding to the house and y sensations corresponding to the tree—for instance, 189 house and 124 tree sensations. Observation merely shows us a house and a tree. Even if we admit that we have exactly 189 house and 124 tree sensations, the fact still remains that phenomenally we have the characteristic *gestalt* of a tree and of a house. The fact remains that we cannot have $x - a$, for instance, 170, sensations and $y + a$, for instance, 143 sensations.'

---

[1] Cf. *Gestalt Probleme und die Anfange der Gestalt Theorie* (1924).

[2] A contribution to *Psychologies of 1925*, p. 167.

[3] In a supplement to Murphy's *Historical Introduction to Modern Psychology* (1930) entitled 'Contemporary German Psychology', and to which I am greatly in debt in this chapter.

The experiments undertaken along the lines of *Gestalt* show many examples of characteristic configurations and wholes, in the field of the recognition of a tune, for example, which is always more than a succession of sounds, in examples of *alternative* judgements or arrangements of things visually seen, and in the ordering of experiences in the light of some prior judgement or expectation. A judgement of a colour, for example, will depend not upon the coloured plane itself but on the colours of contiguous planes. In one setting it may be described as possessing a colour it obviously does not possess in a second. In all this evidence Köhler and Koffka see the mind as possessing permanent structure and as operating as a medium of judgement and of interpretation, apprehending first of all wholes to which the parts form simply conditions and/or variations. *Gestalt* arguments can result in a conception of psychophysical parallelism not dissimilar perhaps to that in the mind of Schrödinger—to the argument that there is an exact configuration of psyche to the body, but that the two are nevertheless separate.

Analysing-psychology, like analytical science, seeks the final explanation or meaning of things in their irreducible parts. To Köhler, as in a somewhat similar way to Lloyd Morgan, it became clear that the real significance or meaning of things had to be sought in terms of *wholes*. And though later he was to retreat from this position, Köhler sought at one time to show how *gestalten*, unique wholes, were experienced in chemistry and in physics—e.g. even in electrolytic processes—as much as in psychology. That he strove so earnestly to build up a metaphysic of 'wholes' indicates how deeply he felt the need to seek a philosophical basis for his psychological theory. In this sense *Gestalt* is also a philosophical argument and it is typical of a whole movement in psychology and in philosophy—the turning away from a strictly empirical basis, away from the atomization of events and objects towards the appreciation of the whole —and wholly real—person by which or in which events are manifested.

Indeed, Sander wrote:

'Ehrenfels' concept of *gestalt* quality, Wundt's principles of creative synthesis, Dilthey's structure concept [and] in a certain sense Freud's thesis of meaningful determination, all belonging to the same decade, have this in common, despite their varying

theoretical potency—that in them was heralded the vanquish-
ment of the refuted view of the aggregative character . . . of
immediate experience.'[1]

It was inevitable that from the examination of the power of
the mind to grasp wholes sooner or later a psychologist would
come forward with the intention of interpreting the peculiar
mind-body whole which is the *person*. There arose the personalistic psychology of Stern. He took his stand to begin with
most consciously upon personalistic *philosophy*, which he defends
vigorously.[2] For him the procedure common to nearly all
schools is erroneous. There is not on the one hand *consciousness*
and on the other *behaviour*, there is only *person*. The person is an
undivided totality. What we perceive as a person is not a consciousness joined to a body like a flag to a pole, but a purposive
individual unity seeking to reach certain ends. The whole
person, the only really perceived unit of psychology, seeks as
one whole to pursue certain ends. The encountered whole person of daily life must be the basis of psychology.

He goes on to argue that in a certain sense the *person* transcends both mind and body. The person is 'psychophysically
neutral'. One does not therefore seek to begin with an examination of consciousness or of organism but with what stands above
them and gives unity and purpose to them. It is interesting to
note that consciousness is not central, or critical for his theory.
It is only by an artifice that we divide the person and speak of
conscious control of bodily behaviour. The purposiveness displayed by the person lies *beyond* consciousness and utilizes, if
it is legitimate to speak this way, the consciousness for its ends
just as it does the body by instinctive or other controls. In this
most bold approach one discovers correspondences with the
theories of Driesch, who postulates an ordered and ordering
unconscious soul which is equally 'beyond consciousness', and
also with the arguments of Dilthey concerning the difference
between understanding and knowing, and his view of the totality
of the person. Indeed Dilthey seems to have inspired the theory.

Heinrich Kluver makes this illuminating comment[3] on the

---

[1] I borrow the quotation from the critical study of *Gestalt* by Bruno Petermann:
The Gestalt Theory and the Problem of Configuration (1932), transl. by Meyer Forbes.
[2] *Person und Sache* (3 vols., 1923–4).
[3] *Historical Introduction to Modern Psychology.*

theories of Stern: 'It is, for instance, not the outstanding feature of a so-called volitional act that we have on the one hand a sequence of bodily movements, on the other hand concomitant conscious processes, but that the objective environmental constellation is changed by an undivided psychophysical act of a purposive nature.'

It is necessary to emphasize the indivisibility of the person. One cannot indeed split up the person as one can split up matter. When matter is split into parts one is working and thinking realistically, for the broken-down matter can normally be reassembled and an accurate analysis will enable one to construct, synthetically, the original unity. But to theorize about the 'parts' of a person, 'to split up the person', is purest analogy, moreover an analogy one is never allowed under any circumstances to test empirically, for reassembly or the synthetic construction or reconstruction is impossible. Once the person is seriously taken apart the virtue has gone out of him and what one set out to explore is no longer there. It is not simply that one has destroyed a living thing, but that the destroyed organism is irreplaceable. It is not just any assembly of organic matter which has died, it is, let us say, the unique Mr. Smith, and never again will the person of Mr. Smith be repeated on earth.[1]

This is to outline no more than two efforts to construct a psychology which really deals with the experiences of the person. In both of them we witness the same effort to describe scientifically what occurs in human behaviour without resort to the atomizing methods of natural science. In psycho-analysis, the most influential contemporary theory of the mind, and the analytic psychology associated with the name of Jung, we witness tendencies to develop theories of history, even cosmogonies which are remote altogether from natural science. Analytic psychology, which speaks of the soul and of the collective unconscious in terms close to those of mysticism, and talks also of myths, approaches a religious attitude to the human psyche.[2]

---

[1] See *infra* p. 114 *et seq.* for a discussion of the reality of Mr. Smith.

[2] 'If it were permissible to personify the unconscious, we might call it a collective human being combining the characteristics of both sexes, transcending youth and age, birth and death, and from having at his command a human experience of one or two million years, almost immortal. If such a being existed, he would be exalted above all temporal change; the present would mean neither more nor less to him than any year in the one hundredth century before Christ; he would

Psycho-analysis, the Freudian theory, follows the procedure of natural science in so far as it seeks to resolve the mind into its component parts; nevertheless it is not seriously concerned to find physical or psychical parts. Its preoccupation is with the dynamics of the mind, with the flow of forces which determine human behaviour, and its actual therapeutic practice reveals serious limitations to its own technique of analysis, fundamental though analysis may seem to be to the whole theory.

For the topography of the mind as Freud has constructed it, his plan of the arrangement of forces, is analogical. The mind is held to possess structure in depth. There is a conscious surface and an unconscious depth. Within the 'space' occupied by the mind is concealed a functional system described as *ego*, *id*, and *super-ego*. The *id*, a term borrowed from Groddeck, is used to describe the sum total of the instinctual forces of the individual. It is blind and it responds like a primitive thing to pleasure or to pain. The *id* bumps up against reality and in the process the *ego* is formed—a something which has relation both to the *id* and to reality and is a bridge between them. By a further process of fracture of the original undivided self a *super-ego* is produced, a powerful unconscious mechanism to prevent the acceptance by the *ego* of unworthy impulses from the *id*. It is the inescapable and undeniable human conscience.

The power-plant which energizes the whole system is the libido or appetite—that spring of blind, instinctual forces which wells up in the *id*. The basic psychic experience which causes the materialization of the secondary functional system from the *id* is held to be the emotional or libidinous relationship which develops between an infant and its parents. The male child loves his mother and is jealous of his father. But he also identifies himself with his father and wishes for his approval. The wish to 'murder', to 'do away with the old man' so that he, the child, shall be left in undisturbed possession of his mother's love conflicts with his identification of himself with his father. Out of so powerful a conflict of impulses a permanent mental

---

be a dreamer of age-old dreams and, owing to his immeasurable experience, he would be an incomparable prognosticator. He would have lived countless times over the life of the individual, of the family, tribe, and people, and he would possess the living sense of the rhythm of growth, flowering, and decay.' Jung, *Modern Man in Search of a Soul* (1933).

form or structure is brought into existence to deal with those situations in which the Self disapproves of its own desires. Guilt and conscience, universal human experiences, are thus recognized as essential features of human psyche, yet all the same as emotional states produced by a deeper libidinal anxiety or frustration. Freudian theory exhibits some uncertainty therefore as to whether guilt and conscience and other forms of anxiety are natural or healthy, or whether they are pathological. The psycho-analytical topography prompts even Freudians to feel somewhat uneasy!—indeed, no one can contemplate it without wondering whether it might not be better for the human being if he lived at the level of the *id* rather than at the level of the *super-ego*. If no strong inhibitory mechanism intervened between the desire and its fulfilment one might have a conscience-free life at an animal level. Certainly all *hyper-sensitive* states of the *super-ego* are regarded as pathological and Freudians look with deep distrust upon cultures and civilizations, especially our own, *because* of the burdens they lay upon the *super-ego*. For that reason religion is the most distrusted of all human experiences. The natural instinct is trusted, the rational and disciplinary human activities are distrusted. Charles Berg[1] speaks of a patient who complained that he felt that something was left dead in him because his mother, at his father's prompting, used to leave his infant cot, and comments: 'Fathers who unconsciously wish to destroy their babies would naturally support this policy on the rationalized grounds of proper upbringing, of avoiding spoiling. But I fancy that the good mother's natural instinct would not be to leave a baby to cry itself out. Love preserves life and health; discipline or training, which is often merely rationalized hate, if it does not destroy them, commonly distorts their shape to fit the mould of an already misshapen culture. *And this is the aetiology of all human ills and illness.*' The longing backward glance of all Freudians to primitive life is revealed so clearly in those words!

So much, then, for the Freudian topography. We must note that it is a picture which cannot of its nature be drawn by direct observation; on the contary, it is a 'construct' based upon travellers' tales—rather like those maps of Ptolemy which stood certain countries on their heads. The Freudian structure and

[1] *Deep Analysis, the Clinical Study of an Individual Case* (1946).

functions of the mind or the psyche are 'called into existence', are 'thought up' to account for certain evidence. What is that evidence? It is (*a*) that not all motives and memories are simultaneously present in the consciousness, (*b*) that some are brought into the consciousness only with extraordinary difficulty, for there is a strong emotional resistance to the conscious examination of them, (*c*) that conflicts arise between 'higher' and 'lower' motives and impulses, and illness may arise from such conflicts, and (*d*) that some such conflicts begin as early as infancy and the outcome of them may affect all subsequent behaviour, and (*e*) the evidence of hypnotism concerning the exercise of unconscious influences on a person's behaviour.

That is the kind of evidence which has to be explained. The artificial topography of the mind is not itself the result therefore of direct discovery, but only of the need to construct a dynamic psychical system to account for facts otherwise irreconcilable, much in the spirit that the 'ether' was discovered. Oriental ancients, unable to account for the fact that the earth supported itself in space and did not fall into the void, explained that the earth rested on the back of an elephant which stood on the back of a turtle which swam in a sea of milk. When this is told as a permanent explanation we are compelled to regard it as a myth. A school created to defend and expound it would become an orthodoxy. And even though Freud has spoken of his own system as a construction he was ready to abandon for a better, should a better emerge, there has been some danger of the establishment of a Freudian myth and a Freudian orthodoxy.

Freud once asserted confidently and, in his own words, 'ever more clearly that the events of human history, the interactions between human nature, cultural development and the precipitates of primeval experiences (the most prominent example of which is religion) are no more than a reflection of the dynamic conflicts between the ego, the id, and the super-ego, which psycho-analysis studies in the individual—are the very same processes repeated upon a wider stage.'[1]

Indeed, the *theoretical* patricidal attitude of the infant becomes for him the *actual* antediluvian murder of the 'old man' which was the origin of law, conscience, and God. The psychic process has become hypostatized in a mythical past in which the father,

[1] Sigmund Freud, *An Autobiographical Study* (1936), transl. J. Strachey.

the 'old man', was murdered by his sons in order that they might secure possession of his wives. A hypothesis to account for certain fundamental human dreads (of incest, for example) is projected into history to become there the base of a pyramid of sociological theorizing *held to prove the theory of the mind in which, in fact, it was born.* This is the method of art and poetry, not of natural science, and it is sufficient to speak of it in order to throw into relief the gap between the intuitive processes of psycho-analysis and the methods of natural science.

In the mythology of Freud—in so far as there is one—Fate is once more the master of human destiny. Not for nothing has Freud drawn upon the characters of Greek legend to label the tangles of the mind, for the Greek drama was wholly obsessed with unseen fate. Freud gives us Oedipus back again. The complex named after him—the infantile tussle with incestuous desires—is nothing compared with the emergence of this dreadful and tragic king to power over the world of men again.

Oedipus is not the story of infants and is not about infants. It is the drama of men in fullness of physical and spiritual stature seeking to avert their doom. The father, Laius, is told by an oracle that he will perish by the hand of his son. With the connivance of Jocasta, his wife, he exposes the infant boy, first piercing his feet so that he shall surely die. Oedipus is saved, but is not suffered to grow up in innocence of the fate awaiting him, or indeed there would be no tragedy. No, he too has his oracle which tells him that he will slay his father and wed his mother, and to escape this horror he flees from the foster-parents with whom he has lived in the belief that they are his own blood, and henceforth his effort is directed to escaping the sentence upon him. Yet he does not succeed. Against blood and effort, he kills his father and by his mother Jocasta begets children.

> Wedlock, wedlock,
> You gave me being, you raised up seed again
> To the same lineage, and exhibited
> In one incestuous flesh son—brother—sire,
> Bride, wife and mother; and all the ghastliest deeds
> Wrought among men! But O, ill done, ill worded!
> In Heaven's name hide me with all speed away,
> Or slay me, or send adrift upon some sea
> Where you may look on me no longer!

the Oedipus of Sophocles cries as, self-blinded, he leaves Thebes, accompanied by the loyal and tragic figure, Antigone, the daughter sprung from his incestuous union with his mother. Save for Antigone, he leaves behind his grieving children to mourn him, and his wife and mother Jocasta slain by her own hand. In such terror does the story end. Yet not even there. The blinded Oedipus is a wanderer without home, yet Antigone, who might have reproached him with that incestuous brand he fixed upon her for ever, does not do so, but loyally cherishes him to the day of his death, and continues to her own death, by her own hand in the cavern in which Creon confines her, not simply a figure of tragedy but of the utmost faithfulness and nobility too. If we are to speak of Oedipus as the prototype of man, then for what role do we design Antigone, so loyal in her life to that spirit of man which transcends his disasters?

That is the dread story which Freud erects over us. What happens in our puling infancy is as nothing to what happens in the full manhood of a great king of Thebes. Possessed of all knowledge of his fate and seemingly of the power to avert it, he is yet destroyed by that against which he has most struggled. The Freudian use of the Oedipus tragedy implies that the king does unwittingly what he secretly longs to do. In the Freudian sense Oedipus is the success story of the unconscious, of the *id* accomplishing its private aim against the opposition of the *super-ego*. But the tragedy of Oedipus is not that he does what he secretly longs to do, but the exact opposite, that he does that which he does not want to do, that which he has fought all his life to prevent. It is not a tragedy of the sin of Oedipus: Oedipus is innocent, more innocent than any Freudian babe. He does not know who it is he murders or who it is he marries. He is in the grip of powers too great for him to resist, yet he does resist. The inner and perhaps unconscious meaning of the Freudian use of Oedipus is just this—that man has no power to avert the doom towards which exterior circumstances drive him.

An interesting departure from the methods of the atomizing sciences is to be found in psycho-analysis as a therapy. In the cure of patients psycho-analysis is compelled to treat with the whole mental world of one unique individual, and it cannot therefore regard that world as reducible to separate autonomous elements. Moreover, the vital element in the cure is the relationship between physician and patient. The cure depends upon a conversation between two persons, there is a dialectical relationship, even an *I-Thou* relationship of a tension not to be discovered in the normal physician-patient relation. Indeed a special problem is created for psycho-analysis in this relationship—a problem of *transference* of emotions, or of a new, and quite as dangerous *dependence* as the one from which the physician may be seeking to cure the patient. Psycho-analysis produces the fiction of the physician's objectivity and neutrality. But it is at best a fiction. If one wishes to perceive how terrible and even dangerous is the clash of wills in psycho-analysis one cannot do better than study with care that clinical report, made by Charles Berg, from which I have already quoted.

Psycho-analysis dare not in the course of therapy apply its own laws by rule of thumb. At the best, accepting them as a guide, it can discover the peculiar operation of the mind of the patient under observation. The hope of psycho-analysis of establishing a *science* of the mind which is strictly science, as determinist as physics used to be and as capable of defining the general laws of human behaviour as mechanics is of the laws of engines, is stillborn. There are no laws, only tentative indications of possibilities. The analyst seeks to understand the mind upon which he is working by an intuitive process of identification rather than by the application of a rule. In nothing is this more simply shown than in the ambivalence of nearly all recorded psychic data.

Each mental experience will normally admit of more than one interpretation, quite frequently of opposed interpretations. It is commonly the case that the professional analyst will make many tentative interpretations of the phenomena revealed by his patient before he hits upon one which seems to fill the bill. There is no way of predicting the effect of certain experiences— a premature sexual experience may produce precocity, or its opposite, frigidity: a humiliating childhood may crush a person with a crippling sense of inferiority, or it may generate an insensate ambition, or it may simply be left behind. The critical psychic experience, for the Freudian school, is the emotional relationship of the infant to its parents. If this conflict is not successfully surmounted some injury or malformation may take place. There will be some result, but no one can say *what* result. There may be a fixation *either* upon the father *or* the mother, there may be sexual ambivalence after puberty, or impotence of psychical origin, or sublimation, or illness. There is no certainty about it at all. *Pyschopathia Sexualis*[1] is full of such unhappy histories, most of which appear to originate incidentally in incidents after infancy. But *what* determines that in this child the crisis is successfully surmounted and in that it is not? And *what* determines that when it is not surmounted the libido seeks its alternative expression in this, that, or the other channel? Even when all the facts are known there is no way of making a final explanation of the idiosyncratic individual development. In nothing is this clearer than the inability to decide whether perversion and inversion are of psychic or somatic origin.

It is just at this point that Adler begins to part company from Freud. He discovers disabilities which he calls *organ inferiorities* as the origin of neuroses. What we might describe as sub-standard physique or physical equipment gives rise, he suggests, to psychic compensation or over-compensation. Inferiorities of the sexual organs, such as an undescended testicle or some trace of hermaphroditic constitution, produce an exaggerated desire to excel either sexually or in some other direction. There is much evidence for this in the weaklings and neurotics, the cripples and the disfigured of history taking revenge in the exercise of power over their fellows, or emerging as men of genius. From this argument Adler proceeds to the hypothesis that every neurotic is making what he calls a *masculine protest*, that for his inferiority he desires the compensation of power. Leaving this theory aside, we note simply that what is fundamentally postulated is the relation between certain states of body and states of mind. This is nothing new, of course, but if one were in general to assume that inversion, perversion, and other types of sexual neuroses originate in (as they are surely associated with) certain recognizable physical constitutions then the origin of them in infantile emotional conflicts falls to the ground unless one is prepared to assume a bodily modification induced by the psyche. This is not easy to accept in face of the evidence of heredity.

One must conclude that there is no infallible Oedipus law,

[1] Krafft-Ebing.

no irrefragable formula. The analyst is up against the mystery of the whole mind—or whole being—in operation, and his own analysis may break down over his efforts to separate elements and endow them with a significance possessed only by the totality. It is not simply the totality of the *experiences* of a person which causes him to act in this way rather than that, but the *judgement* of the experiences. And that there is this unique individual judgement is demonstrated by the fact that in the end the cure of the psyche is effected by a guided judgement—the patient is brought carefully to the point where he can make a judgement of his own case, or revise a judgement about himself made on the occasion of an earlier incident in his life, and, most significant of all, his cure cannot be effected without this act, and no one else can perform it for him. The re-integration of the human personality sought by psycho-analysis is nothing more nor less than the restoration of its power of free judgement. The primacy of the person is established in fact, however disguised in theory. But if the final determinant is the unique personal reaction, the unitary judgement, there can be no science. For science, or at least explanatory science, must deal with laws whose variations are the subject of laws too. There can be no science of the mind where the phenomena are 'half slave and half free'.

Yet there can be the most valuable human studies and to these psycho-analysis belongs. Its influence upon art and literature has been more far-reaching than upon science or sociology because like the former its methods are intuitive. It has promoted a sexual liberation in society—the full effect of which has yet to be seen and the history of which has yet to be written—because of its grasp of the ubiquity (and to some extent the normality) of sexual pressures, and a liberation for the arts which has driven them as far as anarchy because of its exaltation of unconscious, hidden, and irrational processes in creation. In surrealism it witnesses the exploitation of its own mythology. One is compelled to conclude that it is merely the accident of its birth at this moment in our civilization, when truths not organized as sciences are held not to be truths, which has compelled psycho-analysis to adopt the protective intellectual coloration of its times.

Under the pressure, nevertheless, to secure the universalization of its 'laws' psycho-analysis enfeebles itself. The principal property of the Freudian mind is libido, the energy attached to the sexual impulse. It is held to express its development through orderly phases associated with oral, anal, phallic, and genital feeling and Freudian theory claims a correlation between the arrested development of any of these phases and psycho-neuroses and psychoses. The conclusions to be derived from the supremacy of the energized appetites of the psyche is that man exists to minister to his appetites and that sickness is the thwarting of their satisfactions, a conclusion so purely utilitarian that it certainly would have secured Bentham's approval. 'The development of the individual is ordered according to the programme laid down by the pleasure principle, namely, the attainment of happiness.'[1] Though it has to be remembered that this principle, this Eros, exists side by side with the Death impulse (very strangely so indeed, though once again we witness the reversibility of psychic phenomena. The libido can be harnessed either to love or death or simultaneously to both!)

Now this conclusion has been reached in a certain way. The technique in physics is to observe the whole, to reduce it to its elements and to demonstrate the nature of the totality from the nature and property of its parts. This is also the procedure of psycho-analysis. The libido is the *primary* impulse, it argues, out of which grew also the conscious and rational powers of the mind. All is, in the end, appetite, even infantile appetite.

If we go back and look at the mind *before* it is broken down in this way, what do we witness? A totality organized in such a way in its normal state that it is constantly adjusting the demands of its appetites to reality and undoubtedly can control even though it cannot abolish its more primitive impulses, sexual and otherwise, and habitually imposes upon them that powerful discipline which alone permits social life. Now it is at least conceivable that we can look at this dominant mind as upon a tree—that the tree sends forth branches and grows leaves and forces down roots into the soil as the imperative condition of living at all. But it is quite different from saying that the roots make the tree and the tree makes the branches and upon the branches appear fruit. All is one totality, one form through which the dynamic living matter organizes itself.

[1] Sigmund Freud, *Civilization, War, and Death* (1939), transl. J. Rickman.

It is at least as reasonable to suppose that the mind organizes itself from the top downwards as from the bottom up.

For it is undeniable that man has capacities and engages in functions which move against the grain of appetite and impulse, that is against the supposed energies of the mind. He is gifted with a passion for truth, for devotion, for sacrifice, for moral and ethical decisions, for the risk of his life in order to fulfil certain ends rendered necessary by conscience. If these come out of appetite, are merely hedonism of a disguised order, then it is difficult to regard ethics, values, and intellectual activities as having independent validity. It is *doubly* difficult for in the first case Freud traces the permanent form of the mind from events occurring at an age when no independent moral judgement is possible, and secondly he derives the energy of the mind for the whole of life from the quite primitive sexual libido. The judgements which emanate from powers determined in such a fashion are going to be purely capricious.[1]

Now R. G. Collingwood has reminded us that 'distinctions like that between truth and error, knowledge and ignorance, science and sophistry, right and wrong, good and bad, expedient and inexpedient . . . form the armature of every science: no one can abolish them and remain a scientist'.[2] Yet the theories of the many schools of psychology which from the early nineteenth century assumed that reason and will were only 'concretions of sense and appetite' involve denial of the independence and reality of the intellectual and moral qualities of man. It is for reasons of this kind that Collingwood writes with considerable bitterness that 'psychology, therefore, regarded as the science of the mind, is not a science. It is what "phrenology" was in the early nineteenth century, and astrology and alchemy in the Middle Ages and the sixteenth century: the fashionable scientific fraud of the age'.[3]

A crisis arises for biology if it is involved in a denial of

---

[1] It is precisely because Freud is thinking in these utilitarian terms that he can write of religion as the universal obsessional neurosis of humanity and say about its 'enormous inflation of love' that 'the fact remains that anyone who follows such preaching in the present state of civilization only puts himself at a disadvantage beside all those who set it at naught'. (*Civilization, War, and Death* (1939), transl. J. Rickman.) It might be argued that it is a spiritual obligation to seek such a disadvantage, but the explanation could only occur to someone who recognized the existence of spiritual forces.   [2] *Autobiography.*   [3] Ibid.

organism, and a permanent crisis has arisen for psychology because the person is inexpressible by the methods of natural science. Over and above these a permanent crisis is created for the whole of science in the degree that psychology 'proves' that intellectual activities have no inherent or intrinsic validity.

III

If the words of Collingwood are hard, they are not ill-deserved. If not fraud, then confusion covers the field. A gymnastic intellectual effort is needed to believe that there is a common science to a psychology which embraces the behaviourism of Watson and Pavlov, the vitalism of McDougall and Driesch, the psychologies of the unconscious of Freud, Jung, and Adler, the *gestalt* of Köhler and Koffka, the personalistic psychology of Stern and Groddeck, and the descriptive or cultural-science psychology of Dilthey, to say nothing of a score of other schools. It is hard to resist the conclusion that they all derive from *a priori* convictions as to the nature of the human psyche or the significance of human behaviour. It is not so much a matter of evidence, as to what, to begin with, one admits to be evidence: in the enormous mass of material confronting the psychologist, he will put emphasis upon that which he is convinced is significant, but he will not find that the evidence alone will decide this for him. He must make resort to an inward scale of values.

Indeed the matter of values is the central one. The values upon which science as a whole rests are subjectively experienced. The person is subjectively experienced. The person is a value. It is the utter impossibility of coming at these experiences by the objective approach of science which creates the chaotic situation which psychological school after school seeks to overcome. Psychology concentrates for us the confusion which has inevitably descended upon the whole of our intellectual life by the decision that science is the only way of knowing, that the only truths are scientific truths. In the field of psychology we witness the hopeless attempt to reconcile two streams of experience in one scientific formulation. The crisis for psychology, then, is simply a focal point for the crisis for knowledge.

All this may seem to carry us far from the original point of departure—as to whether God exists, whether He can be experienced and whether His purposes can be understood. The more so as it becomes clear that science has nothing deliberately to say upon so profound a matter. Science moves, it is true, within a faith of which it is not always conscious, a faith in the rationality of the universe and from which it cannot be dispossessed without bringing science immediately to an end (and if it cannot find that rationality in a self-ordering universe, it will find it in a religious solution, as some physicists now tend to do). That such a faith arises out of Christian doctrines originally is an unconscious tribute to the notion of a just, ordering, and providential God, but faith in God must rest upon more than the crumbs from the scientists' tables.

Whatever the scientist may say about the nature of the universe, however, the ways in which he uses his mind are tributes to the existence of a higher order in the universe than the world of objects, a hierarchy of values which is not definable in terms of objects. Such are the 'distinctions' which Collingwood said were inseparable from the armature of every science. The scientist uses his mind in a qualitative way. He investigates events, attributes to them what he believes to be their inherent order, says that such-and-such a conclusion is the truth as best he is able to arrive at it. These conclusions arise out of a sense of values—that not all events are of equal significance, not all statements are equally true. 'I will show you what is true,' the scientist says. He does not always succeed. His instruments are too blunt, too coarse to unbare the nature of his own creative and analytical acts. The sharpest knife fails to cut itself. But the tremendous assertion, which it never occurs to him to question, at the root of his inquiries is that he possesses in himself a power capable of overleaping the barriers of space and time and of knowing truth.[1]

---

[1] 'It is by looking into our own nature that we first discover the failure of the physical universe to be co-extensive with our experience of reality. The "something to which truth matters" must surely have a place in reality whatever definition of reality we may adopt. In our own nature, or through the contact of our consciousness with a nature transcending ours, there are other things that claim the same kind of recognition—a sense of beauty, of morality, and finally at the root of all spiritual religion an experience which we describe as the presence of God.' Eddington, *New Pathways in Science.*

In approaching the fields he is to observe, the sense of values which dictates the approach (which decides what has to be known, what is worth knowing) is overlooked or taken for granted. The creative act goes unrecognized. Extracting his own mind and desires from the field of observation, the scientist succeeds in a measure of self-forgetfulness.

So far so good, but what is *really* happening? What have we in the whole assumption of a mind 'outside' looking at a world of sense objects in space and time but either (*a*) a physical impossibility, a pure behaviourist illusion, or (*b*) something quite extraordinary, a mind detached or detachable for certain purposes from the material with which it is associated? It seems to me that there are two incompatibles—something timeless, spaceless, and without mass or location, examining things which do have mass or location. But if, indeed, this does occur then the quantitative insignificance of the human being disappears, for it is he who is discovering the nature of things and annihilating the immensities of space and the obscurity of the atom at one and the same time. This capacity to embrace the vastity of the cosmos by virtue of a quality which is not apparent in it can only mean that man has powers belonging to the highest possible order of the universe. Only one power can stand higher than the power to understand the universe, and that is the power to create it. As far as we can see—if we except God— nothing else in the universe is capable of the act of comprehending it.

And even though this capacity for comprehension is discovered to have limits, yet that it exists at all restores man to the dignity with which humanism once invested him. The recognition of the subjective dignity and greatness of man opens the way for true humanism—'humanism indeed, but a theocentric humanism, rooted in what is radical in man: integral humanism, the humanism of the Incarnation'.[1]

Once again, upon the basis of his psychic supremacy, man becomes something quite unique in the universe, that in terms of which the rest must be explained. He is a being standing in space and time and capable of ranging through space and time, a being, as Kierkegaard has called him, at the junction of time and eternity.

[1] J. Maritain, *True Humanism* (1938).

IV

It would be as well at this point to seek to draw some threads of the argument together. Without seeking to make my treatment exhaustive I have selected certain aspects of modern knowledge in order to draw conclusions about the nature of the universe. The aspects selected appear to me to be fundamental —the atomic structure, the space-time universe, the qualities of living, evolving organisms, the idea of the person. Here I might summarize them.

Certain physicists find that what has been known as 'matter' is so elusive as to be indeed most probably immaterial and from this are inclined to draw spiritual or deistic conclusions. The school of Einstein, misnamed relativity, finds space finite, the speed of light a 'ceiling', and space and time a connected continuum. I have made the not unreasonable assumption that time might prove to be finite too, and in this I am supported by the probability that space and time are properties of the elusive matter of the universe and without matter they might cease to exist. To the nature of human life and the evolution of organisms belongs the idea that time has a *direction*, which is the same thing as saying that it is irreversible or creative. A finite time would support the idea of a creative process in the universe more easily than infinite time, for infinite time (if matter is limited) is by its nature reversible time. The popular notion of time has to be finally abandoned.

An examination of the nature of the organism, so inexplicable in atomic terms, leads inevitably to the idea of discontinuity in the universe and to the argument that belief in evolution as a process leading to and justifying man is an act of faith, for the cosmos is not on the side of evolution or of life. To decide that life and man are important one must decide that the cosmos is unimportant. The dismissal of the cosmos raises at once the problem of the significance of life and an effort is made to show, by biological evidence, that life depends upon will and purpose active in an anti-cosmic sense, that is, as seeking to maintain the unity and form of the organism against the universal tendency to disorder. I then seek to show that the notion of discontinuity in the universe makes it impossible to explain all phenomena by the means of one science and that science is made sterile when the phenomena of one field are reduced to the order belonging to another. In behaviourism we witness such an effort and this is typical of many which have produced a crisis for psychology. The revolt against 'atomizing' methods in psychology produced such typical schools as *gestalt* and personalism, but in psycho-analysis too the unique individual person is discovered to be the subject of its therapy if not of its theory. The crisis for psychology is held to centre round the subjective experience of the person, for subjective experiences are not scientifically verifiable or explicable. Therefore, though it has not been said so far, but now must, psychology is faced with the choice either of remaining faithful to psychical experience and ceasing to be a 'science', or abandoning the person in favour of some 'scientific explanation' of him. This was the conclusion implied by my assertion that psycho-analysis was nearer to art and poetry than science in its methods. The crisis for psychology is really the crisis for the whole of knowledge—what is the meaning for knowledge of subjective experiences? Into this I will eventually go, but for the moment what conclusions, one may rightly ask, may be drawn so far as to the nature and reality of God?

These: consider the metaphysical order we arrive at in an objective sense—matter basically inexplicable, space finite and time creative, and the defiance of the cosmos by living organisms. It is an order which vividly suggests a creative act, or a series of creative acts. A universe moving through its own time to its own end is a created universe. The unifying principle this demands is God. Not simply the Natural Power or Sacred Reality of Huxley, the Creative Process of Bergson, the Veiled Being of H. G. Wells, the Life Force of G. B. Shaw, or the Great Being which for the J. B. S. Haldane of the *Science and Human Life* 'may be a fact as real as human consciousness'—but God in a transcendent sense. For it is not to be conceived how or why such a universe shall have called itself into existence to move creatively towards its appointed end unless we are attributing to it qualities of omnipotence and omniscience commonly attributed to God. And if it did not call itself into existence, what then? For an infinite universe of indestructible matter existing through eternity, one has perhaps little need to suppose a *Creator*. By the same token it is impossible to attribute to it any *process*. For a finite universe containing an evolving movement one is compelled to seek a creative cause.[1]

I follow Berdyaev that eternity is timelessness, not infinite time. Time belongs to the nature of the cosmos, not to what preceded it or will follow it, for no sense of 'before' or 'after' can belong to a state for which time has no existence. We have no more conception of what that state can be in which there is no time than the unconscious stone at my feet has of the time in which nevertheless it endures. Therefore we have no need to ask why the universe should be brought into existence at this 'moment', or why one should exist at this 'moment', rather than at some other 'moment', for the alternative to this 'moment' is not strictly for us another 'moment', but that timelessness, that mode of pure being independent of substance and change of which we can imagine nothing. But we have each one of us a curious hint of the experience that awaits us, for we must all die. And for the living thing, born into this 'moment', it is the annihilation of continuing-to-be in this 'moment'. The world of time vanishes for it, its parts cease to adhere, they 'forget' their purpose, the living principle which compels them to adhere in a united, autonomous whole is lost. The 'being' is annihilated out of time into eternity.

Yet further evidence of the created nature of the universe comes from a consideration of all those factors which have given rise to the theory of emergence—that new wholes appear to have arisen in the process of time in the realm of organisms, wholes which certainly could not be predicted from the qualities and characteristics either of their predecessors or their parts. It is beyond dispute that there is more to the tiger than to the amoeba, that there is more to written language than to speech, more to articulated speech than the grunts and cries of animals.[2] What is this 'more'?—without which there would indeed be no

[1] 'The more orthodox scientific view is that the entropy of the universe must for ever increase to its final maximum value. It has not yet reached this: we should not be thinking about it if it had. It is still increasing rapidly, and so must have had a beginning; there must have been what we may describe as a "creation" at a time not infinitely remote.' Sir James Jeans, *The Mysterious Universe*. Cf. notes on entropy, p. 40.

[2] Professor Richard Albert Wilson brilliantly illuminates this in *Miraculous Birth of Language* (1942).

need for a theory of evolution—what but the emergence of newly created things? And if this is to be accepted, what then is the meaning of the appearance of creation in a cosmos which is *materially* complete, as far as we are able to judge?

So much indeed for the objective evidence leading to God. But we have noticed, especially in considering psychological theory, the pressure of subjective experience. There is a sense in which subjective experience could be held to be all—that the geometries of relativity, the immaterialist theories of modern physics, the hypotheses of science in general are of subjective origin. Whether this is so or not is perhaps not so important as that it *looks* as if it could be so—for it plainly points to the side-by-sideness of objective and subjective worlds. The position of the person, who experiences both worlds, is central to the task of understanding them and is perhaps the key to the relationship of God to His creation.

Let it be said, before I pass on, then, that the conclusion is pressed upon me that the universe is 'called into existence' for a creative purpose. What ultimately that act means I may only learn if I discover the purposes of God, and existence and movement in time for ever prevent the exploration of the Being who exists without them, yet is able to move in them. Yet in my own being, and in all others of the same nature that I observe, there is this effort to understand the universe, to transcend its time-movement processes in which matter and organism are caught and see the whole of it as though one stood beyond time, space, and movement (this is not a mystical idea—it seems to me the actual process by which the mind operates). In that I conceive that one approaches the nature and reality of God Himself. For moving among the unconscious material processes, comprehending them, but comprehended not, is my mind. Time, space, abstraction are only partially barriers. In the same way I conceive that God moves in the order time-space-matter-mind. The consequence of the movement of the mind of man in the universe is creative: the physical consequence of the habitation of the planet by man, to put it simply enough, is the constant adaptation of it to the needs of man. The movement of God in the order comprehended by time-space-matter-mind is the fundamental creative impulse in the universe.

It must now be said that the world of popular, post-Darwinian imagination does not exist and never has existed. Infinite time is an illusion. Infinite continuity is an illusion. There is neither continuity nor homogeneity in the universe but on the contrary organization and reality at different levels—at the level of matter, at the level of organism, at the level of spirit. The new intellectual task is to see this sharply and strongly. This new intellectual vision causes the notion of the human person, the formulator of it and in a degree the transcender of it all, to loom ever more hugely until it dwarfs for us the vertiginous cosmos. The unification of a discontinuous cosmos, the imparting of a meaning to it in the sense of the necessary relation between its parts, calls for a creative justification—for God. From a metaphysical examination, then, of certain important aspects of modern knowledge one may arrive without straining the evidence at the notion of a creative God who must also be eternal and transcendent since He exists in timelessness apart from His created universe. Quite simply one may say then that it is rather more rational to believe in God than not to believe. One may enjoy the irony of this situation, however, that in the view of our times rationality inheres in atheism and God is nothing but the invention of subjectivity.

Chapter Four

THE PERCEPTION OF REALITY

I

The examination of the findings of science so far made has been based broadly upon two assumptions, the first that there is a real objective world about which my senses tell me, and the second that there is a real Self in perceptual relation with it. Now it does not follow that either of these assumptions is true, and modern empiricism has doubts about the (simple) Self and idealism denies the existence of the objective world. With both hypotheses we must first of all deal before any arguments can be marshalled concerning the subjective experiences of the person. Philosophical idealism says that it is not true, or not proven, that there is an objective reality for the first and most obvious reason that all one can have awareness of is one's perceptions. These perceptions may be of events which we call mental (which take place entirely in the mind and are not dependent upon 'external' stimuli and of which a dream is an example), or of events which are physical, as that my corn hurts, or of events or objects 'outside' my mind and body, such as that I look out of my window now and see, not unexpectedly, that it is raining. Yet all these perceptions—the dream, the painful corn, the intimations of the Second Deluge—are events occurring in my mind. That is how I 'know' them. And as I do not ever know them for 'events-in-themselves' how can I be sure that they are not indeed all products of my mental being?

In its most absolute, or subjective form this is solipsism, the theory that my individual self is all that exists and that the persons and things appearing in it have no independent existence. 'In the case of absolute idealism', Whitehead writes, 'the world of nature is just one of the ideas, somehow differentiating the unity of the Absolute: in the case of pluralistic idealism'—

104

the less extreme variety—'involving monadic mentalities, this world is the greatest common measure of the various ideas which differentiate the various mental unities of the various monads.'[1] In either case it is by perception that we know all and—*esse est percipi* or *percipere*, being is being perceived or perceiving.

Idealism has the enormous intellectual advantage of unity. Professor A. A. Luce in *Berkeley's Immaterialism* points out how materialism, or 'matterism' as he describes it, has to contend with two separate orders of being, which Berkeley himself describes as 'a twofold existence of the objects of sense, the one *intelligible*, or in the mind, the other *real* and without the mind'. And Professor Luce shrewdly comments, 'This duplication of the world and of every single thing in it puts a palsy in the thinker's mind. He tries and tries again to consider sensible and material as existing side by side, like Humpty and Dumpty; he tries and tries again to consider the material as real and the sensible as unreal; both notions are too ridiculous for words.' The physicist who finds that his own investigations into the substantiality of matter lead him into a cul-de-sac where matter becomes so inexplicable that it is less real than a mathematical formula about it, or who finds that the order of the universe is comprehensible by *any* logical geometry, and therefore conforms, it appears, to the perceiving of the mind rather than to laws of its own is easily driven to the conclusion that all is idea or thought, and matter an illusion.

We come indeed by this route to the argument of Kant that the 'thing-in-itself' is unknowable and recall that Kant argues that space and time are so to speak properties of the mind—'*a priori* intuitions which are the condition of, and antecedent to all our knowledge of particular objects in space and time'. Space and time are therefore transcendently ideal: they are experiences of the mind, it is true, but not properties of objects perceived. Kant differentiates mental events in themselves as transcendental in origin and sensuous in origin. One cannot lodge all existence in the mind without lodging space and time there too, of course. Now I spoke of space and time as attributes of matter rather than as properties capable of existing independently of matter and against which, or in which, matter moves

[1] *Science and the Modern World.*

and has its being as fishes swim in water. Out of the argument of finite space and finite time came the conclusion of a creative universe in which time played the creative role. If one now moves a stage further and argues that space and time are *the properties of the mind* and have no independence of the mind—no more independence that that of perceived objects—then by a logical necessity the creative process itself is lodged within the human mind. The whole of reality now dwells in the mind of the perceiver. A monstrous egocentrism descends upon thought, as outrageous as the dualism Luce condemns as ridiculous.

We have three systems of thought from which to make choice, if we ignore for the moment the variations to which they are subject, and they are materialism, idealism, and dualism, and each carries with it considerable philosophical disadvantages. The grounds upon which a rejection of absolute idealism is to be made are not easy to elaborate, but if they are not made then the argument concerning the nature of subjective experience cannot proceed. If all is subjectivity then the contrast between objectivity and subjectivity is no more than formal.

One must first ask—When I say I am perceiving, what am I conscious of? The answer is that I experience my own mind, my own consciousness. This is my most real and immediate experience, perhaps my only experience. When I look at my hand, however, I am conscious of it as an object and at the same time *it* is sensible of the pen it holds. Considering my hand, my consciousness has a dual reality to grapple with. But I do not experience my mind as a *thing* in this way, I experience only its *contents*. It is as if I were to have a hand holding a pen but experienced not the articulating hand but only the pen, like the Invisible Man.

What are the contents? They consist of the mind's inner processes such as its oppositions and conflicts and ideas, and of a material body, and of an external world with which both mind and body are in relation. This twofold or even threefold nature of the mind's contents does not appear to be arbitrary. It seems to be determined simply because there are experiences coming from three or more sources: purely mental experiences, bodily experiences, and experiences of events external to body and mind. Without the power to differentiate between them there could only be undifferentiated reality. Or perhaps no experienced reality at all, because no means of handling it.

If I see a bus starting up and a man running towards it—that is the extent of my *visual* perception. My mind reflects on these two phenomena and relates them, and decides that the man is trying to catch the bus. As the man reaches the bus my mind enjoys another kind of experience—that of sympathy: I want him to catch the bus, and my muscles respond so that I feel in myself an echo of the physical striving of his body. My mind may be quite mistaken as to the proper reading of the phenomena, for having reached the bus the man may run past it to a fire alarm, and then my mind has to think again. All this may happen in the open street as a matter of present reality: or it may occur that I see this incident on the screen at the cinema, and, though aware of it as an illusion, yet go through the same mental and physical processes about it: or it may happen in a dream, and so belong to still another order of 'real' mental experience.

These examples help to illustrate that the consciousness I examine is a differentiated reality. It is in no sense a mind in which the phenomena are consistent or uniform in nature, or self-explanatory, any more than it is a mind unconscious of time. The idealist must admit that the mind, that which does the perceiving on which all turns, is *real*. Indeed, for him nothing else is. Now truthfully we do not merely mean that the mind is real, simply and solely in the sense of being a real instrument, we mean that it is also real in the sense that its contents are real, are real contents. We do not genuinely consider the mind as real in itself while continually experiencing *unreal* things. Let me put this difficult point another way—the *experiences*, not the *structure* of the mind constitute its reality. For we perceive nothing but the experiences. We have absolutely no consciousness of structure—of the mind like a glass holding 'thoughts' as the glass holds water. All consciousness is consciousness of mental *events*. But if the mental events are real because they are events I directly experience in my mind, is that not a prima-facie argument for considering *the content of those events as real*? Thus if it is real to say I perceive a tree, because perceiving is my reality, is it not also true to say that the contents of my perception must also be real, and if the content of my perception includes the phenomenon of a real external tree, then that tree is really external *in exactly the same degree that all mental events are real events.* And it is this appearing to be externally real which distinguishes certain mental events (the perception of a tree) from others (the dream of a tree). Reality cannot be reality at the same time that it is illusion of reality. What idealism so often seems to do is to ascribe one order of reality for the mental event *qua* event and another order of reality for its content—argues, that is to say, that the event is real, but some part of the content is imaginary. But that division is illusory, it is a formal device of the mind; all we know is the content, as direct experience. One cannot say, 'Yes, I experience or perceive an objective tree, and there really is a tree, but it is not objective', without destroying the whole foundation of knowledge.

This raises the problem of the differentiation of the experiences of my mind which, we say, knows three orders of events —mental, bodily, and external. If the contents of the mind are real, then this differentiation is real also. It is difficult to see how content and differentiation can be real, and not be 'reality', and still more difficult to see how content can be real and differentiation not. In a sense idealism tends to produce against its will a new *substance* called 'mind' or 'mental events' or 'perception'. It objectifies mind which then becomes a buffer between 'I' and 'reality'. It says in effect that I perceive my mind and my mind perceives something which it thinks is external reality but which is only its own processes.

The error arises with the idea of 'I perceiving my mind'. I do, indeed, perceive the mind, or at least its contents, when it is already in possession of them. That is to say that I can think of, or perceive, the contents, images, and associations which my mind has gathered in the course of its life. I can say to myself, 'Ah, yesterday I saw a swallow'. What I am then perceiving is not the swallow, but a memory of it and of my mental act in acquiring the memory. I look back on a picture of the past. But when I saw the swallow, I did not perceive *my mind* perceiving the swallow. There is no such act of separation as this implies in the immediacy of perception of external reality—despite all arguments about the mind in infinite recession perceiving itself —it is merely the tautology 'perception perceiving perceiving'. No, *I perceived the swallow.* That is the act, complete and direct.

'Consciousness cannot go behind itself', Wilhelm Dilthey has written. There is only 'I perceiving reality' or 'I perceiving the contents of my mind' or 'I perceiving my body', or all these together; there is never 'I perceiving my mind perceiving reality' or 'I perceiving my mind perceiving itself'.

One may urge too that the mind appears to be an erring mind. We know that from time to time we correct its errors and adjust our picture of reality with pain at error or pleasure at the discovery of the truth. A process of judgement of perceptions continually takes place. One must say that this, too, is a prima facie case for the adjustment of one reality to another reality, and not for the residence of the whole of reality in the one perceiving being for whom error can only be an unnecessary self-torment.

II

Idealism seems to raise more problems than it solves. For example, we have seen how a theory of knowledge becomes difficult for it. If one consents that all is idea in the mind of the perceiver then we have the perceiver carrying the world around in his head with him, as J. B. Watson said in connection with the behaviourist brain. All is there and, by implication, known. And it is *all* there, in such totality as it possesses. It cannot part be there, and part absent, part known, part unknown. It is difficult to see how therefore one could discover movement in the totality, whether in the form of change or of new facts, save by the assumption of the changing self bringing new facts into existence—that is to say still further differentiating its own being. And one has to ask why this should occur and with the illusion of occurring about an order independent of the mind.

No small confusion arises because the totality is so consistently imagined to be what is *visually* held in the mind. The visual image has that kind of nature which makes it easy to think of it in two ways—either as a real thing standing out in space, or as a portion of the total perception of the mind. The materialist makes the first assumption and the idealist the second. Let us accept for a moment, to illustrate this point, that there is a chimney pot standing out there in space, beyond me, beyond my room. The chimney pot and my image of it seem one and the same thing—though one is, in the terms Professor Luce ridicules, real, and the other only an image. In visual images we do tend, however, to accept a complete identity. But that is not so indeed, for then we should have to accept that when there is a fog and the chimney pot is obscured—no rare occurrence— there is no chimney pot. Or imagine an air-raid siren. I hear the siren at night, when the siren itself is invisible. Or I hear it in the daytime at the back of the house, when it is also invisible to me. I do not imagine the *sound* of the siren to be the siren as I imagine the *sight* of it to be. I tell myself that a noise I hear is produced by something I have seen, but never that a sight is produced by something that I have heard.

William McDougall makes an acute analysis of this point in his *Outline of Psychology*: 'For, when we hear the stroke of a bell or the humming of an engine, no one would be so foolish as to maintain deliberately that the sensory experience is the bell or the engine; or that the odour of a skunk is the skunk; or that the warmth we feel on approaching the fire (or on going out into the sunshine) is the fire (or is the sun). In all these cases *the sensory quality of experience resulting from the sense-stimulation is clearly not the physical object itself, but only a sign of it, an occasion for our thinking of the object; it is a sign of the presence of the object, a sign which may suggest it to the mind, or may set us thinking of it.* It is seldom that a simple sensory quality suffices to determine us to perceive, or to enable us to recognize, a physical object.'

Martin Buber speaks of the genesis of the hegemony of the visual sense over other senses as that 'which appears among the Greeks for the first time, as a tremendous new factor in the history of the human spirit, the very hegemony which enabled them to live a life derived from *images* and to base a culture on the forming of images [and which] holds good in their philosophy as well. . . . But it is not before Aristotle that the visual image of the universe is realized in unsurpassable clarity as a universe of *things*, and now man is a thing among these things of the universe, an objectively comprehensible species beside other species. . . .'[2]

Even the idealist acknowledges the existence within his field of perception of an elaborate apparatus for perceiving. It

[2] *Between Man and Man* (1947).

consists of sense organs linked by intricate chains of nerve cells to local centres and to the brain. Not every received impulse is communicated to the brain: there are autonomous centres in the spinal column capable of dealing with local impulses— especially those which arise from such self-governing functions of the body as the circulation of the blood. This system is intimately linked with that which carries impulses or instructions to the organs of the body. Here then we have a delicate instrument *within* our perception. By a variety of means—touch, taste, smell, sight, hearing—it receives a bombardment of sensations and secures the adjustment of the body to them. Moreover it is a selective instrument, as we have already seen. Not all impulses are received, or registered. To the whole of external reality the body does not respond, and what it does respond to are not the things themselves, but *signs* of the things from which it builds up as best it can a picture of reality, like an aeroplane flying by instruments through fog. Assuming the existence of external 'things' it is a picture of them which lacks completion by reason of two facts—that it does not respond to all impulses, and it receives in any case signs and not the things themselves. The total reality which results is a personal structure. To this degree the subjective idealists are right. But the *sense* of this complicated system would seem to be a personal picture constructed of a reality with which the mind and the senses are grappling and which may therefore be assumed to have an existence independent of my perception. And the fact that the totality we experience is deliberately limited by our sensory apparatus, but is open to the utmost analysis and systematization by the mind, suggests that its very limitations are designed to produce for us the most *real* picture of reality—as the painter gives us in a few broad strokes a picture of the essentials of a scene which better tells us what is there than if he were to attempt to include every detail.

I must state as a belief what is probably not susceptible of a logical proof, though it is the primary impression of my direct experience, that the world contained in my consciousness is a real world, that it is not mere consciousness *in vacuo* 'thinking-up' a world to demonstrate its own existence, but just in this simple sense that consciousness has reality, what it is conscious of has reality too, and if that reality contains the appearance of objects external to me, there must be a real state of externality to give rise to this idea in relation to the objects of which one is aware. Unless this is so, there is a sense in which mental phenomena are pointless, and the things of experience—the tree, the sky, the London Transport omnibus—are pointless, and the struggle externally with nature and internally with conscience are pointless. Why should what is a unity impose these sufferings upon itself and suffer for the unreal and unnecessary the sensation of the real and inevitable, even the tragic?

III

Now with the notion of monadic idealism there is inevitably less to reject. The independence of a multitude of 'ideas' of the universe arising from 'perceiving minds' involves the acceptance of that 'reality' which is common to them all. Between such minds a spiritual correspondence is possible and so far nothing is denied of that native and uncritical experience with which all thinking must begin. To the general argument of immaterialism, which is not to be accepted as the same as idealism, it is more difficult to make resistance. For immaterialism does not necessarily say that all is idea in the mind of the perceiver; it simply says that the argument that there is matter and mind, the argument of duality, is not tenable. There is no 'matter' as opposed to mind: all reality is the same kind of 'stuff', is perceptual reality. It is upon this point that Professor Luce defends Bishop Berkeley. There is not material reality but a sensible reality, but that reality is real, not notional. It is not intermittent with my acts of perception but is perceived by other spirits and all is perceived by the mind of God. 'For though we hold indeed the objects of the sense to be nothing else but ideas which cannot exist unperceived; yet we may not hence conclude that they have no existence except only while they are perceived by us, since there may be some other spirit that perceives them though we do not. Wherever bodies are said to have no existence without the mind, I would not be understood to mean this or that particular mind, but all minds whatsoever.'

Such immaterialism as this—which seems an afterthought, as much as anything else, on Bishop Berkeley's part—is not hostile to the idea of a 'self' and a 'not self' and indeed it demands 'subject' and 'object', 'perceiver' and 'that-which-is-perceived'; it demands (or appears to, for on this point it is ambiguous) an inner reality corresponding to an outer reality, or a total, differentiated reality of which one's own is a knowing, but subordinate part.

Yet something is begged—the nature of *being*. In the common-sense view perception is a relation, and reality cannot of its nature lie solely in the relation. What must be primary to the relation are the things which can be related. For God to 'be' in so far as He is perceived makes Him conditional on the perception of others. For His creation to be real only in the degree that it is perceived makes it a conditional, a projected reality sans essence of its own. It is useful to take a common-sense view and to say that though we do not know any being which cannot be perceived, nevertheless we should not even know perception were there nothing upon which it could be exercised. Perception is a kind of affinity. If we accept an outer reality and say that we perceive it, we are saying that we are in contact with something which has sufficient affinity to us to 'register'. And affinities, like perception, are 'between' relations, they are states which exist between things. Being must be primary, must precede and be the condition of perception. If one is going to say that being is something else—for example that it is not substantial—one ought not, despite Berkeley, to say that it is a relation, *esse est percipi* or *percipere*. It might well be argued that being is the ultimate about which nothing can be predicated except that it *is*, the more especially if we think of the reality which physics perceives as the extension of 'something' in space and the movement of 'something' in time. The 'something' which is expressed in this way is in itself apparently unknowable. And towards the Kantian conclusion of the unknowability of things in themselves modern physics tends to move. Being is then the ultimate, the 'beyond', the ground—of which what we call reality is what we are able to perceive of it, and this in its way produces another monism—of a universal being or substance somehow differentiated. For Spinoza there was only one substance, God or Nature, and individuals or persons he argued were parts or aspects of that universal whole. Such universal stuff or substance must of necessity be common both to the perceiving Self and that which is perceived. Perception is the apprehension of one by the other. All possess the same kind of reality and the separateness of the person or individual from the objective world must be in some degree illusory, for the same Being is poured into both. *Una eademque res, sed duobis modis expressa.*

Modern physics, not unnaturally, tends to assume that since the 'something' which lies beyond the events it observes is not to be known and that since all that is perceived are events, then there is no cause to assume the existence of any Spinozian ground or being or stuff. If what is observed are events, events are all. It is of the same order as the behaviourist argument already examined that since all that is experienced are stimuli which produce responses, *stimulus-response* is the formula for the reality of behaviour, and that to assume self, consciousness, will, and instinct is as old-fashioned as assuming entelechies and ethers to explain what you do not know and cannot guess. The empiricists in philosophy follow them.

Bertrand Russell writes[1] that '"Substance", in fact, is merely a convenient way of collecting events into bundles. What can we know about Mr. Smith? When we look at him we see a pattern of colours; when we listen to him talking, we hear a series of sounds. We believe that, like us, he has thoughts and feelings. But what is Mr. Smith apart from all these occurrences? A mere imaginary hook, from which the occurrences are supposed to hang. They have in fact no need of a hook, any more than the earth needs an elephant to rest upon.'

He pursues this extraordinary argument about the reality of substance (it seems to me more an argument about the meaning of experiences) in his stimulating *History* from time to time, arguing that he would define matter 'as what satisfies the equations of physics' and that if there is no satisfying them then either physics or the concept 'matter' is mistaken. Matter, he says, will have to be a logical construction. A mind 'must be some group or structure of events'.[2]

He finds Hume's repudiation of the Self of great importance. He goes a long way with him and even declares that 'all

[1] *History of Western Philosophy.*   [2] Ibid.

psychological knowledge can be stated without introducing the "Self"'. The Self is nothing but a bundle of perceptions—it is not a 'thing' in any generally understood sense of the word. Now a generally understood sense of the word *thing* is of something substantially existing, and so the Self is not substantially in existence. Bertrand Russell finds the argument that the Self is only a bundle of perceptions so overwhelming as to make it impossible for the Self to enter into any part of our knowledge. This conclusion, he remarks, is of importance in metaphysics, theology, and the analysis of knowledge, since it abolishes substance and soul and shows that the categories of subject and object are not fundamental.[1]

It is perhaps not surprising that Bertrand Russell has remarked elsewhere that he has never been able to understand why existence should be preferred to non-existence.

The principal objection to idealism in common sense is that in ordinary experience—and the most extravagant philosophical systems seek to justify themselves upon the basis of ordinary experience—it is not true that perceiving is the same as being. There is no lived monism of experience: on the contrary, there are substantial pluralities. And the empirical argument of the non-existence of substance and the non-existence of Self belong to the same order of the belittlement of lived experiences as idealism. The world of the common man and the world of the empiricism of Bertrand Russell do not belong together, for the simple reason that there can be no *man* in Bertrand Russell's universe but only equations with which matter has to agree or so much the worse for matter.

It is as necessary to demolish the position he occupies as to escape the impasse of idealism. Indeed there is little fundamental difference between the two positions—for idealism says that all is idea, and Bertrand Russell that all is events. The sub-

[1] Ibid. 'It does not follow that there is no simple Self; it only follows that we cannot know whether there is or not, and that the Self, except as a "bundle" of perceptions, cannot enter into any part of our knowledge. This conclusion is important in metaphysics, as getting rid of the last surviving use of "substance". It is important in theology, as abolishing all supposed knowledge of the "soul". It is important in the analysis of knowledge, since it shows that the category of subject and object is not fundamental. In this matter of the ego Hume made an important advance on Berkeley.' This paragraph is preceded by the acknowledgement that 'any thoroughgoing empiricist must agree with Hume' that the Self can be nothing but a bundle of perceptions, etc.

stantial difference would appear to be that ideas belong to a person or to God, but that events belong to no one: they are neutral or impersonal, so much so that one cannot even connect them to a substance to which they occur any more than in idealism one can connect perceptions with objects which provoke them.

However, Bertrand Russell does not mean that all is illusion. In place of the substantial Mr. Smith which we are mistaken enough to imagine exists there are at least the *events* which stand for what we believe we experience as Mr. Smith. The events really occur, and they are real events. All that we have then is the negative proposition that mind and body are not *correctly* described as substance, a lame conclusion, for it leaves Mr. Smith exactly where he was before the philosophers began to abolish him, real but inexpressible. This is marking time furiously in order to give the impression of walking fast.

The events theory is consummately vague. It begins with the proposition that one cannot know substances apart from their properties, and that therefore what you really know are properties, and the properties are not the substance. There is no substance, therefore, only properties, and modern physics tends to show properties as series of events. We cannot therefore say that matter is, or even events *are*, only that something happens. But some*thing* imports the illegal notion of substantiality which has just been outlawed, that there is a *thing* to which events occur. Therefore all that we may say is that *happenings* happen. Yet remembering Schrödinger's 'waves of probability' and the fear that the constructs of the physicists might be taking place only in their heads, we should add the necessary note of dubiety and say 'happen happenings happen'. This is realism.

If we remain faithful to lived experience, the theory of nonsubstantiality has another oddity. It is that we know quite well what we mean by substantiality. It is rather like that definition of a solid as something which offers resistance to a deforming force. Substantiality is a universally known and understood experience where such concepts as soul, being, knowledge, and logic are not. I am quite certain in daily experience that a baby or even a fish encounters a substantiality like my own. I am able to infer that the fish distinguishes between the substantiality of land, water, and air and that man experiences many more degrees of it. They are at the root of his relationships with nature as the resistance of other wills is at the root of his relationships with persons. He discovers land that supports him, the current against which he cannot swim, the water on which he may not walk short of a miracle, the air which will not bear him up, the gale which blows him over, the avalanche which destroys him. If one considers, not philosophically but practically, that against which his energy is constantly pitted in his material environment, it is indeed its substantiality. The sweat of the reaper, the sinew of the miner, the exhaustion of the trawler-man, the fatigue of the housewife are called forth by just this obduracy of things. Did man's environment not oppose what he experiences as substantiality to his sweat all things might flow by the act of willing. If we assume that all is *events* to which no substance can be attributed, the problem is to account for the experience of substantiality—or to explain it—in any non-substantial universe. Either we must make this effort or simply exchange the term substance for another which means precisely the same but sounds different.

Now we have the situation of a mind-body A without substance and a material environment B without substance, and into the relationship between them the experience *substance* enters. This is strictly miraculous if by miraculous we mean that what could not exist, exists, and that what could not occur nevertheless occurs. If there is a man without an apple living in a universe without apples and he eats an apple, this is a miracle. For the experience of substantiality to intervene between two non-substantial events is a miracle. It is useless to retort that the concept energy could account for all that the concept substance possesses. If that is so one has immediately to account for the experience of substantiality encountered in energy.

The more logical one's proof of insubstantiality, the more miraculous becomes the experience of substantiality. The more clear it becomes that we can abolish the Self of Mr. Smith, the more wonderful does it become that we ever managed to imagine that he had one. Why indeed should I embark upon the exercise of inventing a Mr. Smith as a hook on which to hang the bundle of events which goes in place of him? And why should I do this in such detail and continuity that I can distinguish one Mr.

Smith from a score of others, to say nothing of the Browns, Robinsons, and Magillicuddies, and believe that he is a person so real that I know what will grieve or rejoice him, and can myself suffer and rejoice with him. *Where* does all this come from so miraculously if Mr. Smith really does not exist? *Is it possible that the fact that there are signs, or events, signifying Mr. Smith means that there is a Mr. Smith making signs?*

Leigh Hunt wrote:

> Jenny kiss'd me when we met,
>   Jumping from the chair she sat in;
> Time, you thief, who love to get
>   Sweets into your list, put that in!

What did *I* experience of that? Nothing. Jenny, I am sorry to say, did not jump from the chair and kiss me. This pleasant event happened to someone else long ago dead. How do I know what happened? Was I present? No. Has someone who was an eye-witness communicated this to me by speech? No. I know of this event only because on the page in front of me are these signs—

> Jenny kiss'd me when we met,
>   Jumping from the chair she sat in, etc.

They are angular, cramped, and formal devices in black on white paper and as matters of direct experience absolutely nothing else. They are not even pictograms: 'Jenny' does not, I hope, look like the living Jenny, nor does 'chair' look like anything one can sit upon. But they are also *signs* and through them in their role as signs I construct a reality otherwise utterly closed to me and which, though not a matter of direct personal experience, is accepted by me as possessing, or having possessed, a reality as real as that of my direct experiences. The reality I construct is the recollection in the mind of a poet growing old of a tender relationship with a child. The manner in which he chooses to communicate to me this happy incident enables me to reconstruct it in my own mind in some of its original warmth and intimacy. But only because we are agreed on common symbols, for I repeat that all I experience directly is this black and white device on paper beginning:

> Jenny kiss'd me when we met.

It is made ludicrously patent that the symbols in themselves are nothing without prior agreement about them if I now write:

CO BESOSO PASOJE PTOROS
CO ES ON HAMA PASOJE BOAÑ.

Whether the reader knows the origin of this couplet or not, it is certain to be without rational meaning for him, for it was intended by its author to be meaningless. It is a remnant of that poetic secret language which Stefan George invented as a boy to convey a richness of sound denied to him in German and which as a mature writer he uses to communicate the alien incantation of a barbaric and intoxicating anthem out of the past:

> Süss und befeuernd wie Attikas choros
> Ueber die hügel und inseln klang:
> CO BESOSO PASOJE PTOROS
> CO ES ON HAMA PASOJE BOAÑ.[1]

of which the beauty would be spoilt were meaning to be attached to it. This, however, is by the way, the important point to be made is that the signs in themselves have only the meaning that is attached to them by the mind of man. It matters not that the meaning of language is arbitrary (as that one man can have many symbols to represent him) and that the gestures of Mr. Smith are not arbitrary in the same sense (he cannot use the expression for grief as a substitute for the expression for joy) for the kernel of the argument is that reality is really communicated by signs. *It is of the nature of human beings to construct reality out of the signs of it which are given to them. And signs might stand as a synonym for events in this context.* One must go on to ask which is the *reality*—the tangible, visible signs on paper or the experience, invisible and intangible to me, for which they stand? In the case of Mr. Smith, which is the reality—the signs or expressions, or the sign-maker?

If one persists that there is no Mr. Smith simply because all

[1] From Stefan George's *Urspruenge*. Carol Valhope and Ernest Morwitz's translation of it (in Stefan George's *Poems*, 1944) runs:

> Sweet and inciting as Attica's chorus
> Over the hills and the islands flung:
> Co Besoso, etc.

one has of him are signs and he is not to be discovered immanent in one, assertions of the most profound philosophical
importance are being made—and nonsense of the most socially
dangerous sort is being talked. It is worth saying, I think,
though a digression, that one cannot defend Mr. Smith from
the consequences of tyranny and oppression, or encourage him
to virtue, to creative and responsible acts, and tell him at the
same time that he does not exist, but is simply a hook upon
which it is convenient to hang certain events. Before long it is
not the events which are hanging upon the hook, but Mr. Smith.

Just in the same way that there is not an amorphous flux of
organic matter, but only organisms, which are individual lives,
so there is not a flux of events or perceptions at large, but only
the presence of perceptions in relation to unique and quite
separate cores of personality. Despite Bertrand Russell's assertion that 'There is no reason why every event should belong
to a group of one kind or the other, and there is no reason why
some events should not belong to both groups; therefore some
events may be neither mental nor material, and other events
may be both'[1]—there is just no knowledge of events occurring
out in the blue. If indeed he means that events can take place in
independence of substances or structures or groups and that
perceptions can take place without a perceiver or a perceived
then we have indeed reached the final metaphysical chaos.

The contrary assertion has to be roundly made that there is
not in personal experience anything more real or immediate
than the consciousness of Self, and so far from psychological
experience being explicable without the conception of Self, no
psychological experience has any meaning whatsoever apart
from this term.

The argument that matter is a structure and/or succession of
events is an argument for a succession of incidents or occurrences without participants; the argument that the Self is a
bundle of perceptions is an argument that it consists of relations,
for perception is a relation. Neither argument can be accepted
as it stands, certainly not without strict inquiry into the significance of the terms 'structure' and 'group' in relation to
matter, and 'bundle' in relation to mind, all of which point
to the acceptance of a unifying principle underlying events and

[1] *History of Western Philosophy.*

giving meaning to them. Are they not simply synonyms either for 'substance' or for 'person'? Much of what is rejected in substance—the idea of a firm structure, for example—is smuggled into the argument by these terms, which Bertrand Russell frequently repeats. The charge that we misunderstand the basic nature of mind, matter and person, or that we are probably for ever incapable of understanding them properly, must be allowed to stand. But that does not oblige us to deny their existence. Should we do so nevertheless we are brought face to face once again with the philosophical *reductio ad desperandum* of our times. It is probably no accident that Bertrand Russell sees progress and hope for philosophy in the field of syntactical exactitude but deplores its union with affirmations concerning the nature and destiny of man. What has no existence has, of course, neither nature nor destiny.

I must conclude this chapter by laying emphasis once again upon the unique wholes which do in fact constitute our immediate experiences of organisms. If one says that *really* these wholes do not exist, either in their mental or material being, one cannot stand there but must go on to explain why the illusion of them should be so powerful. One is under exactly the same obligation in relation to the Self. The more successfully it is demonstrated to be illusion, the more urgent it becomes to explain why it is at the heart of all our experiences and that to which they *belong*. The rise of subjective schools of religion and philosophy—'subjective madness', laments Bertrand Russell—is due to the failure of empiricist arguments to do anything save annihilate immediate experience.

The annihilation is only theoretical fortunately. The lived experience remains and at the centre of it the strange and important being which we call a person emerges. The more abstract thought becomes, the higher must grow the consciousness of the experiencing person. The logical success of empiricism compels its dismissal. For if indeed it cannot account for the most central fact of existence it must contain a serious fallacy. It is a fallacy that can never be discovered by logical analysis, any more than one can hope to disprove the world green by examining it with green glasses, but it may be discovered if one turns back to lived experience and asks what this tells us. Since it gives us subjective experience of the Self—a self known only in inwardness—the next most necessary step is an examinatio.. of the nature of inwardness.

Before we proceed to that, of course, the observation must be made that we do not experience 'person' or 'subjectivity' as substance. Side by side with the experience of the substantial world is the experience of an insubstantial world. I experience my Self as something more than my body, for it is able to observe and experience my body. The events which occur in my mind may occur in relation to substances, whether of my body or of objects, but they may happen purely in relation to themselves, that is in their insubstantial mental form, as when I work out in my head a mathematical equation, think out an argument or enjoy a dream. My body exists always in immediacy, in this moment. There is no such thing as my body carrying its past material along with it. What it is, it is only as it is now. Its rejected or used-up atoms and molecules are so completely severed from it that they do not belong to the body any more, and can no more be recalled than the breath which I exhale at this moment. But this is not the case with the mind, which carries all its past experiences along with it—certainly all its significant past experiences. The hypothesis of the unconscious is of the theoretical availability of all mental events: nothing is discarded. Some inner unconscious instrumentality makes all available for my mind as it is required, though not in the pristine accuracy of the original experience. There is an element of distortion and suppression, even of spoiling, in the remembered experiences which yet does not prevent recognition. If I am asked—'Do you remember the dog we had which died?' then my memory calls up two figures. I reply, 'I remember two.' Then, if I am told, 'The one we called Paddy', I know which is which though I do not see Paddy as clearly as in life. From this point I may pursue deliberately or accidentally all my associations with Paddy and explore a tract of experiences believed forgotten but which obviously my mind has carried along with it for thirty years. If one were to ask for a physical equivalent to this it could only be the impossible hypothesis of my body refusing to discard a single atom which had ever become organically associated with it, and so growing to a stupendous size. But my mind, being insubstantial, has no difficulty in carrying the whole of its past along with it. It would, however, be inconvenienced by the act of carrying it along in consciousness. That it should nevertheless carry its past along in *unconsciousness* is even more remarkable, and it suggests how little indeed we know about it. Yet this is not the end. Unerringly, out of all past experiences, the *right* one I search for is produced. Upon its production it is *recognized* as right. What do we mean by *right* and *recognition* here? 'Do you remember Tom?' Immediately a picture of Tom springs to my mind. The rightness of it is never in question. In complicated political and philosophical theories the acts of the mind are even more involved. Intricate judgements are formed upon the basis of an assembly of experiences of all kinds over a lifetime. *One is compelled to recognize the existence of an understanding and controlling power standing behind the more conscious acts of knowing.* It is as though this knowing or understanding power, which silently summons up the right picture for 'me' to recognize, needs to carry along with it all accumulated experience and so to transcend time. Hans Driesch has called it the soul. 'There is only one concept in normal psychology which is quite final: *My ordered and ordering unconscious soul.*'[1]

Let us be quite clear as to where we have arrived, for it is vital to the whole argument of this book. We have arrived at the idea of a reality standing behind the reality signalled to us by our senses. We have arrived at the idea of an invisible and intangible reality which is superior to the visible and tangible one. And we have come to this point *without* the destruction of the reality of the immediately experienced material world. We are at the portal of pure spirit.

[1] *The Crisis in Psychology* (1925).

2

THE NATURE OF SUBJECTIVITY

Chapter Five

KNOWING AND UNDERSTANDING

I

When Job cried aloud in his misery 'Why didst thou ever take me from the womb? Why could I not have died there in the dark?' he is answered, after the moral consolations of his friends have failed, by the most glorious rhapsody concerning the majesty of God.

Whereupon are the foundations thereof fastened? or who laid the corner stone thereof;
When the morning stars sang together, and all the sons of God shouted for joy?

.   .   .   .   .

Canst thou bind the sweet influences of Pleiades, or loose the bands of Orion?
Canst thou bring forth Mazaroth in his season? or canst thou guide Arcturus with his sons?
Knowest thou the ordinances of Heaven? canst thou set the dominion thereof in the earth?

Look at Me, the Lord says, confront Me like a man. Regard My majesty and omnipotence, My unfailing presence in creation and be silenced. Why darken My design with a cloud of thoughtless words? It is poetry of such breath-taking elan as never to have been equalled since, and Job is hushed by it, his complaining ego is humbled. Yet it is strictly no answer to his questions (save in the sense that all poetry by which we transcend our iron egotisms is an answer) for it demands of him that he shall see God working through creation with a poet's eye— as Wordsworth did—as something so sublime and aesthetically satisfying, so full of wonder and mystery that the troubles of one brief individual man become of little account.

Yet what concerned Job was an inner conflict, not an external glory. The tension of his inner disharmony was made the more unbearable by that glory. He was ill and afflicted, and neither morally nor aesthetically a pleasant sight and the very majesty of God was therefore an affront. For if his physical misery and spiritual despair were the consequences of the glory of God—then 'How is a man to get his rights from God?' he is forced to demand. What is *his* share of the glory?

Why does God give sufferers to light, and life to men in bitter despair?

This lamentation corresponds ill with the miraculous choir of creation worshipping its Creator in which Job is asked to join. So the questions of Job are begged until the New Testament answers them by deeds. They are our own questions, too, and they rise spontaneously in us from the experiences of life. They remain unanswered by all efforts to construct God out of nature. This is not to say that the natural world is of no significance, or that it is alien to, or reveals nothing of God, or that His presence is not to be found there, but that nature is impersonal and man is a person, and the impersonal, natural God cannot answer the cries of Job or of anyone else concerning his personal afflictions.

One can decipher, in the natural world, plan and organization and direction. In the atomic world of the physicist (assuming it to be more than subjective) construed in terms of forces, waves, geometrical patterns, and mathematical formulae, one reads an aesthetic majesty to which the unknown poet of Job would undoubtedly have paid tribute too, had he known of them. From the miraculous nature and organization of living things, the same aesthetic delight can be derived. One cannot consider the interlocked, created whole without a sense of wonder that the access of knowledge increases rather than diminishes. From such aesthetic experiences it is easy enough to pass to pantheism, as Goethe and Wordsworth did.

God is in nature:

—In which all beings live with God, themselves
Are God, existing in the mighty whole,
As indistinguishable as the cloudless East
At noon is from the cloudless West, when all
The hemisphere is one cerulean blue

or else the universe is an organic whole from which God is emerging. Yet in the loftiest Hegelian idealism the nature of God is lost in the monism it establishes. In permeation He loses identity. In the unity which any such monism establishes God has to be all, the misery as well as the glory, the evil as well as the good, or He has to be nothing at all. And it is quite logical, therefore, to discard Him in favour of an abstract principle, in favour of a *process*.

The physical weight and spatial immensity of the universe (that material pressure of the 'gross and carnal'[1] of which science has made men so conscious) caused materialists and idealists alike to believe that nature is all, and that if there is God, He is finally to be found embodied in it, and presently to be made known in its forms and laws. But the rub is that such a God is unreachable and immovable by the fact of dispersal throughout nature. He is essentially inert. Even to call him the Source, the Fount, the Frame, the Form does not mean that one can make Him *responsible*, for responsibility is a property which belongs to organisms and to persons in the degree to which they are capable of action and decision in the sphere of freedom.

One has to seek the meaning of God as *person*, and in relation to human *personality*. Our analysis of theories of the natural world has driven us more and more to examine the mystery of the person, and the mystery of God cannot be severed from it. Martin Buber has asserted unequivocally that 'God cannot be inferred in anything—in nature, say, as its author, or in history as its master, or in the subject as the self that is thought in it. Something else is not "given" and God then elicited from it; but God is the Being that is directly, most nearly, and lastingly, over against us, that may only be addressed, not expressed.'[2]

If this is not the whole truth, it is the necessary point of departure.

---

[1] Speaking of Hegelianism Dr. Hugh Ross Mackintosh wrote in *Types of Modern Theology* (1937): 'Absolutism has no love for unique persons. In its secret heart it feels that history essentially is gross and carnal.'

[2] *I and Thou*, English transl. by Ronald Gregor Smith (1937).

II

In that Atlantic of scientific thought and metaphysical speculation which occupied the first four chapters there has been no way by which God as a Person might be discovered by patient distillation and extraction as the Curies reduced radium salts with infinite labour from mountains of pitchblende. But the harder we stared into the mystery of externality, the more implacably we came up against the certainty of inner being. In the dark glass we began to divine our own face.

The affirmation of the Being of God implanted in the heart of Buber's transcendentalism *throws light upon the nature of human beings*. For they cannot be 'inferred' from something else. About them, too, 'something else is not "given"' in order that they may be elicited from it. They equally are 'addressed'. They are a matter of direct experience, though that experience is far different in nature from the experience of material things. They are, for all of us, the accepted reality which cushions us round and by which we begin to form our lives from birth, and which we normally accept without question, as the working biologist accepts that there is life and that the concept life is not capable of reduction into constituents.

If then we have to reject an attempt to 'construct' God from nature—though without the intention to alienate God and Nature, for 'God is not to be outlawed from His creation'—then we are compelled to look inward. What do we understand of the relationships of persons or beings? This is not so much a matter of the understanding of God at this moment, as of that which precedes it, of that approach to subjectivity which provokes us into another view of our sources of knowledge and understanding. Martin Buber has most sharply distinguished between what he calls the *I-It* relation and the *I-Thou* relation. For the moment I will simply say of this distinction that it implies that our knowledge of nature is *of a different order* from our knowledge of persons. We know natural things impersonally, as objects which exist beyond us and are impenetrable by us; but we do not know other persons with whom we are intimate in this way—we meet and address them, they live in us and we in them.

This clear intellectual distinction Buber makes, in that small work of his (so radiant with the love of God and which has had so marked an influence on our times) is curiously anticipated by one who said of himself that 'the possibility of living through religious experiences in my own person is narrowly circumscribed'—Wilhelm Dilthey, the German philosopher-historian to whose theories reference has already been made.[1] Because he realized that it was impossible to formulate our knowledge of *other beings* in the same manner as for *things*, Dilthey was led, following in the footsteps of Schleiermacher, to advance a philosophy of the understanding which can be summed up in his own words—'Die Natur erklaren wir: das Seelenleben verstehen wir' ('We *explain* nature: we *understand* mental (or spiritual) life').

He approached this problem from a rational standpoint, from the need to establish a genuine science of the human studies, a genuine psychology rather than one which laboured to fit human beings into the categories supplied by natural science. Of his work he wrote to his friend Peter Yorck that he felt himself 'moving in an unknown country' towards a new way of philosophizing, for he saw with clarity and argued with a cogency his times on the whole distrusted—for it had come to devote itself to the opposite solution—that the methods of natural science could not be applied to human studies. The 'units' of natural science were themselves hypothetical, they could not really be known or experienced or assumed to be final. The perceiving mind observed events in nature—events among things—and by such objective examination—this act of looking through the window at what was going on inside the room—made inferences as to the composition, structure, and

---

[1] Wilhelm Dilthey (1833–1911)—the humanist, philosopher-historian, biographer of Schleiermacher and one-time Professor of Philosophy at Basel. He attempted to construct a new methodology of human studies and his main works include *Einleitung in die Geisteswissenschaften* (1883), *Das Erlebnis und die Dichtung* (1905) *Das Wesen der Philosophie* (1907), *Der Aufbau der geschichtlichen Welt in der Geisteswissenschaften* (1910), *Die Typen der Weltanschauung* (1911).

His *Gesammelte Schriften*, the first nine volumes, were published between 1914 and 1936. The only book in the English language known to me is Professor H. A. Hodges', *Wilhelm Dilthey, An Introduction with Selected Passages* (1944). My own debt to this work is patent in the pages which follow, but as Wilhelm Dilthey is less known in this country than many German thinkers of lesser standing I would venture to say that English learning as a whole is greatly indebted to Professor Hodges.

laws of matter. But the knowledge of the units of human studies is of quite a different order, for the units *are* known, they are human minds of whose inner life we cannot be unaware, for it is exactly of the same order as our own.

I regard the tree, and what I come to know of the tree depends upon the extent and care of that regard. Through this act of observation I know the tree and can explain it, but I never understand it. I regard a person, but I see only—and in this Bertrand Russell is right—a series of disconnected expressions and actions—and these are externals which are only relevant in the degree that they enable me to understand that person from the inside, as if this other person were myself. I know the tree from the outside, I understand the person from the inside.

In human studies we are dealing with a range of experiences into which we can imaginatively enter, and by the act of entry influence or change our own being. Therefore to argue, as the optimistic positivism of Dilthey's times tended to do, that human nature and the human studies were to be understood and knowledge of them increased by an extension to them of the methodology of the natural sciences was to overlook this most vital distinction between 'knowing' things and 'understanding' beings.

Something occurs—this is clear enough already—in the act of understanding of another mind which is quite absent in the cognition of objects. A meeting of like and like, a recognition of like and like takes place. We witness an exchange, a converse between minds, absolutely alien to the events of the natural world, absolutely fundamental to human relations. In the meeting with another mind we know the laws to which it is subject, for the impulses and motives which move it are kindred to those we experience in our own mind. About this process Dilthey 'set speculative questions aside' and studied 'the process of sympathetic understanding soberly and scientifically'.[1] And I should grossly misrepresent him were I to attribute to him anything but the purest scientific motives. Yet his conclusions in effect transcend science if we mean by it what is understood in foundational sciences like physics—agreed concepts, strict laws, the experimental verification of hypotheses objectively demonstrable.

[1] Hodges, *Wilhelm Dilthey.*

KNOWING AND UNDERSTANDING

The *understanding* which Dilthey squarely opposes to mere knowing is, like that power to read a higher reality from a pattern of black and white marks on a page which has already been discussed, 'the process in which, from signs given outwardly to the senses, we know an inner reality' or 'the process in which from signs given to the senses we come to know a psychic reality whose manifestation they are. This understanding extends from the apprehension of a child's babble to that of *Hamlet* or the *Critique of Pure Reason*.'[1] The child's prattle and Hamlet's speeches, like the marks my pen makes on paper, are *expressions*. All the experiences of the human mind give rise to *expressions*. We know ourselves by expressing ourselves, and we observe the expressions of others and interpret them in the light of our own. If we see expressions of joy or grief upon another face, we do not argue that here is a special configuration of the face associated with certain events called human joy, or that here is a secretion from the tear-ducts associated with certain events called human grief. Such a conception of the knowledge of another's inner experience is monstrous to suppose. For we do not simply recognize another's joy or pain in the objective way that we watch a traffic light change from green to red, we *experience* it. Not as our own, though it may make us rejoice or suffer sometimes more acutely than our own, but as belonging without any doubt to another being compounded like us, and capable of the same experiences as we enjoy. We *relive*, says Dilthey, another's experience. It is mirrored in our minds by their expressions. In such acts of understanding the process of experiencing is reversed: in myself experiences give rise to expressions, in my understanding of others my observation of their expressions reflects in me their experiences. I have no difficulty in dissociating the two types of events—the reflection in me of someone else's experiences is bracketed-off (*Eingeklammert*).

Into another's being, then, we *project* ourselves. What we are saying to ourselves in observing their expressions is that if these expressions were mine I should be passing through such and such an experience. According to our interest and sympathy we are involved in the act of *reliving* the experience of another. This is the unmistakable purpose of *projection* into the life of

[1] Dilthey, *The Rise of Hermeneutics* (from Hodges).

another. But the means whereby we are able to do this are not limited to the actual immediate intercourse with other beings. The immediate expression is an objectification of an inner experience. Such objectifications can become or be made permanent, and about this I will have more to say presently. Suffice to say, at the moment, that our knowledge of human history is bound up with our interpretations of objectifications which have been given permanence, and, over a much longer period of activity than the purely scientific spirit has been manifested, men have been perfecting their arts of interpreting by poetry, art, myth, legend, sculpture, song, history, the inner spirit of their fellow-men. 'This art of interpretation has developed just as gradually, regularly, and slowly as, e.g., the art of questioning nature by experiment.'[1] 'The secret of the person invites us of its own accord to ever new and deeper attempts to understand. And in such understanding there is opened up the realm of individuals which embraces human beings and their creations. Herein lies the most characteristic service rendered by understanding to the human studies. Objective mind and the power of the individual together determine the world of mind. History rests on the understanding of both.'[2]

Following Dilthey, we find that what indeed we are conscious of in this meeting with other beings is a sense of their wholeness. We do not regard our friends and neighbours as bundles of faculties tied up with psychological string or as series of instincts pulled along like a string of sausages by a bulldog of a libido. The sense of the absoluteness of their being is always with us whatever we may feel of its quality or detect of the parts which constitute it. It is indeed 'the only intrinsic value that we can establish beyond doubt' and the human beings with whom we have relations take up 'a considerable space in our lives, in forms that are noble or mean, vulgar or foolish'. In living experience we do not break up the mind that confronts us, we are in contact with the totality upon which, we perceive, events and experiences are acting. We are faced with an indivisibility of being which made Dilthey declare that he was led 'to make

---

[1] Dilthey, *Rise of Hermeneutics* (from Hodges).
[2] Dilthey: from an essay *The Understanding of Other Persons and their Expressions* (from Hodges).

this whole man, in the full diversity of his powers, this willing, feeling, thinking being, the foundation for explaining even knowledge and its concepts . . . however much it may seem that knowledge weaves these its concepts only from the material of perception, imagination, and thought'.[1]

III

One has only to watch the growth of the consciousness of a baby to see how it develops, not as a dissociated group of appetites and impulses severally satisfied until, by a process of neuro-physiological conditioning, it is constructed into the illusion of an independent, thinking being, but as, from its very birth, from its first protesting cry, a person sharply cut off from all others. It is a being from its birth: it shows immediately will and feeling, and is shaken, startled into consciousness not by encountering first a breast to feed it, or a hand to control or a bosom to nurse it, or a body to move it from place to place, but by a leap, by coming with a suddenness which can be seen in its eyes upon awareness of other beings like itself and with whom a correspondence of feelings is possible. Often the presence of a mother beside the cot is sufficient to still a child's crying. 'I am not alone, I am not deserted', one may read in the child's face. 'These *other beings* are here.' Mothers and fathers, watching their infants, look first for the growth of this consciousness until it becomes a recognition of actual persons. By the fact that the 'understanding' child smiles or makes a gesture intended to evoke an answering sign—a process which a child does not make except in play to inanimate nature—we are brought to understand that the child is approaching that which it apprehends as essentially the same as its own being.

In *The Crisis in Psychology* Hans Driesch discussing the argument of Scheler that man has within him an innate capacity for the recognition of a *you*, that is of another being compounded like oneself, speaks somewhat in the manner of Dilthey of the strange human faculty for the understanding of the faces of

[1] Dilthey, *Introduction to Human Studies* (from Hodges).

other people and for the imitation of their expressions and gestures and argues that such faculties have by no means been studied to the extent they deserve.

He continues:

'It seems, in fact, as if the young human child, the real "baby", possesses the ability, firstly, to interpret the expression of the faces of other people with regard to the feelings they represent, and, secondly, to imitate in its own face what it has seen. Both abilities are quite wonderful and not very easy to explain by ordinary methods.

'The faculty of interpretation may be explained, however, in some such way as this: When the mother smiled the baby got something good; when she looked angry, it was, perhaps, beaten. But even this would not explain the introjection of a *feeling* into the mother.

'But the faculty of imitation is not even "explainable" in part. The baby has seen other faces smiling but never his own; yet it can imitate smiling, nay, quite specific movements of a face which it has seen, as for instance, rolling out the tongue, and pouting the mouth. And even if it had *seen* its own face smiling or rolling the tongue or pouting the mouth, how can it know how all this is motorially performed?'

The infant, we must say, is born into a world of like beings and this is the primary fact of its existence and development. The most important experiences by which the infant grows into a mature human being occur in the confluence of its mind with other minds. Dilthey speaks of the childhood self receiving nourishment from its earliest days from the world of objective mind. The arrangement of a room, the planning of a street or a square, 'the gestures and looks, movements and exclamations, words and sentences' which always confront it in the same form and bear the same meaning, in all these circumstances the child discovers the working of minds akin to its own, and in and through these things and the persons from which they emanate *it discovers itself*.

Martin Buber has written, 'The development of the soul in the child is inextricably bound up with that of the longing for the *Thou*, with the satisfaction and the disappointment of this longing, with the game of his experiments and the tragic seriousness of his perplexity.'[1] The child is roused from the sleep of his consciousness 'in the flash and counter-flash of meeting'.[2]

The Freudian theory of the development of a child makes the highest powers of its life appear in themselves pathological. For what happens according to this theory? The infant is involved in an agonizing emotional conflict with its parents— it has a libidinous attraction to one and is jealous of the other. It is forced to a violent act of distortion of its primitive instinctual loving self, it must repress and deny and distort itself, and out of this is said to come the higher powers of the mind (conscience, in particular), the origin of which is so mysterious.

There is at least a cogent argument that something quite different occurs, that the spirit is not repressed into existence but *called into existence* by the encounter with other beings and the dialogue which occurs between those other beings and the child. In another work[3] Martin Buber speaks of the child living in a world of things. And then suddenly the child begins to speak. 'How does the child tell what it tells? The only correct designation is *mythically*. It tells precisely as early man tells his myths which have become an inseperable unity composed from dream and waking sight, from experience and "fantasy" (but is fantasy not originally also a kind of experience?). *Then suddenly the spirit is there. . . . The child "has spirit" for the first time when it speaks; it has spirit because it wants to speak.*' The spirit is an almost miraculous happening in the intimate life of a group of persons.

The feral children of which history provides examples, those unfortunates abandoned or lost in infancy and suckled by wolves or bears or gazelles, and living like them an animal existence in caves or woods do not become human: they never properly awake from a deep animal sleep into a discovery of their humanity. The intelligent Mowgli is nothing but a charming fiction. The sordid reality is the little girl Kamala, of whom we have records, taken from a wolf cave with her younger sister when she was ten. When caught she was completely bestialized —she squatted on all fours, went naked, howled like a wolf in the night, ate carrion, and refused human company. At the end of seven years of human intercourse, that is, just before her

[1] *I and Thou.*   [2] Ibid.
[3] *Between Man and Man.* Italics mine in the last sentence.

death, she had learnt to walk upright and to refuse carrion, to speak with a limited vocabulary and to respond to human affection. She liked to wear frocks and wept when the children went without her to market. It is true that exposed children such as Kamala would have died without animal care and were suffered to exist only by the grace of some animal being which recognized likeness even across the void of species,[1] but when restored to their own kind they are never able to arrive at full stature because they have failed to discover themselves in the converse of truly like beings. Because of this deprivation they are destroyed. When caught, they can seldom recover. They go on all fours, they have no use for sex organs, their less-than-Freudian libido is directed to eating, drinking, sleeping, and escaping. They remind us of how little of our essential nature rests upon its material needs, upon water and earth, air and food, or even upon hereditary equipment, and how much is called into existence by the realization of ourselves in the minds and lives of others whose essential identity with our-selves constantly illuminates our inner being.[2] The peculiar

[1] In the conversion of animals into pets which abandon altogether their natural state and deny their impulses for the sake of the relationship of dependence which they have established with human beings we see the opposite and much more common process at work—the adoption of animals into a communion with human beings.

[2] *Note on Wild Children.*
Of the many authenticated cases one may note these:
1. Peter the Wild Boy of Hamelin who was brought to England by George I and became a popular 'show' and was educated by Dr. Arbuthnot.
2. Victor, the savage of Aveyron, who was brought up by the physician M. Itard who wrote a useful paper on him. Victor never learnt to say more than three words and was probably mentally deficient.
3. Mademoiselle Leblanc, captured in the eighteenth century at Soigny in north-east France was a girl of twelve or thirteen, clad in skins and armed with a club and able to give a good account of herself physically. It transpired that she had been living with another girl in the forest and that this girl had died. She was never reconciled to the confinement of human society and never lost the taste for blood, human or otherwise.
4. The frog-boy Stephen of Kapuar in Hungary whose effigy, shown in the act of swallowing a live frog, was to be found in the palace of the Esterhazys. Though caught and christened he escaped and took to the marshes and was never recaptured. He perhaps was nine or ten.
5. Kamala and Amala, brought up by the Rev. Singh in the Midranapore Mission between 1920–7. The story of Kamala is told in Arnold Gesell's *Wolf Child and Human Child* (1941), which is based on the Rev. Singh's diary and contains photographs of Kamala. Arnold Gesell's preface makes mention of a

horror which attaches to insanity and which cannot be removed simply by changing the name of the disease or of institutions for its cure, does not derive from ignorance or stupidity, or not from these alone, but from the severance of human intercourse which insanity produces. The truly insane is *incommunicado*.

In short, without other beings we are dwarfed and incomplete. We need to be in corporate and spiritual communion with them. But if we are not, that is not to say that we are aware of the nature of our loss, any more than the wild children seem to be. Is it not just so, then, of our relation to God?

In the correspondence with other minds we are limited in what we learn by the extent of our interest. The meeting is never absolute—in the language of Buber the *I-Thou* relation constantly becomes *I-It*. Yet in the full love of two human beings there are no intentional barriers for there is the desire, alas never completely to be fulfilled, for the merging, not simply the meeting of two beings. A process of mutual exploration and identification takes place which lifts the loving experience far out of the realm of physical acts, for even parting does not involve an absolute separation. The *presence* of the other is carried about in the human mind while ever the love endures, enriching and

---

complete study of some thirty-nine feral children in preparation by Professor Zingg of Denver University.

One may quote Dr. Thomas Jarrold's comment in *Education for the People* (1847): 'An animal, after a short interview with its species, owns a relation; but a deserted child, when captured, watches as earnestly, and with more perseverance, an opportunity to escape, than a bird shows when caught in a snare. So extinguished were Peter's faculties, that, in a long life, he never exchanged a sentiment, or acknowledged an obligation, or felt an affection, or sought an associate! His mind was shut to knowledge, and his heart to sympathy; the forest was his favourite home, and the twigs of trees his food. Leblanc, after some time spent in civilized society, displayed a thirst of blood not common to the most savage tribes of men, which desire she must have gained from the influence of her animal associates. To such cases nature has no parallel; no order besides of created beings manifests a like disposition.'

The degradation of human nature in feral children can be evaluated in two ways —the behaviourist interpretation would presumably be that the children received that kind of conditioning which made it improbable that they would ever break free of it and become conditioned to human society. Yet I would suggest that the alternative interpretation, of the failure to realize themselves in like beings, is the true one. As Dilthey has said the human being is incapable of realizing himself simply by his inward states—he needs the reflection of them in others to discover their meaning to himself.

fulfilling life despite absence, so that to fall out of love in the *company* of the loved one is a more desolating experience—a spiritual truncation—than to love and be parted. How true, at least, this is of first love which can be experienced as a consummation so intense as to make death preferable to life without it. This no one has better understood than Shakespeare in *Romeo and Juliet*.

I have already spoken of Dilthey's important argument about the objectification of expressions—the process of *fixing* of expressions, as the salts of the developer fix the transient impression of light upon the emulsion of a camera plate. For inward experiences do more than result in gestures, speech, and expressions of the body and face—they objectify themselves also in human institutions and products—in art, literature, science, laws, learning, industry, commodities, towns, homes, history, and so on. There is created round men and by men an environment with two aspects—there is the physical impress of the ideas and desires of men upon the form of things as in the manufacture of tools and implements, the building of homes and making of fields, and there is secondly the environment of signs which are fixed means of communication—letters, figures, symbols, sculptures, pictures and sounds whereby men interpret to each other their inner life, almost as surely as if they were in living contact with each other. The most immediate reality for men is that they find themselves not in a hostile cosmos, not in a world of nature against which they fight, but in a world already shaped for them by the human mind, and which begins almost at man's first breath to communicate with them. Nature and the cosmos are never experienced at first hand (at least in the first place) but always to begin with through the media provided by the man-shaped world.

Both aspects of the world *communicate* to men. Such communication is of the most extraordinary importance and the spiritual, or scriptural importance of art rests precisely upon its revelation of the nature of men and the inner and otherwise incommunicable processes of their being to each other. With Othello we suffer the pangs of jealousy, with Lady Macbeth our hopeless guilt grows, with Hamlet we endure humiliation and indecision, with Socrates we face the bowl of hemlock, with Christ and His disciples the Passion—because men *can* communicate their inner life and constantly do all in their power to extend and deepen the means of communication and in so doing permanently heighten human consciousness and understanding.

Dilthey speaks of reading Luther's letters and writings, and the history of the Reformation, and experiencing vicariously 'a religious process of such eruptive power, of such energy, in which the stake is life or death, that it lies beyond any possibility of personal experience for a man of our day', and thus man 'can live in imagination through many other existences. Before man limited by circumstances there open out strange beauties in the world, and tracts of life which he can never reach. To generalize —man, bound and determined by the reality of life, is set free not only by art—as has often been shown—but also through the understanding of history.'[1]

In the laws and institutions of our own and other lands we read men's motives, we discover what they value and what they disapprove. The slogans of parties, the causes of revolutions, the theories of history, the distribution of property, the doctrines of morality in other times or places reveal to us the minds of men of the same basic pattern as our own. We can comprehend them, and comprehend too where they fail and why they have to fail without ceasing to understand nevertheless why men accepted them and even died for them.

All this is placed in relief by Dilthey's *hermeneutic*, or theory of the understanding, as standing over against a mere epistemology, or theory of knowledge. Reference to this has already been made and there is no need to repeat the explanation of the weight that he attaches to the *Understanding (das Verstehen)*. *What needs emphasis at this point is that to him the act of knowing is performed by a limited part of the mind, but the act of understanding is the movement of the whole Self, of the whole powers of the Person.* Explanation (*erklaren*) is purely an intellectual process, but understanding demands the co-operation of all the powers of the mind or being—feeling, intuition, will, and so forth. In the act of understanding we begin with the whole, we are in contact with the system of the whole which is a living reality to us (*der uns lebendig gegeben ist*) and we seek to make any particular

[1] Dilthey, *The Understanding of Other Persons and their Expressions* (from Hodges).

part intelligible to us in terms of this given whole. No better simple explanation of this could be given than the attitude of a young child to the arrival of a new baby. Quite often it does not bother to inquire where the baby comes from, or is satisfied with a perfunctory explanation, especially if it has noted the arrival of babies in other parts of its environment. It has accepted, perhaps for a very long time, a whole human picture which includes *as a given part* the arrival of new babies.

In the function of knowing, the function of what Dilthey describes as the intellectuality of inner perception, the mind seizes upon the relevant aspects of particular events, abstracts those aspects and arranges and explains them before the totality to which they are, so to speak, summoned. This is not necessarily a process which takes place in that immediacy in which things are simply understood. It is often with extreme difficulty that the significant is singled out to be *known*. Quite often the events that we come eventually to know (in that we can describe, explain, or interpret them) are long past before we can undertake this. Yet when on reflection we do so, and we know them intellectually, we often know, too, that when they occurred they were nevertheless perfectly understood. 'We understand', in the great paradox of Dilthey, 'more than we know.' 'Understanding here can never be transmuted into rational comprehension.'

Confirmation is given to this by the modern subjective psychologies, for which Dilthey's work was in some ways a preparation. The whole argument of the presence of hidden motives in the unconscious is, of course, an attempt to say that some part of the being is aware of the circumstances of a situation and what it is fundamentally desired to do about it, and the act of knowing is either not accomplished at all or is wrongly accomplished—the knowing is achieved in such a fashion as to disguise or deny what is nevertheless perfectly understood somewhere. Psycho-analysis aims at the revelation of 'forgotten' circumstances and it is the whole point of such revelations that initially they were only too well understood and have somewhere remained so. Amongst much that is problematic or schematic in the subjective psychologies, this enlargement of the area of the understanding beyond the function of simple intellectual explanation must remain important.

Something, Dilthey says (in effect following Kant), quite extraordinary occurs in the inner lived experience which bears no resemblance to what takes place in inanimate nature. In the performance of an act of thought, a multitude of the most diverse inner facts and experiences is drawn together 'in the indivisible unity of function'. The supreme power of the mind is just this ability to knead into a synthesis the scattered and unrelated experiences it receives. We constantly experience combinations of facts within us, and we continually read 'combinations and connections' into the stimuli of the senses. The reasonable conclusion is to be drawn that there is *something* doing the combining and connecting, a given power of the mind. Experience is necessary to knowledge, but, in the words of Kant, 'though all knowledge begins with experience, it by no means follows that it arises out of experience'. There is to be found that pure ego or self, that inner unity or identity, without which no part of experience is cognizable.

Speaking of the whole composed of minds and bodies and 'each of which is a world', Dilthey says, 'indeed, the world is nowhere else but in the consciousness of such individuals. This immensity of a mind-body whole, in which in the last resort the immensity of nature is contained, can be illustrated by the analysis of the world of ideas, where from sensations and ideas an individual intuition is built up, which then, whatever wealth of elements it may comprise, enters as only one element into the conscious combination and separation of ideas.'[1]

IV

Dilthey succeeds in enlarging our conception of man. The human person is not to be understood as a pyramid, at the base of which is the blind instinctual self and at the summit of which we find the monarch reason enthroned. We might better picture the person as a dark and semi-transparent globe. A shifting point of light upon its surface would be reason or intellectuality: the area under the glow would be the part of the whole under conscious examination, but the real and indispensable

[1] Dilthey, *Introduction to Human Studies* (from Hodges).

totality would be the entire globe. There is a knowing function within an understanding whole.

Schleiermacher, before Dilthey, enlarged the nature of religious experience in the same way. And, of course, in doing so influenced Dilthey considerably. The eighteenth-century Goddess of Reason seemed implacably opposed to religious experience, to acts of faith and worship. In the light of reason many religious experiences appeared delusions or deceits. Many religious practices seemed indefensible superstitions or acts of plain idolatry for which no explanation could be found except the primitive darkness of minds under priestly influence. Organized churches appeared to be conspiracies to delude and defraud simple folk. All Protestant churches in the nineteenth century were themselves under the pressure of this critical tendency and not only joined themselves in the denunciation of 'superstitions' but sought to cleanse their own religious services of irrational procedures. Sacramental worship fell under suspicion or into desuetude, simply because it appeared to have no rational basis. Moral teaching was all.

In such an intellectual climate it was difficult to prove that religion was anything but a mistake, its power over man an inheritance from an infantile period out of which he was now growing. The future belonged not to irrational religious processes but to science and technics, to the task of increasing the domination of intellectual procedures over life and matter, and eventually over human society too, which was to be purged of all irrational, impulsive, and uncontrollable elements. At the very time, of course, that this thesis was being advanced intellectually it was being denied aesthetically, in the Romantic Movement. Schleiermacher was a romantic. The power of the Romantic Movement was eventually to penetrate philosophic and even scientific thinking, but that is another story. The point to be made is that in the nineteenth century, and often still to-day, human progress was regarded as the extension of rationality, as the heightening of the intellectuality of man's perception. The nihilistic revolt against the 'rationality' of history, of which Nietzsche and Sorel became the spokesmen, was not taken seriously until our time.

We are chastened to-day, after the eruption of powerful irrational movements in Western civilization, and attach less importance to this thesis of the extension of rationality. Certainly we find it difficult to believe in its inevitable growth. Indeed, the opposite theory has now become fashionable—that the advance of man's intellectuality at the expense of his instinctive life may produce a dangerous and explosive recoil in man and society. Freudian thinking is saturated with this feeling, that man belongs to forces other than those of his intellectuality.

The greatness of Schleiermacher (or so it appears to me[1]) is that at the time of the triumph of the arguments of enlightenment, when religion appeared to be quite without any intellectual basis and was to be equated only with ignorance, he prepared the way for the view that religious experience was a natural, an organic need, as much a part of man as any other admitted instinctive drive such as sex or self-preservation. And just as these other instinctive drives stood obviously apart from reason and morality, drawing their force from something which was prior to them, from life itself, so it could be argued that the religious urge of man sprang from a like source. Apprehension of the Divine was *an immediate experience*. Religion, which so many of its supporters insisted upon presenting to the world simply as organized morality, became by the arguments of Schleiermacher to be more than reason or morality, and it did not stand or fall by them. Religious experience flowered out of an inner being beyond the reach of rationality and was not to be plucked simply by taking thought.

'Of God himself no man can think', wrote the author of *The Cloud of Unknowing*. 'And therefore I would leave all that I can think and choose to my love that which I cannot think. For why; He may well be loved, but not thought. By love He may be gotten and holden; but by thought never.' The validity of mystical and intuitive experiences and acts of worship returned to theology through Schleiermacher. It began to be understood that, if this was not all that had to be said about religion, at least it could be conceded that the religious experience was a *valid* one, was at least something more than delusion.

It is the aspect of immediacy which Rudolf Otto develops in *Das Heilige* (*The Idea of the Holy*). He takes the concept of divina-

---

[1] The famous work in which he develops his thesis of the naturalness of religious experience is 'Addresses on Religion to Cultural Despisers', *Reden über die Religion* (1799).

tion which is at the core of Schleiermacher's theology and develops a new natural theology around the idea of the evolution of man's instinctive and direct apprehension of God. The God of Otto's non-rational theology is the majestic dreaded Being, the object of awe and holy fear. Awareness of the *mysterium tremendum* is, for Otto, the primary religious experience, one without necessary connection with the moral and intellectual elements of the Godhead, and indeed prior to them. It is by virtue of this inward power that we learn of God: discovery of His other attributes is a later experience. Though this Being is unknowable, it undoubtedly confronts us and before it we feel not merely sinful, but humbled, not only fallible, but profane, not simply beings, but creatures, abashed by our creatureliness.

God crushes us with His awful might and mystery and we cannot dissociate awe and dread of Him even from our love. This emerges powerfully from Otto's reasoning. Yet we long also to be taken up by God and to have His spirit breathed into us. This is the 'enthusiasm' of the ancients and the ecstasy of the mystics. The mystics 'smite upon that thick cloud of unknowing with the sharp dart of longing love'; they seek to be lost in the Presence, and in the intensity of such an effort the external world may be annihilated for them.

Now there are grave objections to 'natural', 'organic' theories of religious evolution. A religious 'evolution' carries with it the notion of inevitability. Without the effort of man or the grace of God there is a gradual exploration and realization of His Being. The inescapable intellectual destination of such a theory is Julian Huxley's *Religion without Revelation*, that is, religious experience as an end in itself, an end which does not require even a Godhead.

Yet when that has been said, what remains of the theories of man's natural awe and reverence before the Holy is not negligible, and is to be ignored only at the cost of denying an elemental human experience. It is that religious experience contains a relation to an unknown which cannot be resolved under the headings of rationality or morality, and that it contains ecstatic and dread experiences. A constant of the confessions of mystics is the longing for Godhead, for annihilation from the world and the flesh. Not a longing for the total destruction of outer reality necessarily, but certainly a longing to live absolutely, without counting the cost, to live from the very fount of one's being and to annihilate the minutiae and trivia of daily life which appear so destructive of the spirit. The Bacchae of the ancient Greek cult who spent nights in intoxicating dances or in abandoned rushing hordes on hillsides sought such an emancipation. They sought ecstasy even through lust and debauchery, and they desired to be possessed by *something*, if not by God, and to live, even if evilly, beyond themselves.

It is a passion to be found in our own time. It is present in the novels of Dostoievsky. It is in the plays of Jean-Paul Sartre. It is in the mysticism of Richard Jefferies. It is a factor of contemporary history, and is certainly to be found in Fascism, for example.

In 1920 in Thuringia, the New Throng of the Wandervögel danced its way into the countryside. A Dancing Saviour had appeared, a youth called Muck-Lamberty, who appealed to youth to throw off the present and strike into the blue. His was no manifesto on paper, but a physical leadership, for he sang a song 'Spirit is Fire' and danced the 'Rundinella' so infectiously that young people followed him, as in legend the children had followed the Pied Piper. Wherever the New Throng stopped and danced and sang the respectable burghers left the inns and cafés, and the hausfraus the cooking-stoves and danced until whole towns stood idle. Even the police sent to stop the abandonment danced too.

The ecstasy was shortlived and it had no definable religious objective. The element of possession in it is not to be overlooked. Such ecstatic possession is to be found in revolutionaries too, for whom the revolution is not a means to a better society but in truth an end in itself, an opportunity to live without counting the cost. The ecstasy of the New Throng, the abandonment of the Bacchae point indeed to the need to be possessed by God. The awe and dread of which Otto speaks give us an impression of man abased before God and wanting, but unable, to procure a means of communion with him. It does not follow that from any of these experiences man will find God. The possession for which he longs may, when it comes, turn out to be demoniacal, almost certainly so where the religious experience is demanded but God is rejected as in so many irrational modern movements. The arguments of Otto and Schleiermacher

147

reveal to us the hunger of man for God, but they do not reveal God. There is more to religion than the evolution of God-perception, and more to God than man's awe and dread of Him, as I hope presently to show.

V

In Dilthey we find a phrase which curiously anticipates Buber—'Understanding is a rediscovery of the *I* in the *Thou*'. And with this we return to the conception of the twofold attitude, the duality of experience on which Buber lays so much stress. For him, as for Dilthey, we perceive nature, but we experience mind or being and these two processes are in no sense identical, nor can one methodology be applied to the examination of such disparate acts of comprehension.

Buber writes:

'The attitude of man is twofold, in accordance with the twofold nature of the primary words which he speaks.

'The one primary word is the combination *I-Thou*.

'The other primary word is the combination *I-It*.'[1]

His argument, already briefly touched upon, is that with objects we have an *It* relationship—we address them as *It*—and this subject-object relationship implies one consciousness examining or appropriating a world of objects in the being of which it does not share. They are *other*. But a *Thou* relationship, more truly an *I-Thou* relationship, cannot belong at the same time to the *I-It* class, for it is not a subject-object relation at all, but a *meeting*. It is useless (argues Buber) to apply the term

---

[1] *I and Thou*. The anticipation turns out to be less curious but more important than I had thought, for in *Between Man and Man* Martin Buber pays a tribute to Wilhelm Dilthey, *his teacher*. This was for me an exciting confirmation of the connection to be discerned between the thinking of these two men.

In the course of the most important essay in *Between Man and Man*, entitled 'What is Man?', Buber traces the origin of the *I and Thou* phrase to Feuerbach's sentence, 'Man's being is contained only in community, in the unity of man with man—a unity which rests, however, only on the reality of the difference between I and Thou.' He quotes, too, Karl Heim's initial approval (subsequently withdrawn) of the discovery of the *Thou* as *the Copernican revolution of modern thought*, bound to lead to a new beginning, and pointing out for man a way beyond the Cartesian conclusion. Not *cogito ergo sum*, we might then remark, but I am because thou art, or in a sense still more profound, I am because *Thou* art.

'objective' to the *I-It* relation and 'subjective' to the *I-Thou* meeting for there is a real sense in which nothing could be farther from the truth. In the *I-It* relationship nothing could be more subjective than the existence of a single realizing subject cut off from the objects it is experiencing by the barrier of difference in kind or incongruity of approach, and in the *I-Thou* relationship nothing could be more objective than the meeting of like beings in the territory between them.

If once we grasp the tremendous import of this idea, so profound and so simple, it cannot but change our understanding and our lives. For, as Buber points out, the relation to the *Thou* is direct. 'No system of ideas, no foreknowledge, and no fancy intervene between *I* and *Thou*. The memory itself is transformed, as it plunges out of its isolation into the unity of the whole. No aim, no lust, and no anticipation intervene between *I* and *Thou*.'[1] The meeting, the encounter, is in the real present, and it is pregnant with responsibility—'love is the responsibility of an *I* for a *Thou*'.

Yet man has, of necessity, to live in a twofold world. He is compelled to encounter the world of *It*. The *Thous* of his meetings become *Its*, they slip into the world of objects, acquire history, and become the past. Even in the very process of meeting this continues to take place and by no means can be avoided. Yet, 'in all seriousness of truth, hear this: without *It* a man cannot live. But he who lives with *It* is not a man.'[2]

Martin Buber does not exclude the world of objects from an *I-Thou* relationship. He appears to find that such a relation comes into existence in an aesthetic approach. Consider, for example, his poem about a tree (for a poem indeed it is) in *I and Thou* in which after considering the ways in which a tree may be an object of observation, as picture, as movement, as part of a species, he says: 'It can, however, also come about, if I have both will and grace, that in considering the tree I become bound up in relation to it. The *tree* is now no longer *It*. I have been seized by the power of exclusiveness. . . . Rather is everything, picture and movement, species and type, law and number, indivisibly united in this event. . . . Let no attempt be made to sap the strength from the meaning of the relation: relation is mutual.' It seems to me that Buber, who is on the whole suspi-

[1] Martin Buber, *I and Thou*. [2] Ibid.

cious of mysticism, here seeks to reveal an essentially mystical relationship between man and nature, or man and objects when linked by a creative approach.

The *I-Thou* argument is fiercely illuminated by its practical consequences. To treat those to whom we should have a *Thou* relationship as objects is to degrade them and to degrade ourselves. It is to use or exploit them. The most terrifying aspect of the contemporary revolution is that it seeks just this: it has crowned the capitalism of *Money* by the capitalism of *Masses*. The *scientific* resolution of the movements of history is the effort to resolve human beings—human masses—into objects governable by predictable, unvarying laws manipulated to produce certain ends. Whatever opposing ideological groups find to fight about, this is the common ground of agreement between them they are mostly too shrewd to admit.

When men take the road of compelling human affairs to conform to the scientific laws applicable to objects of the natural world, we shortly fail to discover the freely-willing person who possesses divinely appointed rights and discover instead the social unit, the biological end-product, the target of economic laws, the unit in a column of statistics or the rump of neurophysiological processes.

'Whether it is the "law of life" of a universal struggle in which all must take part or renounce life, or the "law of the soul" which completely builds up the psychical person from innate habitual instincts, or the "social law" of an irresistible social process to which will and consciousness may only be accompaniments, or the "cultural law" of an unchangeable uniform coming and going of historical structures—whatever form it takes, it always means that man is set in the frame of an inescapable happening that he cannot, or can only in his frenzy, resist.'[1]

Though therefore we may seem to move with Buber in the realm of pure mysticism (which he himself would deny), in pure adoration of Being, yet that is not so, or not only so. That which he teaches is concerned, in the earthly here and now, with this kind of relationship—'If I face a human being as my *Thou*, and say the primary word *I-Thou* to him, he is not a thing among things, and does not consist of things'.

[1] Martin Buber, *I and Thou* (1947)

The human person who is supreme for Dilthey becomes sacred for Buber.

VI

God is also *Thou*. Relationship with Him is of the same pattern as the meeting with other beings to whom we have said *I-Thou*, yet with this exception, that God can never become an *It*. Even though we speak of Him in the third person, this is merely a convention of communication. We have to address Him, we cannot express Him.

In all meeting there is communion. Dead sticks and stones lie side by side, neither giving nor taking from each other, but in the meeting of persons there is not this exclusiveness, this incommunicable side-by-sideness of things, there is an exchange. Like passing ships, persons hang out signals of recognition and fire salutes or broadsides, they communicate feelings, knowledge, emotion, and meaning through those forms of expression of which Dilthey has made us conscious. We are aware of differences in the value of such meetings. Some are no more than curious glances exchanged in a crowd or a half-smile across a crowded bus. Some are of much greater import, they affect our whole lives, they lift us up or depress us, they fill us with hope, and deepen our knowledge. Our very being is quickened and made significant by them. How much more so then with God. There too is a meeting which is not measurable, which is even less explicable than that altogether strange communion with other persons which we take for granted only because it is the common and accustomed ground of our lives.

God transcends us. He is more than immanent, He is beyond us and outside us. We may *meet* Him. In the meeting with God, Buber says, man receives a Presence as power. There is a real mutual action and it results in the confirmation of the meaning of being.

For Dilthey there is only universal being or becoming of which man is part, but for Buber there is a real and transcendent God, a Sovereign Lord by whom man is 'raised up and bound in relation'. The difference is crucial. No one has demonstrated more sharply than Dilthey the superior reality of persons and personal relationships or illustrated more exhaustively the unique processes of understanding in man. There is not to be discovered, if Dilthey's arguments are followed, any higher or finer reality than the personal life. Even the necessary and enriching objectification of man's mental being through art and society is inferior to the real inner life and meetings of inner lives from which it is derived. But universal being or becoming is *inferior* to man, *inferior* to his personal life, for it is simply a process. It is the 'sublime fermenting vat' or 'automaton' of Thomas Hardy, 'unconscious of our pains' but which somehow permits man to come out supreme. The man of an evolutionary movement looks back at that which has thrown him up. He has passed beyond it already and is quite alone. The process which produced him cannot suffer, it cannot rejoice, it cannot know pain or evil or the struggle against them. It is therefore alien to man's most rich and exalting experiences. Is one to conceive of anything greater than man? If there is nothing greater then one has to cover up his torn, divided, and anguished nature, for it is inexplicable. But if it is to be conceded that there is something greater than man, then by a leap of the understanding one perceives that it has to be something which can stand over against the *person*—and nothing save the Sovereign Lord, the Lord God, the Subject which transcends my own subjectivity can stand over against me. Only this gives my person meaning.

The significant thing about the relationship with the Absolute as Subject is that the meeting with God is in inwardness and in faith and that this is of the very nature of my experience of other personalities.

I have reason to despise my own personality: I know its littleness and misery, yet my knowledge of it is of a uniqueness so isolated that I cannot imagine it in any way interchangeable as a whole or in parts with any other human personality. Nor can I imagine it re-created in some incredibly distant future with all its present atoms but without its memory. My being I share with other beings, but my existence stands alone and cannot be replaced. Even my knowledge of myself, then, has affinity to the manner in which I may know God. My own spirit tells me of the spirit of God.

'It would be strange', Dr. William Temple wrote,[1] 'if He acted only in the inorganic and non-spiritual, and dealt with spirits akin to Himself only by the indirect testimony of the rest of His creation.'

In my spirit I may see, and in my heart know, God.

[1] *Nature, Man, and God.*

Chapter Six

IMMANENCE AND TRANSCENDENCE

I

God must be distinguished from His creation, but may not be alienated from it. This is the profound paradox which closes every approach to His being. It compels us to look once again at immanence, to understand it. To embody God in His creation, a yeast in the dough, is to make Him indistinguishable from it. He is lost there. He is all creation equally irrespective of its quantitative and qualitative variations and temporal changes. Nevertheless the immanent God is a concept peculiarly fitted to a teleological view of evolution. Out of it is born the pantheistic idea that God is to be found in the evolutionary process or *is* the evolutionary process and that He is, like matter or mind, engaged in a process of self-discovery of which the end is beyond doubt. On assumptions like these matter becomes life, life becomes man, man becomes God. God is the cosmic current against which it is not possible to swim. It is a thesis which deeply influenced Christian apologetics in the last century. What is subsumed here under the word God is an organic or absolute power moving under the impulse of its own inviolable laws from an ascertained past to a predictable future—that is to a future which could be rationally predicted if one could see and know all. Within such a monolithic process the tragedies of human life are meaningless. Upon some higher plane they are resolved into a harmony along with all other things in the Divine Purpose. Strictly, it does not matter what we do because everything we do must conform to the preordained movement.

Now evolutionary theory, whether God is resident in it or not, is the outcome of a need to account for the fact of development—for that 'more' of which I spoke in Chapter Three. It

154

IMMANENCE AND TRANSCENDENCE

seeks to replace the notion of a static creation, of things created 'once and for all' by the notion of a developing creation and in its most grandiose conceptions speaks of a cosmos moving from one state to another by a kind of interior volition. The concept of a static creation produced many intellectual difficulties, not the least of which was to account for structural resemblances except on the basis of transition from one species to another. Yet the idea of evolution in its creative aspect (as concerned with the appearance of new properties or qualities in creation) has also its intellectual difficulties. Not the least of them is how one is going to account for the appearance of something new without admitting to an act of creation, irrespective of by whom or what committed. Whatever evolution as a theory may point to, science cannot admit to any new creation without overthrowing its determinism to begin with. Things or events cannot at one and the same time be the consequence of a chain of causation and on the other hand be freshly created irrespective of what went before. Besides, the chain of causation, in strict scientific theory, is not independent of its material. The causation inheres in the material. And it is in the nature of evolutionary argument that every thing develops from something else. The word evolution means unrolling or unfolding. The flower is simply a developed, an unfolded bud. What is observed at the end was potential at the beginning. The observed changes therefore can only be relative changes—they occur in the relations of certain *given things*. They are a re-arrangement of existing material. They do not (save by the theory of emergence, which is a theory of the intervention of God, strictly speaking) introduce anything completely or absolutely new.

It is because the theory of anything absolutely or completely new is scientifically intolerable that mind must be reduced to organism, organism to a chemical arrangement of matter, and a chemical arrangement of matter to a physical arrangement where conceivably one reaches rock bottom (but if not one descends still farther to 'waves of probability'). Evolution contains its own opposite, that is to say it contains not only the idea of the development from the simple to the complex, but the idea of the reduction of all complexities to the irreducible simplicities of matter: evolution contains counter-evolution in the best dialectical sense. And over the need to contain its own opposite,

155

even at the price of sterilizing its own theory, it is continually stumbling. For it is compelled to acts of intellectual contortionism, of standing on its head and saying, in physics, that this is a physical arrangement of matter and these are its laws; and in biology, this is an organic arrangement of matter and these are its laws, *nevertheless* this is a physical arrangement of matter and its laws are physical laws.

'What can this mean?' asks Kierkegaard, in a similar case.[1] 'Is it possible that by contemplating the consequences of something as they unfold themselves more and more one might by a simple inference from them produce another quality different from that contained in the assumption? Is it not a sign of insanity (supposing man in general to be sane) that the first proposition (the assumption with which one starts out) is so far astray about what is what, that it errs to the extent of a whole quality? And when one begins with this error, how shall one at any subsequent point be able to perceive the mistake and apprehend that one is dealing with another and an infinitely different quality?'

In the pertinent simile which follows he says that it is as if one noticed that along a path something had passed, and assured oneself that it was the print of a foot, then observed after all that it was the mark of a bird, then finally the sign of a spirit that had passed that way.

The intellectual problem is to account for the arrival of new properties or qualities, like life or mind or language, if an evolutionary theory is adopted. And this belongs just as much to the evolutionary theory which contains an immanent and unfolding God as one which thinks of evolution as the product of 'The viewless, voiceless Turner of the wheel'.

Either the immanent God is by acts of creation adding to the extent and intricacy of His own being, or He is revealing what exists eternally. In the first case, though one does not understand why God should seek to do this, new acts of creation occur and the causal chain is therefore broken. In the second, nothing occurs except new arrangements of existing things.

But we are still without an explanation for a *creation* which is freely-moving and itself freely-creating. One needs here to lay

[1] *Training in Christianity*, transl. with an Introduction and Notes by Walter Lowrie, D.D. (1941).

emphasis more and more upon the word creation. One must seek a process beyond prediction because to the degree that it is creative it involves the not-predicated. And this involves the notion, paradoxical as it may seem, not of an immanent God but of God suffering and experiencing in the world of free creation and for whom this participation, as for men, is creation. The created universe shares creation with God.

This is only to be understood if God in the sense of a process is abandoned for God as a person. For it is only, strictly, in organisms and above all in persons that we can understand creation. For man, creation is so normal a function that his life and achievements are not intelligible save in the light of it. Man is an anti-evolutionist in his living. He does not wait for events to proceed in his direction or for time to function on his behalf. He proceeds to compel events: he wills that which he wants and transcends his circumstances by creative acts. He does not wait for the raspberries to evolve into jam, or for the bricks in the course of years to form themselves out of clay and build him a house. There is an absolute affinity between rasp-berries and jam, between clay and bricks, yet no possibility of an evolution of one into the other, however much one is 'potential' in the other. Corn gives us bread, yet not in a million years does corn become bread. What is needed to produce one from the other is manufacture, a gross and violent intervention upon the part of man with the processes of nature, but one which is above all his normal procedure for grappling with the problems of his existence. Inherently these are acts of creation, or the repetition of them. What is incorrectly described as the evolution of man is full of these dramatic, self-revealing acts against his environment and even against himself—acts which cannot be inferred from what has gone before but deny or upset what went before. If they are not predictable as the acts of an inviolable law, they transcend law. They are their own law. For man discovers and uses fire, which no animal has ever done. He makes tools. He invents an articulated language which, with its arbitrary associations and infinite combinations, is so unlike the unformed cries of animals as to deserve to be considered a miraculous birth.[1] He caps this by an altogether inconceivable development, the association of arbitrary written signs which

---

[1] Cf., of course, *The Miraculous Birth of Language*.

tally with spoken signs which stand for things. Not in a million, million years could these things have occurred by an evolution. Not even looking back, wise after the event, is it possible to say 'Of course they *had* to happen'. If one says it had to happen to man, then it had to happen also to all gregarious groups of animals who stood, and stand, in just as much need as he of perfected means of communication. These things happened not by law, but by creative acts.

Beyond man, too, we discover events in evolution which mark just as sharp and as unpredictable a break in the course of things as the miraculous birth of language—the very appearance of life, its divergence into a myriad forms, the perfection of its instruments. I cannot see in these happenings anything but a series of violent creative acts, of things or powers called into being by God—the bestowal of *gifts* by God or by His creatures through Him.

One might speak of them as a series of revelations of God—of acts of intervention in His universe. In this sense creation continues and the universe is apocalyptic and non-rational. Yet what happens is not against reason, or even undermining reason, but beyond reason, as genius transcends reason, because genius creates, and God creates, and where indeed we come most surely against Him and are most conscious of finding Him is in being called to creation. 'Creation happens to us, burns itself into us, recasts us in burning—we tremble and are faint, we submit. We take part in creation, meet the Creator, reach out to Him, helpers and companions.'[1]

Not in a thousand years could I hope to express it more vehemently.

II

When we speak of the universe as non-rational there is an immediate hesitation. And even though we take up the word *non-rational* and play upon it and say that we do not mean it as something idiot or anarchic, but as something supra-rational, creative, there is still a doubt. One must say first that there is a difference between *intervention* and *creation*. If a small boy

[1] *I and Thou.*

158

arranges his toy railway lines on the carpet and sets his engines running and then leans down and moves switches to cause crashes, that is an act of intervention, and there is nothing not rational in this simply because the railway engines are unable to perceive the exact form of intervention which has taken place. This is simply 'the occasional breach in the causal nexus in nature by a Being who himself instituted it and must therefore be master of it'.[1] For all we know this intervention in the world may constantly take place and must always take place rationally and naturally. Now suppose the boy leans down and says to the engines 'Fly' and they rise up and fly. That would be an act of creation. A new content has been introduced.

Beethoven's Seventh or Bach's Mass in B Minor and rationality have nothing to do with each other, for Bach and Beethoven do not enter upon explanations, they make revelations. They do not analyse or manipulate a given content, they make a new content. Perhaps once more we must call upon the experience of love. Falling in love is not a rational experience, but a creative one. What occurs in love has little to do with the procreation of children or the establishment of home and family however well it may serve these ends ultimately. The jealousy sometimes a part of it is no instrument to the living of a normal and rational life, but the whole experience creates a new meaning and content for life not to be predicted from what went before, unless what went before was also love.

We do not *know* a loved one, not as we know a book or a multiplication table—indeed we face a tremendous unknown. But we are identified with the loved one. We succumb to an imperative beyond ordinary considerations. This transcendence is accepted in our lives and we hardly realize its implications, though in the most spiritual and enduring form of love, as a power beyond bodily passions, in the love of children, or of parents, in the love which is a deep compassion for the suffering and helpless, we experience a power which changes our lives.

The creative process is love. That God is love, that so often made declaration, so meaningless when it is assumed to mean that God is a mere kind of indulgence, a sugariness which excuses or mollifies the harsh reality of the world, an oversweetness unwelcome to the stringent modern palate, acquires

[1] Rudolf Otto, *The Idea of the Holy*.

a new meaning when it is understood to be *really* like love, and really not like fondness. For to be really in love is to suffer enormously, even unendurably, to care nothing and yet to care all for oneself, and, however painful the experience, to know quite well that it is infinitely beyond ordinary life and that though one goes through it with anguish one would not relinquish the anguish. For it has the same aspect of liberation and fulfilment which the artist experiences and is compelled to experience at the cost of his life and his comfort, for to be creative is to be free and to be free is to suffer. The genius really loves—with pain and hardness and clarity and without sentimentality. God is love, but God is not sentimentality.

'The Lord is the Spirit,' Saint Paul says, 'and where the Spirit of the Lord is, there is liberty.' Christ comes to set men free. They are to listen to the voice of God within them, and rise above the forms of the law. It is a call to creativeness which fills men with hope and with dread—hope of redemption from the futility of their days, dread of getting above the safe ruts of the law into that realm where man is free and must constantly act from the decisions of his own spirit.

'Freedom is creative energy,' writes Berdyaev,[1] 'the possibility of building up new realities. The ethics of law knows nothing of that freedom. It does not know that the good is being created, that in every individual and unrepeatable moral act new good that had never existed before is brought into being by the moral agent whose invention it is. There exists no fixed, static moral order subordinated to a single universally binding moral law. Man is not a passive executor of the laws of that world order. Man is a creator and an inventor. His moral conscience must at every moment of his life be creative and inventive. The ethics of creativeness is one of dynamics and energy. Life is based upon energy and not upon law.'

Life, for man, we might also go on to say, is based upon decisions. Upon the living of decisions arrived at in inwardness and not upon exterior laws or abstracted universal principles. Yet when we talk of love, of creative acts, of decisions arrived at in inwardness we are presupposing persons who possess the capacity to love, who can engage in creation, to whom decisions

[1] Nicolas Berdyaev, *The Destiny of Man* (1937).

relate in that they affect their actions and dispositions. We are asserting (once again) a supremacy to persons, we are attributing to man and to God those things that belong, as far as we are able to see, *only* to organized personalities. We are saying what, after all, has been affirmed all through these pages that God is a Person, and that it is only as a Person that His dual aspect of working in, yet being separated from the universe becomes comprehensible to us, because it is of the same pattern as the relation of our minds to nature: our minds work in and through nature and leave their impress upon it, but never *are* nature. That is to say that we behave sometimes as God acts continuously—creatively.

When we distinguish God as a Person (or as Three Persons) we separate Him from His Creation and make this relation intelligible. At the same time we identify Him with His creation —it is *His* creation. He is not alienated, nor is He—for as a creation it is free—equally responsible for all its quantitative and qualitative variations. If it possesses the attributes of an independent Creation, it cannot at the same time be denied independence.

Nor does God by the act of independent creation lessen Himself or limit His sovereignty: paradoxically He enlarges both. For God does not give over part of Himself to be in a measure independent of Himself. The creation is not tied to the creator by part of the creator remaining in it. In the passage in Kierkegaard's *Religious Discourses* which Theodor Haecker so wisely praises[1] this is said—'The greatest good which can be done to any being, greater than any end to which it can be created, is to make it free. In order to be able to do this omnipotence is necessary. That will sound curious, since of all things omnipotence, so at least it would seem, should make things dependent. But if we rightly consider omnipotence, then clearly it must have the quality of so taking itself back in the very manifestation of its all-powerfulness that the results of this act of the omnipotent can be independent. . . . Omnipotence alone can take itself back while giving, and this relationship is nothing else but the independence of the recipient. God's omnipotence is therefore His goodness. For goodness means to give absolutely,

[1] In *Soren Kierkegaard*, transl. with biographical note by Alexander Dru (1937).

yet in such a way that by gradually taking oneself back one makes the recipient independent.'

Finally, let it be said that the conception of God as a Person resolves that other dilemma, the effort to come at God by means of cognition. For let us recognize that there is a sense in which all beings transcend one another and can veil themselves from one another at will. Human beings constantly do this because they must—because it cannot be endured that their motives and feelings shall remain always known and under scrutiny. No life could exist in such wretched transparency—could ever belong to itself. Only to God are we prepared to concede that all about us is known. How much more so must God veil His person from us, not from reasons of its limitations indeed, but because we could not endure to know all that He is. As Kierkegaard saw, the circumstance that the 'finite spiritual person' can conceal himself if he wishes and that no 'system' can compel him to reveal himself or can read him if he chooses not to be read is the final overthrow of all Hegelian systems by which the whole nexus of time, universe, and God is in the end to be transparently revealed.[1]

---

[1] Theodor Haecker, *Soren Kierkegaard*. 'What was a spiritual person to a system giving itself out as the final and highest knowledge of mankind, and not only that (an outrageous hybrid) but as the knowledge, the self-knowledge of God? Kierkegaard's answer was a roar of laughter, but one that produced the powerful pseudonymous works. Kierkegaard found a system which, helpless before the finite spiritual person whose secret it cannot penetrate in an age if he does not divulge it, proposed to understand the secrets of the infinite and unfathomable God who moreover, expressly demands of man faith and not knowledge.'

Chapter Seven

INWARDNESS AND FAITH

I

The existentialist argument turns sharply inward. For existence, in the significance which Kierkegaard attaches to it, concerns man in his most profound inner decisions. In his deepest being man is not concerned with assessment of proof but with the gravest of choices, the most binding of beliefs, in which the consequence is not an academic assent to theoretical propositions but the movement of the whole being in the acts of life. 'Existenz', Brock has written, 'is not real in being known, it is real only in being effectuated, in the remembrance of it, and in resolutions for the future which are taken to be absolutely binding.' This is reminiscent of the dictum of the phenomenologists of the school of Husserl that life is not a problem to be solved but a reality to be experienced. Life as a problem, as an intellectual problem that is, is that which has already occurred, which has already sunk into the past and which may be examined objectively, its laws determined and its motions described. But life as lived in 'this instant' is not spread objectively before us like the past, but presents us with the dark unknown of the future and from moment to moment confronts us with new, unexpected situations and permits new vistas and calls for new decisions.

Hugh Ross Mackintosh speaks of 'existential thinking' as 'a mode of thought which concerns not the intellect merely but the whole personality of the man who awakens to it and adopts it. To think existentially, therefore, is to think not as a spectator of the ultimate issues of life and death, but as one who is committed to a decision upon them. . . . Kierkegaard would have said that the chief defect in Hegel's philosophy is the definite lack of such thought.'[1]

What *is* existence? It is possible to essay a brief philosophical answer which will at least put the word in perspective. To answer the question, What is existence? we must oppose the concept *existence* to the concept *being*. Existence has priority over being, for being (or essence) is simply that of which a thing *is*. A man is a human being: *all* men are human beings: their human essence is what they have in common between them, it is that of which they are composed. But to say that a certain man is a human being tells one nothing about him. That he has two eyes, a nose, hair, legs, and so forth, as well as other human characteristics is the least important thing about him in a sense. The *most* important thing is that he is John Smith, or Adolf Hitler, or Jean-Jacques Rousseau.

We do not experience 'human being', though we know quite well what it is; we experience only unique individuals. We understand what we mean by wood, but we do not experience *wood*, we experience only individual things—articles of furniture, pencils, trees, twigs, planks, boxes, matches. Being can only realize itself in existence, or rather in individual existences, the existences of concretely realized things. We cannot know the essence of things which do not have existence: existence is necessary for the realization of being. Only with God is it not possible to separate the concept of His Being from His Existence. God is: or God is God.

Modern existentialism (if one can speak of a general philosophy rather than a series of personal attitudes) is not concerned philosophically with the world of things but actually with the concrete human experience. And the human experience is of the absolute uniqueness of existence. Over and above my common being, the basic nature which I share with others of my kind, is my personal *existence*. The solitary man has communion with himself, and with himself only, for his subjectivity is the glass into which everything is poured. His existence is not merely his most immediate experience, it is in a sense his only experience—even his prison.

---

[1] *Types of Modern Theology*. Dr. Mackintosh is seeking a definition of 'existential' in order to make clear the origins of 'The Theology of Paradox'. The saying of Brock, above, is borrowed from the same source.

INWARDNESS AND FAITH

In communion with himself man experiences profound emotions of guilt and of anguish. He listens to the call of his conscience. Whence come these experiences? That is like asking—Whence comes his existence? The call of his conscience has no meaning outside his existence. His conscience is the call of his existence to itself—the self-summons to the freedom of a complete self-realization. Man is free to answer this call, but he is also forsaken. He is alone. The world is stolen from him. God is dead. This is what appears (to me) to emerge from the elaboration of existentialism at the hands of Heidegger, Jaspers, and Jean-Paul Sartre. The existential man is absolutely alone and absolutely free and must make the most absolute decisions, a void of nothingness all round him.

This is the viewpoint of the later, 'systematized' existentialism. So much does it conflict with the Kierkegaardian existentialism from which it was derived that Berdyaev sought not long ago to describe Kierkegaard's thought in a new way in order to distinguish it especially from the aridity of Heidegger's. He said that Kierkegaard's thought was not existential but 'expressionist'—the expression of an existence.[1] And no doubt he sought this definition because he sees Kierkegaard as seeking *the expression in life of his faith*. Kierkegaard stands in his thought before God, with whom he has a binding relation, and

[1] Jean Wahl's *Petite Histoire de l'Existentialisme* (Paris, 1947), concludes with a report of a discussion of Jean Wahl's thesis in which M. Berdyaev took part. Seeking to distinguish the viewpoint of Heidegger from that of Kierkegaard he says 'la philosophie de l'existence de Kierkegaard est une philosophie expressioniste . . . on pourrait dire: est l'expression de l'existence de Kierkegaard'. A most important exposition of Berdyaev's view is contained in *Dialectique Existentiel du Divin et de l'Humain* (Paris, 1947). *Existentialisme Chrétien*, by Gabriel Marcel (Paris, 1947) should also be consulted.

Jean-Paul Sartre's *L'Être et le Néant* is the immense and unreadable exposition of J.-P. S.'s view: but his short and vigorous *L'Existentialisme est un Humanisme* (Paris, 1946) is his best brief defence. A valuable historical account is to be found in *L'Existentialisme* by Paul Foulquié (Paris, 1946). Jean Wahl's book contains an appendix which seeks to trace a relationship between Kafka and Kierkegaard. A similar effort to unearth the literary roots of existentialism is to be found in Paul-Henri Paillou, *Arthur Rimbaud: Père de l'Existentialisme* (Paris, 1947).

Two critical analyses are now translated in English: they are (1) *Existentialism* by de Ruggiero (1946) with a thoughtful introduction by Rayner Heppenstall; and (2) the paper on 'What is Man?' in *Between Man and Man* by Martin Buber. Guido de Ruggiero opposes existentialism from the standpoint of idealism: Martin Buber opposes to it the *I-Thou* concept with which we have already become familiar, and the light of 'the Copernican revolution of modern thought' shines through all his words.

the atheistic existentialism of this decade would be to him precisely that despair to which, of necessity, faith is the answer.

In the sense that the existentialism of Kierkegaard conceives of movements of the whole being it has affinities with Dilthey's concept of the understanding as greater than mere knowing, but it turns away from—though it does not deny—the objectifications which Dilthey speaks, whether the objective world of nature or the objectifications of man in society. This raises the most profound, yes, the most existential questions, as I hope presently to make clear; at the present it is sufficient to say that Kierkegaard thinks only of the approach to God. For him there can be no objective way to God whether in the human society or in the natural world. 'God is Subject, and therefore exists only for subjectivity in inwardness.'[1] He is *necessarily* Subject for the very reason that He is *necessarily* nearest to that which is most real in existence: and what is most real in existence *is* existence. It is that inner being, that profound and mysterious Self which Berdyaev calls 'the unrepeatable unique personality of an existential centre'.[2] It is useless to oppose the universe or universal order to the individual. Useless first in the sense that man is not to be counted a *part* of the swooning immensity of the cosmos, for he is not a part, he is a person, he is not a unit of something else, he is *himself*. And secondly because his Self is of a higher order of reality than the cosmos. Kierkegaard speaks of it in this fashion: 'The paradox of faith is this, that the individual is higher than the universal, that the individual determines his relation to the universal by his relation to the absolute, not his relation to the absolute by his relation to the universal.'[3]

Berdyaev speaks of man's relation to the objective world less abstractly, but in a way which leaves no doubt as to his meaning: 'What value does the very idea of world order, world harmony possess, and could it ever in the least justify the unjust suffering of personality? The idea of the harmony of the whole in the world order, is also a source of slavery of man. It is the power of objectivization over human existence The so-called world order and the so-called harmony of the world whole

---

[1] *Concluding Unscientific Postscript* (1846). Quoted from Walter Lowrie, *Kierkegaard*.
[2] *Slavery and Freedom* (1934).
[3] *Either/Or* (Lowrie, *Kierkegaard*).

was never the creation of God. God is certainly not the construc-
tor of the world order, or an administrator of the world whole.
God is the meaning of human existence.'[1]

And so the applecart is upset. Man turns his back not only
upon nature, but upon five centuries of rationalization of human
and universal relations. The crushing immensity of the universe
is lifted, the burden of its empty space, its milling star-clusters,
and the infinite unrolling of its years is thrown aside and avails
absolutely nothing before the concretion within me of my
existence. Here within me is my existence, compelled to the
most fundamental choices about its life, standing before God.
That is the reality for Christian existentialism or personalism—
not the picture of man as an ephemeral figure in the world
procession or world history, not even if you call that history
universal reason and grant man a role in it. It is no wonder that
Theodor Haecker speaks of Kierkegaard as seeking to reverse
the order and procedure for philosophy and thought. 'He
wishes to go from the person over the things to the person and
not from the things over the person to the things.'[2] He seeks to
shift the European speculative balance, perhaps for all time.

II

The existential centre (to keep for the moment the phrase of
Berdyaev's) we already know is a mystery. We perceive our
limbs, we possess our five wits, but behind the screen of our
activities is that which is most real about us in just the degree
that it is invisible and intangible. It is the subject which is unknowable and dwells in unknowability. It is beyond objectivity,
it is pure subject. And if God is beyond that, not as subject, but
as eternal Subject, how shall it be supposed that one shall ask
of Him for proof or evidence in the objective world which He
cannot enter without ceasing to be Subject and becoming
Object, without ceasing to the Infinite and Eternal and becoming Finite and Temporal? How can He be discovered then in
the historical and material world? It is the paradox of man,
however, that *he* stands at that point in which he is both object

---

[1] *Slavery and Freedom.*   [2] *Soren Kierkegaard.*

and subject, at the point in which he is in nature and yet is a spiritual being.

Kierkegaard asks us, in an extravagant analogy in his *Concluding Unscientific Postscript* to suppose that God should take upon Himself the form of a rare and prodigious green bird with a red beak and perch upon a tree and chirp noisily. Men, he says, could not then fail to observe Him. Paganism, he goes on to point out, consists in just this, that the apprehension of the divine takes place through just such a limited and tangible form which men can witness. But the spiritual conception of God demands that God shall be experienced in spirituality, in the inwardness of that 'existential centre' of which we have spoken. God does not pretend to be invisible, He is invisible. His divine subtlety is such that one does not need to *notice* that He exists, but if one is to find Him it is not by searching the objective world with microscope or telescope, but precisely in His invisibility, through the inwardness of man, through man's *own* invisible spirituality. That which is most real and immediate in man is most invisible, that which is most real and immediate in the universe is most invisible—the experience of the continual presence of God.

The objective world, the world of nature, it can be argued, is determined and conditioned. The spiritual realm, which is the creative realm, is not simply *beyond* the objective world, it is also *free* from it, free from necessity and free from law. It stands in its own relation to God. This was the relationship which Kierkegaard above all sought to establish in his life and in his writings—to stand alone before God in his inwardness, to sink or to swim with seventy thousand fathoms beneath him out there in his faith before God. This was the immensity of his personal choice. 'That God could create free beings', he wrote in his *Journal*, 'apart from Himself is the cross which philosophers cannot bear but remain hanging upon.'

The search for God does not yield us objective proof of His existence either through nature or through the person. When we consider the qualities of existence we are deprived of the props of external evidence. For if existence is describable it is not measurable. Existence is something experienced in immediacy and is not to be contemplated from afar off. It is in the nature of my *I* and your *Thou*, in the direct personal experience of one's self which must be for ever beyond proof or argument. Because of this it must trouble us less that God is beyond proof in exactly the same way. He cannot *be* and not be related to the nature we experience in ourselves, even though He must still be, as Kierkegaard is at pains to emphasize, qualitatively far removed from man. We may remind ourselves again that Dr. William Temple wrote that it would be strange if He 'dealt with spirits akin to Himself only by the indirect testimony of the rest of His creation'.

If to our neighbour's being we must address ourselves, accepting implicitly the existence of that of which we have only signs, then how much more so must we address ourselves to God, accepting implicitly God's existence? We are not compelled to seek a meeting with our neighbour: we are not compelled to address ourselves to God. We have the choice which belongs to free beings. But without the willed act to seek a personal experience of Him we cannot believe in Him. Faith is an act of will and of choice. Knowledge of God is in inward experience. Once it has taken place there can no longer be any problem of 'whether it is so or not'. It is so! But if the approach has not been made, then proofs are irrelevant, much as if one were to seek to prove that there are soldiers advancing towards one by exclaiming that the flashes on their shoulders are of such and such a Division when one's colleague is not only too short-sighted to see, but is looking in any case in another direction, at the mountain no soldier can scale. Proofs will not produce or conjure up God. At the most the dialectical approach such as Kierkegaard makes, such as I have sought to make on different grounds, can compel a person to pause and search his own heart and to ask himself—Is it possible, is it conceivable that I am mistaken about the meaning of my own existence? Can I, and should I make that inward movement towards God?

Nothing else suffices—

'For one may have known a thing many times and acknowledged it, one may have willed a thing many times and attempted it, and yet it is only by the deep inward movements, only by the indescribable emotions of the heart, that for the first time you are convinced that what you have known belongs to you, that no power can take it from you.'[1] God is revealed in 'the deep

---

[1] Kierkegaard, *Either/Or*, transl. Walter Lowrie.

inward movement', in 'the heart's indescribable emotion'. There is no longer any question as to the meaning of human existence. 'God is the meaning of human existence.'

III

The deep inward movement is a choice. But not in the sense that I toss a coin and agree to abide by the result of its spin, or in some other way remain passive while the choice is in fact decided for me by external acts or pressures such as the piling up of evidences. For such a 'choice' is in effect a decision not to choose, but to allow the choice to be made for me. And what Kierkegaard means by his either/or is not that one decides for or against something in the first instance, but that one decides whether one is going to choose 'choice' or not choose it: whether in other words one is going to think existentially and move in the free realm of spirit to which absolute choices belong, or whether one is going to be ruled by objective necessity. 'My either/or does not first of all designate the choice between good/or evil; it designates the choice of choosing between good and evil/or excluding such an alternative.'[1]

In so profound a choice of freedom/or necessity the totality of the being is involved, and not the least part of it is the heroic effort of the will. In the movement of being, in the indescribable emotion of the heart the decision is made. And unless it is made in such completeness, Kierkegaard would say, it is not made, or it is better not made. This is the leap of the soul.

To speak thus means perhaps little unless one is able to show in the lives of men of what one speaks. One might instance in the first place so simple a person as that Richard Weaver of

[1] Kierkegaard, *Either/Or*, transl. Walter Lowrie. Judge William in *Either/Or* also says 'But what is it that I choose? Is it just this or that? No, for I choose absolutely, and the only way I can manage to choose absolutely is by not choosing this or that. I choose the absolute. And what is the absolute? It is myself in my eternal worth. Nothing else but myself can ever choose absolutely, for if I choose something else, I choose it as something finite, and so I do not choose it absolutely. . . .

'But what is this self of mine? At first sight, and as the first expression for it, I would answer: It is the most abstract thing of all, and yet in itself it is at the same time the most concrete thing—it is freedom.' Ibid.

whom William James writes, the miner and pugilist who became an evangelist—and who might have been the model for Shaw's recanting Christian martyr, Ferrovius, in *Androcles and the Lion*.

Though converted to Methodism, Weaver had more than once become a backslider, even to the point of breaking a man's jaw. This, says James, makes his later conduct the more remarkable. For one day, in the mine, he found a fellow-workman seeking to deprive a boy of his wagon, and so of his earnings, by force. Weaver remonstrated with him and stopped him and gave the wagon back to the boy. The miner swore at Weaver and called him a methodist devil. Then, after argument, he said to Weaver, 'I've a good mind to smack thee on the face'.

The story continues in Weaver's own words:

'"Well," said I, "if that will do thee any good, thou canst do it." So he struck me on the face. I turned the other cheek to him and said, "Strike again". He struck again and again till he had struck me five times. I turned my cheek for the sixth stroke; but he turned away cursing. I shouted after him, "The Lord forgive thee, for I do, and the Lord save thee". This was on a Saturday; and when I went home from the coal-pit my wife saw my face was swollen, and asked what was the matter with it. I said, "I've been fighting, and I've given a man a good thrashing". She burst out weeping, and said, "O Richard, what made you fight?" Then I told her all about it, and she thanked the Lord I had not struck back.'[1]

Yes, of course, it goes without saying that this is a naïve story of a naïve and stubborn man. A man who might perhaps just as easily been a Luddite as a Christian evangelist. A man whose very pacifism contains the belligerency of half a dozen Ferroviuses. Yet when all is said and done this simple man had made a decision which had deeper roots than mere obstinacy. He had made a decision which came out of a profound conviction about what his life ought to be under God. Such behaviour can only spring from an absolute certainty of choice. It contained no half-decision. Saint Augustine shows the worthlessness of the half-decision when he confesses that he prayed 'Grant me chastity and continence, but not yet'. How alike Kierke-

[1] William James, *Varieties of Religious Experience* (1919 edition). James borrows the story from J. Patterson's *Life of Richard Weaver*.

gaard and Saint Augustine are in the intensity of the experience of such an inner conflict is shown by these words, which though they come from Kierkegaard might just as well have come from Saint Augustine—'I must either cast myself into despair and sensuality or choose religion absolutely as the only thing— either this world on a scale that would be dreadful, or the cloister'.[1] That these are words foreign to the contemporary world arises from the belief that the power of choice is irrevocably lost. In a set of aphorisms designed to illustrate the axioms by which modern man lives, collected by Professor Emil Brunner, I[2] note these two—'I cannot help being what I am and how I am' and 'There are laws of destiny which determine everything'. There is no choice of choice because we have inherited the world on a scale that is dreadful and the mass of men are no longer conscious of a spiritual cloister in which its fatal nihilism can be rejected.

The inheritance of 'the world on a scale that is dreadful' is regarded as pessimistic and exaggerated by that shallow optimism of our times which defies the reality of actual events and assumes that automatically 'history is on our side'. The exhaustion and despair of two great world wars and several revolutions, the nihilism of science as expressed in atomic warfare, the extinction of individual rights in totalitarian systems, the massacres of whole peoples and whole cities—all these somehow are argued to be simply unfortunate deviations from the rule of genuine human goodness and genuine social progress. Upon the worst aspect of them Julian Huxley manages to base his hopes of real human religion that we discuss later.

The French poet and patriot Péguy became in his thirties, after a youth of atheism, a Catholic once again. We discover from his friends how difficult and rending a decision this was for him. He was visited one day by his lifelong friend and intimate, Lotte, who was also at that time a non-believer. This is what Lotte wrote:

'In September of each year I used to go and see him. In 1908, I found him in bed, worn out and ill. All that immense

[1] *The Point of View*, transl. by Walter Lowrie.
[2] Collected for the World Council of Churches. Cf. *Christian News Letter*, No. 278, 22 January 1947.

burden borne without faltering for twelve years had got him down at last. I myself had gone through very unhappy days. He told me about his worries and weariness and longing for rest, for a small philosophy class in some secondary school a long way off, somewhere near me, in the heart of the provinces, where, without obstacles or troubles, he would at last be able to produce what he bore within him. . . . At one moment he raised his head and leaning on his elbow he said, with tears in his eyes: "I have something more to tell you. . . . I have got back my faith. . . . I am a Catholic." It was as though a great storm of love swept over me; I felt my heart melt and with warm tears, head in hands, I said, almost in spite of myself: "Ah, well, old man, we are all in the same case."

'We are all in the same case. What made me say that, when a minute before I was still an unbeliever? What slow, dim, deep principle had been at work? At that moment I felt I was a Christian.'[1]

Conversion did not mean the end of Péguy's troubles, rather the beginning of a worse phase: it made him look ridiculous, the man approaching middle age, in tears for the love of God, who 'prayed incessantly as he walked from one end of Paris to the other, or on the tops of "omnibuses" with his beads in his hands and tears running down his face'.[2] He had married an unbelieving wife and his three children were unbaptized. What could he do? He was not married at all in the eyes of his Church. Here he was, a Catholic, and unable to live as a Catholic in obedience to his Church. Yet few have cast themselves on God with the absoluteness of his leap. A year before his death in battle, one of his sons fell dangerously ill with typhoid. Julian Green tells us, 'Péguy did what a medieval Frenchman would have done, because he was a medieval Frenchman, he spoke earnestly to Our Lady about his unbaptized children, one of whom was in danger of death. He could not look after them. "I have enormous responsibilities", he explained to the Queen of Heaven. "You must do something

[1] Daniel Halévy, *Péguy and Les Cahiers de la Quinzaine*. M. Halévy does not give the source of this quotation. See also my 'Portrait of an Angry Saint', *Ashridge Quarterly*, October 1947.

[2] Julian Green in the Introduction to Charles Péguy's *Basic Verities* (1944), transl. by Ann and Julian Green.

for my children. I place them in your lap, I give them to you, and now I am going away before you can give them back to me.'''[1] When the sick child recovered, Péguy showed no surprise. He knew how to ask, comments Julian Green.

In moving words Saint Augustine tells of his conversion. Ponticianus visits him and tells him of servants of the Emperor who have abandoned all to follow a life of cloistral meditation. The news is shameful and unbearable to Saint Augustine, who has been hovering on the periphery of Christian action, for it reveals to him his own agonizing vacillation in contrast to the completeness of the decision of these others. Augustine is only thirty-one, a vigorous, proud, and sensuous man, and all his life he has been pursuing truth—but not alone truth—with passion. The decision *intellectually* to become a Christian is already made, but he is not helped by it, for what he shrinks from are the total consequences of becoming a Christian. Not the arguments of the intellect but the decisions of daily life affright him. Again Kierkegaard speaks exactly for him, for his long years of reflection precede just such a radical decision as that which Augustine is being compelled to make. 'It is surely because Christianity is *a radical cure* which one shrinks from . . .' that persons 'lack strength to take the desperate *leap*'.[2] In the grip of a horrible and confounding shame Augustine cries out to his friend Alypius, 'What is wrong with us? What is this that you heard? The unlearned arise and take heaven by force, and here we are with all our learning, stuck fast in flesh and blood! Is there any shame in following because they have gone before us, would it not be a worse shame not to follow at once?'[3] He cannot control his emotion and goes off into the garden, his dumbfounded companion at his heels. He is in such a torment of irresolution that he cannot control his bodily movements. The inability of his mind to decide for him is beyond him. 'And what is the root of it? The mind gives the body an order, and is obeyed at once: the mind gives itself an order and is resisted. The mind commands the hand to move and there is such readiness that you can hardly distinguish the command from its

[1] Julian Green in the Introduction to Charles Péguy's *Basic Verities* (1944), transl. by Ann and Julian Green.
[2] From his *Journal* (Lowrie, *Kierkegaard*).
[3] *The Confessions of St. Augustine*, transl. by F. J. Sheed (1943).

execution. . . . The mind commands the mind to will, the mind is itself, but it does not do it.'[1]

'Such things I said, weeping in the most bitter sorrow of my heart. And suddenly I heard a voice from some nearby house, a boy's voice or a girl's voice, I do not know: but it was a sort of sing-song, repeated again and again, "Take and read, take and read."' He accepts this as a sign to read the Gospels and what he finds there seals his conversion as though 'a light of utter confidence shone in all my heart, and all the darkness of uncertainly vanished away'.[2] 'My whole nature is changed,' says Kierkegaard of his own conversion. 'God has run me to a standstill.'

For neither of these men is conversion the beginning of ease and relaxation, a comfortable way out, any more than it was for Péguy. The essential dread of Saint Augustine and Kierkegaard is that it will impose new obligations and new responsibilities and is for them the end altogether of a soft life of self-indulgence. Henceforth they are completely responsible for their own souls. It is an event for Kierkegaard of world-shaking importance, 'of incomparably greater importance than a European war or a war which involves all the corners of the earth, it is a catastrophic event which moves the universe to its deepest depths'.[3]

The existential choice is the choice which determines one's life. If we do not choose, a choice is nevertheless made for us by forces within us or without us, but beyond our control. Because we are dealing with existence, and not with formal, logical patterns produced by the intellect, we are dealing with paradox, with absurdity. Existence itself is a paradox (it is full of antinomies), as it is in the nature of God to be a paradox (He is immanent and transcendent), and of Christianity to be a paradox (for one has the interruption of the temporal process by the eternal). In one's choice, therefore, one has to accept the dialectic, the paradox, the absurdity of existence and choose nevertheless. Faith by virtue of the absurd, cries Kierkegaard. Faith is a recoil from the utter despair of unbelief.

Yet for Kierkegaard it must be remembered everything is

---

[1] Ibid. The helplessness of the intellect unsupported by the will, by the movement of the whole being, could hardly have been better put.
[2] Ibid.   [3] *Journal* (from Lowrie).

before God. There is even a strange darkness in his works from this very isolation of himself before God which tends to alienate him from his fellows. His person is humbled before God, aware of the tremendous qualitative gulf between himself and God.

An act of worship is a prostration in complete unworthiness before God. Before God we are always in the wrong, Kierkegaard exclaims. We are fallen creatures and we are full of disobedience. We must approach God in fear and trembling, in anguish and dread, ready to suffer for our unworthiness, for in the hand of God the final judgement awaits man.

No judgement of Kierkegaard's Christian existentialism may ever be made which does not recognize his awareness of the Presence of God as the justification of his belief. The leap of faith is, for him, a leap not into the dark or into despair, it is a leap into the lap of God. It begins and ends with the certainty of God's existence and of man's relationship to Him, and of the truth of Christ's appearance and revelation and eternal presence in the world of men.

I emphasize this in order to separate Christian existentialism from the non-Christian kind which was earlier forced upon our attention. Existentialism divorced from Christ is demoniacal. If one says, forgetting God or rejecting Christ, I think existentially, in the heart of my inwardness, making the most profound decisions there, it is not merely that one rejects God, but that no external constraint at all is recognized. One thinks with the blood, one makes a decision because one is impatient of not making decisions, and the decision may carry with it a calculated defiance of men and God.

Nietzsche and not Kierkegaard is the prophet of this existentialism. Listen indeed to what Jean-Paul Sartre has to say.[1] And when one speaks, he has argued, of desertion, an expression dear to Heidegger, we wish to say only that *God does not exist,* and that we must suffer the consequences of that to the very end. The existentialist is strongly opposed to a certain kind of lay morality which wishes to suppress God with the least possible trouble. In the eighties certain French professors sought to build up a lay morality after this fashion—God is a useless hypothesis we are going to get rid of, but we have got to have all the same

[1] What follows is a summary of the argument contained in Jean-Paul Sartre's *L'Existentialisme est un Humanisme*

176

a morality, a society in which certain values are taken seriously, as having an *a priori* existence. It is necessary *a priori* to be honest, not to lie, not to beat one's wife, and to beget children. We are going to show that these values exist all the same, written in heaven, even if God does not exist.

This was the tendency, Sartre explains, which belonged to all that was called *radicalism* in France—nothing is changed even if God does not exist, and one can hold on to all the norms of honesty, progress, and humanism and make of God simply a marginal hypothesis which can die quietly and alone. The existentialist, on the other hand, believes that it is troublesome that God does not exist, because with His disappearance goes any chance of discovering values written in the sky. There can be no *a priori* morality, because there is no Infinite and Perfect Conscience either. We exist on a plane on which there are *only* men. Dostoievsky has written that if God does not exist *all is permitted*. That is the point of departure of existentialism. If existence precedes essence one cannot explain things by reference to a given human nature: but on the other hand there is no determinism, and man is free, man is at liberty. We are alone and without excuse. That is what is meant by the phrase—man is condemned to be free. Condemned, because he did not create himself and make himself free, and because once thrown into the world he is entirely responsible for all that he does. Such are the arguments of Sartre.

It is hardly necessary to reply to this that there is all the difference in the world between the two statements—I choose for myself, and I choose God. The catastrophe of the West began earlier than Kierkegaard, it began when men commenced to believe what Kierkegaard ever fought with stubbornness, that nothing lay beyond man, that he was supreme, and that his law was the highest law. Out of this everything can be justified, and by it every barbarity can be reconciled. This is the direction in which the appalling 'nightmare shape'[1] of contemporary atheistical existentialism is moving. The actual choice not to know God leads to the special despair the world is experiencing.

[1] Cf. the introduction by Rayner Heppenstall to Guido de Ruggiero's *Existentialism*.

III

Existentialism stands contrasted with relativism. 'The knife of historical relativism', said Wilhelm Dilthey, who nevertheless continued to sit upon its edge, 'has cut to pieces all metaphysics and religion.' If one seeks to show how creeds and doctrines are true only 'up to a point', how they are determined not so much by their truth or falsity as by their serviceability or expediency at given junctures of history, how they serve to conceal the appetites and motives of individuals or groups, and how most certainly those in which one believes at this moment will pass away when they are no longer useful, then one provides material for a universal scepticism. There is no good reason for accepting anything as final or absolute in one's person or in history. Everyone is entitled to his own opinion just because no one's opinion is worth anything at all.

Dilthey was deeply conscious of the relativism of philosophical systems. Though made uneasy by this thought, he could see no way out and faced the conclusions bravely enough. Every system of philosophy belongs to a particular date and a particular situation. It does not deal with immutable ideas or concepts but is just White's philosophy or Black's philosophy. It was the secret burden of present-day philosophy and philosophers that whereas once it had seemed that a system was complete and could stand for all time, now philosophers were ruefully conscious of the lack of permanency or absoluteness in thought and inwardly conceded that their philosophies were only 'valid up to a point'—in the light of the contemporary situation. This led him to two solutions and the first was *to get rid* of philosophy and metaphysics. He would use relativism as a surgeon uses a knife, to cut away the dead parts and replace philosophy by history, by a history of philosophies. (A process to which one cannot very well see an end, for if indeed relativism is the only absolute, then theories of relativity are themselves doomed and must give place to other theories of relativity, or even to theories of absolutes. One might therefore compile in the end not merely a history of philosophies or a history of histories but a history of theories of relativity; or a theory of the relativity of theories of relativity.)

His second solution was to stand on the sidelines and cheer the supple and agile human mind which continually grapples with old and new situations. 'The last word of the mind which has run through all the outlooks is not the relativity of them all, but the sovereignty of the mind in face of each one of them, and at the same time the positive consciousness of the way in which, in the various attitudes of the mind, the one reality of the world exists for us.'[1] As Professor Hodges reminds us this is equivalent to saying that each *Weltanschauung* 'while false as a theory, is true as a record of vision'. It does not do more than give a 'testimony of how the world can appear to a certain type of mind in certain conditions, and how such minds in such conditions can confront their world. . . . This really will not do. It is in conflict with Dilthey's own admissions. For he himself has seen the psychological necessity of a *Weltanschauung* to give unity and direction to a life, and it is obvious that a *Weltanschauung* can only do this if it is not merely toyed with, but definitely held.'[2]

Now this argument of the relativity of philosophical systems makes poor reading for those—and they have been many—for whom it has been a precondition of their acceptance of religious beliefs that they should conform to certain philosophical suppositions. If the prop of the philosophical system is shown to be a rotten one, this choice faces the would-be believer—either religious systems are relative too, in which case I can believe nothing, for nothing is supported for me, or else I must decide to believe or not to believe out of my own inwardness. If I accept the universal validity of relativism then by some new inner path I must decide what is true, I and I alone by good sense or animal faith. This is the existential dilemma even of those who reject existentialism.

[1] Wilhelm Dilthey, *What is Philosophy?* (from Hodges).

[2] Ibid. Dilthey's own words are: 'We only need to be thorough. We must make philosophy itself an object of philosophical study. There is need of a science which shall apply evolutionary conceptions and comparative methods to the study of the systems themselves.' *Modern Man and the Conflict of Outlooks* (Hodges). I am irresistibly reminded of that dig which Kierkegaard makes against philosophers in *Either/Or* and which we might apply here to Dilthey by substituting *Weltanschauung* for the word 'reality' (which I have put in italics): 'The fact that philosophers talk about *reality* is just as deceptive as when a man reads on a signboard in front of a shop "Ironing done here". If he should come with his linen to get it ironed, he would be making a fool of himself, for the signboard was there only for sale.' (Lowrie).

In the same degree it is devastating for all humanist codes and near-religions, like Dilthey's own. For humanism bases itself upon the dignity and integrity of the human person, but in a sense the human person in the light of something above him, the rational. The human person, then, as rationally conceived. What is rational is real. What is the rationally understood nature of man is the real nature of man. Man is a rational being. But if humanism leads to the conclusion that the rationality of thought is only relative, only good for a given here and now and without fundamental truth or validity, why! that is the same thing as saying that thought is irrational, that man is irrational, that humanism is irrational. It then becomes difficult for humanism to hang on to its humanity. It is difficult to refuse to admit that 'truth' is simply the latest belief or that progress is what happens, or that man is only the creature of circumstances.

What humanists profoundly desire is that certain qualities of man shall be honoured and shall triumph. They would wish for the growth of enlightenment, of knowledge, of kindliness, of civic virtues and of moral integrity. But it is a puzzle—even on the basis of the social desirability of this or that named quality —to justify these qualities in the frame of an evolutionary theory or a theory of the relativism of ideas and beliefs. More especially when evolutionary theory in particular deifies ruthless struggle, and, in the world to-day, we are able to witness qualities precisely the opposite of those praised by humanism triumphing, and even producing from a humanist point of view good results.

This is a dilemma which faces Julian Huxley—though he does not appear altogether conscious of it. More aware of human depths and longings than some of his fellow-rationalists he long ago proposed a *religion* of humanity.[1] With an ardour which belongs to the vanishing golden age of humanism he sums up his creed thus—'I believe that the whole duty of man can be summed up in the words: more life, for your neighbour as for yourself. And I believe that man, though not without perplexity, effort, and pain, can fulfil this duty and gradually achieve his destiny.

'A religion which takes this as its central core and interprets it with wide vision, both of the possibilities open to man and of

[1] Cf. *Religion without Revelation*.

the limitations in which he is confined, will be a true religion, because it is coterminous with life; it will encourage the growth of life, and will itself grow with that growth.

'I believe in the religion of life.'[1]

But in the strict evolutionary sense more life means more death. Not merely in the quantitative sense that all living things are mortal and must die, but in the sense of a struggle for existence—the greater the number of living things, in relation to resources, the fiercer the struggle is the classic theory. And in a moral sense, if a belief such as this can be said to possess a moral view, one should welcome the intensifying of the struggle since this will lead to the production of more struggle-worthy types. It is impossible to pick and choose if one decides to believe in the religion of life. Its most relentless qualities are just the ones in the end which seem most worthy of praise if any distinction is to be made at all between qualities. And though Julian Huxley, no less a person after all than the Director-General of Unesco, must find the spectacle of the annihilation of men by contemporary political and national movements as horrifying as do all civilized men, yet perhaps it is not an intellectual accident that he was able to write during the course of the war not so long terminated: 'Meanwhile we are confronted with the spectacle of social movements of a religious nature, such as Communism and Nazism, taking the place of traditional theological religion in large areas of the modern world. I regard this as a symptom and a portent of the rise of humanist religions to pre-eminence.'[2] Can it really be that Hitler and Mussolini and Stalin are the portents of what is to follow, to supersede in the march of progress—*Christ?* God help us all, we are made to comprehend here in startling and painful truth, by the words of an eminent rationalist, the very core of that choice of which Kierkegaard speaks with evangelical fire, for indeed one cannot sit upon the fence and admire, as Dilthey does, the human mind grappling with its problems, or as Huxley does, the endless resource of life seeking to live. One must come down into the arena, but if one does not will to make the choice then it may nevertheless be made even against

[1] Cf. *Religion without Revelation* (Thinker's Library edition).
[2] From his December 1940 Introduction to the Thinker's Library Edition of *Religion without Revelation*.

181

one's will and morality. And if the choice is not to stand before God conscious of one's creatureliness, of one's evil, then it is with equal implacability, even though by default, to choose life, or the world, and not in the tidied-up bits and pieces one can admit to learned societies or the columns of humane reviews but by implication all of it, its sin and corruption and mortality. And if one's choice is indeed that the world is all, then the most copious floods of tears will not dissolve it away. It is this absolute sense that either one chooses to stand before God or one takes all the consequences that cause Kierkegaard to wrestle with God for the whole of his life.

Yet one may do Julian Huxley an injustice nevertheless. What really concerns him is not a quantitative increase but a qualitative increase in life. And that depends upon what one values—those qualities and developments most honoured will be those upon which one will judge the success of a religion of humanity in 'increasing life'. But what is valuable is just what it is quite impossible to determine if all values and beliefs are relative.

It is just the absolute choice of which I have spoken which is beyond many men to-day: even beyond Christians, so that Christians seek sufficiency in a religion of kindness and social reform, and are at a loss as to how to distinguish it from a platonic goodwill to the world which is, unhappily, ineffectual to check resolute evil. Charles Gustav Jung has confessed[1] that among all his patients in the second half of life there was not one whose problem was not 'in the last resort that of finding a religious outlook on life'. He asserts that everyone of them became ill because 'he had lost that which the living religions of every age have given to their followers, and none of them has been really healed who did not regain his religious outlook'. That which they most needed to recover—faith, hope, love, and insight—were gifts of grace, not to be argued into them pedagogically but only to be received by them out of living experience.

When men lose the love of God it does not follow that they find, and can control, *themselves*. For what has replaced God in the modern world is not strictly reason or light, but that fate

[1] *Modern Man in Search of a Soul.*

or destiny of which Buber spoke. That which has come to dominate the lives of modern men, so that like the characters of Greek tragedy no matter how they turn or twist they cannot escape, is the blind, dread movement of events which can in no wise be broken. This aspect of fate Jung also finds. Modern man, he says, is paralysed, chilled with fear in face of blind contingency, in face of the monstrous forces he is incapable of controlling by social or political measures. And if, from the 'terrifying prospect of a blind world in which building and destroying successively tip the scale . . . he then turns his gaze inwards upon the recesses of his own mind, he will discover a chaos and a darkness there which he would gladly ignore'.[1] One may worship life, it seems, only at the price of submitting in the end to its darkness and terror.

Meanwhile, we return to relativism. Now if man is all or if he is—it amounts to the same thing—the highwater mark of evolution, it is difficult to escape the conclusion that the only knowledge and understanding there is reside in himself, and there the only truth lives too. If then one goes on to conclude that he trims his intellectual coat to suit his material cloth as circumstances dictate one reaches inevitably the conclusion that side by side with the Heraclitean flux of matter is the flux of belief. In both, the final reality is change. The logical intellectual conclusion is scepticism.

What is the answer to relativism?

If one rejects relativism and argues that truth is absolute because it must be so, in what sense may this position be supported? To begin with it does not follow that because there is an absolute or final truth that man knows it, or knows all of it. One may very well extend to man's intellectual nature that fallibility and imperfection which so obviously belong to his moral being. Man gets his values mixed, and his motives confused with his moral truths. All this is true and one has maybe got no farther than the admission of relativity from another angle. Yet that is not so: the relativity in this case is *in the degree of ascertainment* of a universal and absolute truth. Man will never by seeking know all of it, but by effort and reflection he may come to know more of it. He is capable in himself of increasing

[1] Ibid.

the stature of his mind and the articulation of perceived truths. In this sense the supersession of philosophies has another explanation—that each new advance in thought calls up new problems of the nature of truth for solution, and shows the need to reach a deeper layer of understanding. There is indeed a dialectic. That men revolve round the absolute truth which is God and of which they can never know the whole is a far different thing from the relativist argument that there is no absolute truth and that therefore there is no truth.

It must not be overlooked that there is a truth in an existentialist sense not simply, as we have been arguing, in an intellectual sense. It is true that there are intellectual formulations to which one can give assent or not, but just as with Dilthey's hermeneutic there is an understanding which lies deeper than knowing, so there is a truth which lies below the assent or dissent of the intellect. It is that truth which is contained in the orientation of our being, in the unrepeatable individual moral and creative acts, in the conduct and the bearing of our lives when we know, not always infallibly, but many times with an inward certainty, that this or that decision or action is the revealed way of truth.

IV

To emerge from the darkness of a metaphysical night, from intellectual flux and formlessness is part of the task of redemption of our age, which must not be supposed merely to be presented with moral problems. And if that emergence nevertheless appears impossible, it is the impossible which must be attempted. This is the paradox of Kierkegaard's thought. Faith is impossible? Then essay it, for it is also necessary.

Kierkegaard was determined to make faith as difficult as possible, so that there could be no doubt in the end that faith was faith and not proof. In his own life he carried this resolution to disastrous lengths. He undertook, as the last act of his life, an embittered campaign against the platitudinous established religion of his own country, Denmark. He was moved to scorn by the ease with which people accepted Christianity without reflection—in the circumstance that everyone called himself a Christian he saw the negation of Christianity. We have seen already how absolute an act faith appeared to him. The acceptance of the Gospel of Jesus Christ was equivalent to an acceptance of contemporaneousness with Christ, and one had to live continually in that sense. To have a moral feeling that Christianity was a good thing, or to share certain intellectual assumptions with Christians which made it possible to be Christian 'up to a certain point' was utterly abhorrent to him. Half-measures were worse than no measures; there had to be, as we have seen, a movement of the total being in the act of faith. In this he had the gift of prophecy. A no-more-than humanist Christianity is incapable of checking the movement of men to find in the world their exclusive habitation, and can only result in the disintegration of Christian society. When philosophers speak of the modern world living upon its spiritual capital, they mean living upon the faith of earlier and less sceptical generations.

It was also necessary for Kierkegaard to make faith intellectually difficult because he saw intuitively that the complexity of life was not to be answered by a plausible gloss which concealed its antinomies and contradictions within a grand system. In face of such antinomies intellectualizing was helpless, there had to be an inner decision about meaning. So he would have no proofs, no 'results' as he called them, no Paley-like contriving of an aesthetic universe of divine design, and indeed, as we shall see presently, he would have no history. All such were nothing more than a substitute for faith. 'Faith is immediacy' —yet not immediacy alone. 'Faith is immediacy after reflection.'

The disastrous element in Kierkegaard's thought springs from an almost unconscious sense of perfectibility: one had to be, it is fair to remark, perfect in the act of faith or one could not be a Christian. Yet Christian doctrine preaches that man is fallible in faith as in all else. Now side by side with this demand for an absolute act of faith, Kierkegaard preaches the distance between man and God in order to thrust home the idea of the unlikeness of God and man, of His absolute and complete transcendence, of God as one 'before whom we are always in the wrong'. It is a doctrine to which many arguments

185

of Kierkegaard point. Let it be said that an utterly base creation, 'always in the wrong', is not capable of perfect leaps of faith.

Christianity, it is hardly necessary to say, speaks not only of man's fallen and corrupt nature but of the Incarnation, of the entry of God into man's world, of man's redemption, of the gathering of the blessed into the Kingdom of God, of man's necessity to strive to 'be perfect as your Father in Heaven is perfect' and from these doctrines may be garnered—yes!—the likeness of man to God, the vision of a God not utterly unknowable and immovable.

It is in the doctrines of contemporaneousness with Christ that the exaggerations of Kierkegaard's arguments become most clear. This argument is central to his position. His belief may be most clearly demonstrated by his own words:

'For in relation to the absolute there is only one tense: the present. For him who is not contemporary with the absolute —for him it has no existence. And as Christ is the absolute, it is easy to see that with respect to Him there is only one situation: that of contemporaneousness. The five, the seven, the fifteen, the eighteen hundred years are neither here nor there; they do not change Him, neither do they in any wise reveal who He was, for who He is is revealed only to faith.'[1]

Each one faces Christ absolutely and contemporaneously. Each one of us must face Christ freshly, as His disciples did, and complete in this meeting the act of faith, as also His disciples did. Then what of the paradox of Christ's earthly life? That He is for all time, past, present, and future has to be reconciled with His appearance in history which is the starting-point of the Christian religion to which Kierkegaard adheres. To this dilemma—of the absolute as against the historical Christ—Kierkegaard returns in many places. That an eternal consciousness appears to have an historical point of departure is of no more than historical interest. How is it possible to base an eternal blessedness upon historical, that is temporal, knowledge? That the eternal truth has come into existence in time, this is the paradox—not necessarily something to be reconciled but to be accepted in faith.

'Can one learn anything from history about Christ? No. Why not? Because one can "know" nothing at all about

1 *Training in Christianity*, transl. by Walter Lowrie.

"Christ"; He is the paradox, the object of faith, existing only for faith.'[1] And as history is the communication of knowledge, from history one can learn nothing about Christ. If He *exists only for faith* history has nothing to do with Him and He does not belong to history.

Speaking of the invitation of Christ, 'Come hither unto me, all ye that labour and are heavy laden, and I will give you rest', he exclaims: 'This interval, rather, all that this interval makes of Him, secular history and Church history, with all the worldly information they furnish about Christ, about who Christ was, and consequently about who uttered these words, is a thing completely indifferent, neither here nor there, which merely distorts Him, and thereby renders these words of invitation untrue.'[2] Indeed He roundly declares that the centuries since the death of Christ 'have contributed with steadily increasing power to do away with Christianity'.

That the 'interval' is a thing completely indifferent, however, comes near to rejecting altogether the idea of *historical* intervention. If God comes into history it is to act in history, not in what becomes a mystical severance from history. The years of Christ's life on earth are not to be severed from all that preceded and all that followed them. To dismiss the historical occurrence upon which Christianity bases itself, or somehow to separate those years of Christ's life from the rest of the historical process is to slur over the miraculousness and significance of the Incarnation, and to lessen the importance of history or the time process for men. For 'the interval' cannot be a matter of indifference to God. It has meaning also for man. Christ commands His disciples to go into the world and preach the Gospel—to move in history and affect history. This is an effort which we witness and by the historical consequences of which we live.

It is true that Kierkegaard exempts sacred history from his general denunciation. Sacred history means both the living tradition enshrined in the Church and symbolized in the laying-on of hands, and the vehicle of the Scriptures. Yet without men moving through both sacred and secular history it is inconceivable how Kierkegaard should be presented with a conception of Christ that can become contemporary with him. Dr. James

---

[1] *Training in Christianity*, transl. by Walter Lowrie.   [2] Ibid.

Moffatt wrote that the first Three Gospels witnessed 'to the firm conviction of the early Church that Christianity was an historical religion, and that all adequate conceptions of Christ must be related organically to the real, historical personage of Jesus. Christianity was not to evaporate in ecstasy, nor to run out into vague eschatology, nor to dissolve into a spiritual mysticism.'[1]

This view both rebukes and confirms Kierkegaard. It confirms him because he seeks, too, the real, historical personage of Jesus (what he is rejecting is a historical *fiction*) and it rebukes him because it witnesses to the connection between Christ and the evangelical movement initiated deliberately by Him in history, which Kierkegaard tends impatiently to brush aside.

Each soul in awfulness dwells alone before God. In the ultimate sense of each man facing God in all his responsibility this is true. But each man also dwells in time, that is in history, in a particular place and amid particular circumstances and he is responsible to God for just those particular acts of his in time. Anything that lessens the significance of this, in that degree depreciates Christian thought and action.

Now Kierkegaard was, as a matter of fact, highly conscious of the hardness of this historical reality. It is out of it indeed that his doctrine of contemporaneousness emerges. What is past, he says in the work quoted, is real, it really occurred. But it lacks for me the final determinant of reality if it lacks *for me*. What is truly real is what occurs *for me* or *for thee*. 'Only the contemporary is reality for me.' But as Christ is also real for him, then *Christ must be contemporary*. That is the purpose of his whole argument. Yet indeed it is to make nonsense of the Incarnation to say that it occurred with the same reality to Kierkegaard as to Peter. For the one was able to see Him with the eye of the spirit alone, but to the other He appeared also in the flesh. To Peter, when he chose to follow Christ, He was really unknown, the Crucifixion, the Passion and Resurrection had not yet occurred and these divine events are part of the furniture of Kierkegaard's mind whether he will or no. Yet Peter, not Kierkegaard, beheld Him plain and spoke with Him.

To dismiss this distinction, to say that Christ appears, because He is Absolute, with equal reality in both cases, is to miss that Christ is in history and accepts the historical limitations of

[1] *A New Translation of the Bible* (1935), Introduction

the flesh because God intended that He should be *incarnate in history*, so that the consequences of His life should work out in history and give it divine significance. The Incarnation affirms to man what is to be found so simply in the Lord's Prayer that in the work of our daily lives, as in worship and contemplation, God's purpose must run. It was an announcement that holiness, not merely evil, dwells in life and is to be discovered in the works of men, corrupt creatures though they may be.

To have said so much and not to say more would be to do Kierkegaard an injustice. By the sign of a man of flesh and blood, the nature and power of the spirit of the Son of God was communicated to those contemporaries of Christ who saw Christ whole and plain. By the signs and intimations embodied in History, in Sacred History, in the living Church is communicated —what? Not in truth a polite fiction or a pleasant story—not these really, but what Peter too discovered in his inwardness, the eternal and immediate presence of the Son of God. *That* is what is discovered. And Haecker has wisely reminded us that Kierkegaard could never have fallen so low as to declare the world illusory. His dismissal of the consequences of Christ's life in history, and of all historical formulations and arguments about Him is more apparent than real, for it arises out of a confusion in his mind between the actual working of Christ in history and *misrepresentations* of it. It is a confusion Kierkegaard is too impatient to notice because he is anxious to plunge ahead with the argument which makes *Training in Christianity* his most important work. He proposes to destroy the bourgeois ease with which Christ was accepted by his contemporaries. He seeks desperately to make men see the living Christ of Galilee. Consider, he asks, what manner of man this was who said 'Come hither unto Me all ye that labour'—a tramp, an illegitimate, a person without home or job or stability, with no place to rest His head. Consider what it would *really* mean to be faced with this call upon faith, that a wandering labourer should announce Himself to you as the Son of God and demand your faith. Which side would you be on—the side of those who followed Him, or of those who crucified Him? You can only understand what it is to have faith in Christ if you regard His life as contemporary and seek to put yourself in the dangerous position of being among those who followed Him.

Kierkegaard, in dismissing history thus dangerously, because it presents us with a reconciled picture, of Christ ascended and glorified and sitting on the right hand of the Father, asks of Christians a tremendous imaginative act, one calculated to make them grieve and tremble. Consider what it really means to face Christ in His incognito, and then answer on whose side you would have been and what you would have done. Would not a Christ in such contemporaneousness be something to cause you to cry out in offence? Would you not crucify Him?

V

It is as well to be reminded at this point of the reality of history. If we begin by speculating about the objective world we come in the end almost with a shock upon the inexplicable nature of the being that we experience in inwardness. If, on the other hand, we concentrate our attention upon that being it draws us, as it drew Kierkegaard, from the world; and it is with a shock of another kind, like coming from the warm fire and lit room into the grey winter streets, that we remember that there is, as the *sine qua non* of experience, the obdurate, objective world. *Nature* then takes the place of spirit as the tremendous mystery. Without the objective world one may conceive of God but not of human existence, not of the lived and changing human experience with which all our cogitations begin, and the stuff of which becomes the vehicle for the parables of Christ.

What is the relation between the two worlds? Here one must say halt, if necessary, to existentialism or personalism if or when they seek either to abolish the objective world or to grant it at most a derisory acknowledgement. The very meaning of existential thinking was for Kierkegaard an honest and forthright acceptance of the duality of experience. Thought is to be reduplicated in existence. There is a real world, he seems to say, and there is my inward spirit, through which I find God. There is a spiritual dualism too, in the sense that I am I and God is God, and there is a qualitative difference between us, an absolute and unbridgeable difference of identity. Acceptance of this human condition would appear to be for him the very root of reflection and faith. Yet in the passage I have quoted from Berdyaev on pages 166–7 the objective world would seem not simply to be resisted but questioned. The theory of the *person* as an existential centre—and Berdyaev is to-day the leading Christian personalist—seeks to demonstrate how those objectifications of the human mind of which Dilthey speaks, the constructions of law, reason, intellectuality, art, and so on, are not final, they are the frame by which reality is perceived and handled and the instruments by which the spirits of men communicate, but they are not themselves the creative or dynamic forces of existence, for these reside only in persons, and persons constantly transcend such constructions. These spiritual forces are the higher reality. It is through them that we transcend law and reach God in faith, and unless we use them to that end we are caged behind the objectifications of our own making from which there is no escape except in frenzy.

It is necessary to remember that when we are speaking of this objective world we are talking of a complicated group of phenomena. Firstly there is the world of inanimate nature, and then there is the world of organisms. These two worlds can exist even where not encountered by man. Then there is the world of these things where encountered and organized by man and upon which he has left the impress of his ideas and his intelligence. Such is the aspect of any inhabited country— where men live together they create for themselves a concrete form of environment. It has visible shape, and to other men, even though strangers, an intelligible organization. The impress of the spirit of man is communicated by the visible social world he creates. A dwelling is a dwelling, a track is a track to any man. The purpose that each serves is immediately known. Over and above these objective worlds is the world of signs, of all those means whereby men communicate deliberately with each other and of which we have spoken at some length in examining other matters—language, symbols, arts, music, literature, telegraphy, laws, codes, formulae, and the inner content of institutions and organizations, groups and castes and so on.

As we have said it is not to be conceived how man shall exist without these worlds. From infancy onwards the social organization cushions the growing man, enlightens and enriches him and provides the humus that he needs. If it were not for society (in this complete sense) then his life would be that of Kamala or Peter the Wild Boy. For this reason many philosophers looking at the integration of man in society conclude that man is a product of society and nowise exists without it. Man is a social being or he is nothing. It is the argument of Marx. Dilthey too, despite the importance he attributed to the person, says 'man as a fact prior to history and society is a fiction of genetic explanation'. Quite soon, when one has decided that man is a social animal, then the social relations and institutions man has established appear to have produced him. He belongs to them, not they to him. And before long he is becoming subordinated to them in fact: the objectifications have obtained mastery over him. It is against this concept of human life that existentialism and personalism protest. It is against this idea that Berdyaev is really speaking. Man does not belong to his objectifications as the apple belongs to the apple tree. Those things that seem so real and so formidable, are indeed unreal and even dead. The objectifications of man are not the reality, they are simply the shadow of a reality. The reality is the inward life of man. It is the inward life that creates them *to communicate and to cultivate that inward life*. And the objectifications are of value in so far as they serve the inward life. It is there that the absolute reality is to be found. Every effort to deny this, from whatever quarter, and to make man the product of nature or the product of his social relations is a blow at the spirit and tends towards the enslavement of man. This is what Berdyaev means; and not that objective reality does not exist. The argument of the supremacy of the person is an assertion too that the living of life is more important than theorizing about it. Existence—choice—imply living life absolutely in the light of the most absolute inner *decisions*, the most prodigal expenditure of spiritual energy. Understood in this sense neither Christian personalism nor Christian existentialism seek to establish another monism, such as the world of pure spirit from which objectivity is outlawed, and in which decisions would be irrelevant.

For in lived experience no complete unity is to be discovered, not even in the person, or it would contain no paradoxes which were not resolved. The tremendous hunger of man to reduce all things to a unity, the aim of nearly all philosophical systems, has not got the evidence on its side. Against subjective idealism, the *reductio ad absurdum* of which is a bare abstract unity, and against materialism, the *reductio ad absurdum* of which is a mere multiplicity,[1] I have raised enough metaphysical objections in the earlier chapters of this book. Suffice to say that I do not wish to establish a personalist monism. There are grave religious objections to *all* monistic conclusions. In the life we live we experience constantly division, incompleteness, opposition. It is shot through with paradoxes, antinomies. In what ultimate sense everything is caught up into the hands of God we shall never know, but in lived daily life we discover a human spirit, torn with inner conflict, engaged upon a pilgrimage through time and space in a real world against which it must pit itself. 'In lived reality there is no unity of being,' writes Buber.[2] And he is hostile to efforts to make the interior life of man self-sufficient. Any 'narrowing of the circle of reality' as in mysticism or monistic idealism he finds results in the denial or exclusion of one part of reality. And, one may add, in the impoverishment of life. Even if, in the most profound mystical experience, we are caught up into the Presence of God, we cannot remain there, but must presently descend and live among men. If we do not see that this is our fate which we cannot ever completely escape in life then we may be taking part in 'the abysmal destruction of reality'. The most rare of mystics return to the life of the world after their ecstasies and some preach that *return* is for them the meaning of their experiences. Saint Teresa prosaically exclaimed that the object of her soul's union with God was *work*. On the other hand the claim of Meister Ecke-hardt that 'if a soul is to see God it must look at nothing in time; for while the soul is occupied with time or place or any image of the kind, it cannot recognize God. . . . Only he knows God who recognizes that all creatures are nothingness' annihilates all for the spirit. Miss Evelyn Underhill speaks[3] of Ecke-hardt as having a 'total disdain for history and succession, a tendency to exile God from His creation'. This is the point made many times before that God is not to be exiled from His creation. To this, too, He belongs. 'God is the meaning of human exis-

---

[1] W. R. Inge, *Personal Idealism and Mysticism* (1907). The phrase is Dean Inge's.
[2] *I and Thou.*   [3] Cf. *Mystics of the Church.*

tence,' exclaims Berdyaev. This is true, but not in the sense that nothing but man's existence has significance. Man exists as spirit, as ego, as identity, as person. A man exists in his '*I*'-*ness*. But his '*I*'-*ness* is not alone, it has relation to many *Thous*, and it has relation to his own earthly creatureliness, to his corporeal humanity, to his mortal and corruptible bodily self. Indeed, the transient nature of that corrupting body tells him that the very special nature of his present existence will soon be terminated, and in that darkness and uncertainty which obscure what is beyond his life.

Now that material being in which his existence is cast has affinity to the whole of nature beyond him. What is man to say of this? The more sharply he distinguishes his personal existence from the *being* of nature, the more imperative it becomes to ask what the relationship is between them. There is a sense, paradoxical as it may sound, in which all being has existence, and that all existence has meaning or significance in the hierarchy of God. The unique existential centre, the person, crowns creation, but does not exclude it. Man's unique position implies for all other 'forms of existence', all material and objective things, a very special relation to men and therefore to God. It is this, it seems to me, which Buber strives all the time to make clear. All things have relation to God, and therefore to each other. God, therefore, is not to be exiled from His creation, and nature is not to be thrust away from man.

The Christian view of man, to which we now come, recognizes this. It does not, like Buddhism, brush all away. It speaks of the journey of spiritual man through the material world. It speaks of the spiritual existence of a natural creature. It speaks of the spirit of man thrust into the world, into a natural existence. By this token it is a religion concerned also with material things. It is concerned with the earth, which the Son of Man trod, with the hardship, poverty, misery, and labour of the earth—and with joy and harvesting in the radiant day. It petitions for man's daily bread and does not seek only the health of his spirit. It baptizes him in cold water as well as calls down upon him the Pentecostal fire.

3

THE MEANING OF REVELATION

Chapter Eight

THE SIGNIFICANCE OF FAILURE

I

God gives meaning to the universe and in a manner ultimately inexplicable is involved in the universe. God stands over and above it and, in the paradox of His being, works within it too. And so in relation to man. God stands before man, but it is the meaning of the spirit that God is to be discovered working within man. Therefore for man there is not simply a twofold attitude, but a threefold attitude. First, the experience of the objective and independent world; second, the experience of man's inner kingdom; third, the discovery of the real and transcendent God. There is a trinity of experience which might be said to correspond to the trinity of God.

The objective world is experienced within, and God is experienced within, but neither the objective world nor God are within—on the contrary both have to be met and faced. That is what Kierkegaard is thinking when he says that subjectiveness is really the most complete objectiveness. In this threefold relation, to nature, to God, and to himself, the being of man is unique. Facing one way man addresses himself to God, of like being with God. He is caught up into relation with God, in the words of Buber. Facing a second way he is within the material or natural world, one entity of its many entities. Turning within, he is conscious of the simultaneous existence of both worlds, the world of God, and the world of world, both with their demands upon him. And this he discovers *in himself*, the third party. In the realization of this spreadeagling, this crucifixion of his being is necessarily suffering. In the inevitable isolation and conflict which it compels even when not consciously understood—exclusion from nature, since man is not wholly nature, and exclusion from God since man is not God but only of His image—lies the whole tragedy of human existence.

Christianity is concerned with the uniqueness of man in his relation to God and to the world and with the suffering and tragedy which belong to that ordained role. Christianity cannot be concerned to explain away that role by simplification, either as that man is all nature, or that man is all God, or that man, nature, and God constitute one organic whole with harmonious parts and that man has no more to do than to discover by intellectual exercise the secret of that harmony. Christianity cannot be so concerned, for *it regards the disharmony of man's position as of supreme significance for his spiritual life*. Therefore Christianity has to face without hesitation or equivocation the *lived* life of man upon which it cannot permit a gloss to be made in the interests of mental or emotional comfort. To this point of view it must ever remain faithful. In that *lived* life, the direct daily experiences of men—pain, suffering, grief, love, joy, worship, truth, beauty, goodness, work, sickness, birth, and death —comprise the supreme realities: they escape their intellectual or psychological explanations. They are not to be exiled or explained away because they are paradoxical. This clarity and honesty makes Christianity a religion concerned essentially with human reality: it has made possible arising out of Christianity a civilization equally concerned with reality, with the real world.

We have looked at many theories concerning the nature of man and his universe. What is missing in nearly all of them is this contact with the real experiences of men. They are constructs of the intellect: they explain the stars, or resolve atomic behaviour into formulae, or tell us of phylogenesis or show why man has the illusion of acting as a free agent. Christianity speaks of the suffering man without the pretence that his suffering is an illusion, or that it can be permanently cured or that it is an unfortunate aspect of a higher harmony. Christianity speaks *to* the suffering man.

II

Man is a fallible being. He is fallible physically as well as spiritually, and if we consider this physical fallibility we perceive instantly that it is a characteristic he shares with the whole of animate creation. Fallibility throws light upon the nature of freedom, for it is only in relation to living things that fallibility has any meaning whatsoever. Error does not, as far as one can see, belong to the realm of the inanimate. There is no such thing as H_2O almost but not quite succeeding in becoming water, or water on the boil almost but not quite succeeding in generating steam. Either it is water or it is not water. Either it is steam or it is not steam. If a chemist is engaged in the effort to manufacture synthetically a natural product and he fails, he attributes the failure to himself and not to his materials. It is not they which have misbehaved, but his calculations which contain error, and real error as against the statistical variation present in the handling of all substances. His formula, probably, is incorrect. When he has established it beyond the possibility of human fallibility then his experiment will succeed and may be repeated endlessly. If in the course of one of the endless repetitions something again fails, it is at once assumed that something vital has been overlooked, or that there has been a purely physical breakdown in the machinery, for example. Is not this then error in the inanimate? No, it is once again human error— the design is faulty, the machinery has become worn out, or insufficient allowance has been made for this pressure or that friction. It is all mathematically calculable, and the chemist, or physicist, knows that if *he* gets his calculations right then the machine or process will function, but not unless.

He does not expect to have to make the allowances that a jockey makes for the behaviour of his horse. He does not expect to conjure up additional effort or spirit from his machinery or it would not possess for him what is its great virtue—the capacity to reproduce or repeat without temperamental variations. The machine which produces ballbearings must continue to produce ballbearings which differ from one another not at all to the human eye: there can be no question of almost but not quite succeeding in producing ballbearings.

The ever-present assumption in the minds of biologists is, however, that there is an innate variability of performance among all living things. Not simply a performance which varies as between one organism of the same species and another, but a variability which is revealed by comparisons of the performances of the same organism at different times. There is a constant search to explain this variability of performance on mechanistic lines: the science of medicine is in part built upon the thesis that chemical and mechanical correctives may be offered to sickness and disease. Here also incalculable factors emerge, such as that some patients respond to certain curative treatments which make others worse, some recover by inner will, and for others nothing avails because it is lacking. And every physician is forced to consider his patient as a whole, to judge not merely of his disease, but of his general resistance and his spiritual determination. Certain failures of medicine led in the end to psycho-therapy and psycho-analysis, to the discovery that some severe and painful illnesses had no discoverable physical basis but were of mental origin.

Whatever its origin, illness has to do with some internal failure. The organism is not completely whole, its harmony has vanished. But there are other failures, more revealing, which have no relation to this kind of organic disfunction but belong to the being's outwardness, to the life of its activities. They are the failures of judgement characteristic of all living things. This capacity to make wrong judgements is estimated by the hunters of prey—the likelihood of the fly to entangle itself in the spider's web, of the insect to walk into the sundew, of the hen to panic, of the rabbit to become paralysed with fright, and of the moorhen to dash from cover to open water. The hunter judges when his prey may be least watchful, or most easily frightened. The Gestapo called at two in the morning. Again there are failures which do not belong to encounters with foes, but to the occasions when the animal or human being is quite alone—the deer which fails in its leap, the dog which misjudges the current of a stream and is drowned, the child which stumbles. Indeed, all living things not born fully equipped for the situations of their lives undergo the period of special protection and training which is called infancy or childhood for just then, when all has to be learnt, the toll on the mistakes of the healthy organism is the greatest, as the road-traffic accident rate demonstrates. Health has nothing to do with it—the healthier they are the more risks they run.

We observe quite often animals and human beings acting in ways which will bring harm upon them. We watch them making errors of judgement, exaggerating this or that event or underestimating another, and often we know only too well what the consequences will be, yet are powerless to avert them. We see these things happening not out of any lack of will to live, or to preserve themselves, or to seek their own well-being, but out of an *excess* of all these desires, out of greed or lust or power, out of a will which outruns capacity or a response which exceeds justification—in all from a surplus of life which cannot secure proper direction.

We can witness exactly the opposite kind of failure—that which comes of too little will or courage—the failure of the total being in situations demanding resolution. Anyone can produce examples out of his personal experience. One who has trained athletes or animals knows often enough the exact moment when failure is coming—it is revealed in a look, a hesitation, a mood in an otherwise perfectly trained specimen. In battle this can produce the complete disintegration of a healthy man. He becomes the pitiful wreck of Wilfred Owen's *Mental Cases:*

> Who are these? Why sit they here in twilight?
> Wherefore rock they, purgatorial shadows,
> Drooping tongues from jaws that slob their relish,
> Baring teeth that leer like skulls' teeth wicked?
> Stroke on stroke of pain—but what slow panic,
> Gouged these chasms round their fretted sockets?
> Ever from their hair and through their hands' palms
> Misery swelters.

Then, in the end, all beings without exception fail, for they die. Death is a process known only to living things. It is completely meaningless in any system of mechanics. To physics and chemistry the term is unknown. The most curious and inexplicable attribute of living things, that which gives meaning to the word *living*, is that they die. Living things possess, if we are to consider them for a moment as mechanisms, an advantage which other machines do not possess. They can renew themselves. The manufactured machine wears out. Its substance is in the end physically worn away, the parts fail to adhere and lose their strength and repair takes place by the decision of some owner or mechanic. If it is too far gone, the machine is scrapped and that is the end of it. It would be absurd to say that it is dead: it has always been dead. But in Schrödinger's vivid phrase the organism sucks orderliness from its environment: it replaces the atoms which have become disordered by orderly groups extracted from its environment and so, minute by minute, renews itself as its parts wear out. This miraculous function might very well, one could argue, guarantee to it individual immortality. Yet it does not. The replacement is never quite complete, the maintained whole, which is constantly being renewed, nevertheless deteriorates as a whole until in the end it loses altogether the function of replacement. It dies of old age.

Death can put a period to life without this creeping destruction. Disease, a violent injury, even a shock which involves no perceptible organic injury may impair the capacity of the system to hold itself together, and the living thing dies. We know almost nothing about what exactly occurs. There may even be an actual decision to die, as in suicide, or a failure of the will to live. One has seen animals, as well as human beings, decide to die. It is of the most extraordinary human significance that Freud witnesses to the existence of a *death impulse* side by side with that Eros which one would have imagined to be the solitary source of human energy, for love and reproduction serve life and defy death and at first thought one might infer that this is the sole justification of living. Yet a death impulse argues that death is necessary and important, that living things need death, that life is only to be completed through death, that it is not a senseless truncation, but a crowning of the edifice. The idea of death as unnecessary, as a hostile cutting-down of the living tree, as a process inimical to us and which ultimately we shall conquer as we hope to conquer disease—the theme of *Back to Methuselah*—must give place to the concept of life-death unity. In the ultimate sense death is necessary to life. 'The wages of sin is death' might be expressed biologically by saying that the payment for life is death.

Yet I confess that the balancing of life's books by the 'payment' of death has a utilitarian ring which obscures the graver note of death. It adds an unreal consolation. That one lives and therefore one dies is rather like saying that if one goes up on a swing one must come down. The events of life *do* have that kind of logic—if one is young, one can grow old; if one is old, then one has been young. There is a *process* about living in which time plays a creative part. It is quite significant that one cannot short-circuit growing-up, that, if young, one must face puberty, sexual life, love and labour before reaching old age, *but not before reaching death.* Death does not belong to the process. To speak of it at all is to admit that one can come down without going up, that one can eat one's cake without having it.

Death breaks into the closed circle of life at any point it chooses. It lies alongside the whole of life, as the waters to the lake shore, as the invisible air fits the whole globe; it is life's other, but unknown, self. The new-born infant cannot pass instantly to manhood, but can instantly die. The existentialism of Heidegger and Sartre presses upon us that we are suspended over death, that our human freedom is freedom-towards-death.

It is the argument of Dilthey that we can live through the experiences of others, and so increase our human stature. But we cannot live through anyone else's experience of death. And we are utterly unable to understand our own dying. For the understanding does not illuminate that which appears to stand for the annihilation of the (worldly) understanding. Nor can we understand by analogy—the entropy which must overtake the universe is not the death we individually face. In universal entropy matter and energy are equally distributed, but they are not lost. In human death man *is* lost, he is plunged out of existence with the same suddenness with which he is thrust into it. Death is not a *modification* of his life on earth, a reorganization of it, but that which stands at the other pole, the absolute negation.

The human situation, in which we are confronted with death, demands that death in its turn shall be confronted by the human spirit. But that is far easier to say than to do. For the present, let us say only that our human freedom imposes upon us the necessity to take death into our reckoning. To proceed to discuss the living man as if he did not have to die is to forget his true human situation, his true anguish.

Failure has no meaning except in conditions of freedom. It cannot belong to any automatism in the sense I am using it— as involving some individual responsibility for the variability of performance. Failure is the necessary condition of living a life: the span between the plunge into life at birth, and the plunge out of it at death, is like the tightrope walker's demonstration over Niagara, it involves a continual risk to the organism to which the organism has no answer without freedom to act. Not an absolute freedom, any more than the tightrope walker possesses it, but a freedom to act within and in the light of the given conditions. That freedom may be of the most elementary biological kind—the freedom to accept or reject substances—or it may be higher still, the freedom to move and to choose a mate, to run or to fight, to migrate or to eat, to nest or to wait. Evolutionary theories are based upon the assumption that no two performances will be equal and that this is the actual mechanism by which an ascent of species is maintained. The theory of the struggle for existence is derived from the capacity of living things to succeed or not quite to succeed. Some will fail where others succeed, some will die where others live, but all must die in the end or there would be no replacement (reproduction) and hence only a static creation. Failure—this term so meaningless save where you might also succeed and therefore where all is not cut and dried in advance—is the root of all biological and psychological theory. And failure means freedom in the sense of there being space to act, or more than one way to act, more than one level of action, more than one possible outcome of action. And it means a conditioned freedom —that is a freedom in which not all acts are of the same value, in which it is possible to foresee an end to be produced by an act of a certain intensity made in a certain direction, as when a leaping deer foresees that one particular leap of a certain length will secure its escape *but not any leap in any direction.*

The living organism is indeed in a double dilemma. It is constantly failing to put forward the effort demanded by its environment, yet it is also constantly succeeding in making efforts 'beyond its capacity'. Stretching itself up to or beyond its limits, it still fails to reach the grapes. The strain of the organism to maintain the effort and the failure of the effort to succeed call down death. Life is given meaning by the effort, death is the reply to failure. But 'effort beyond its capacity', 'Failure to meet the demands of the environment'—how fatuous these phrases are except in the atmosphere of freedom!

However it is not necessary once again to evaluate vital

phenomena. All that is essential at this point is to make clear the fallibility of living things and to show that man shares in that physiological fallibility and that it is of the utmost significance for his existence. Birth on the one hand and death on the other cease to be accidents on this reckoning but partake of the body of the freedom in which living things move. They are just not to be conceived apart from that freedom. Now birth is wasteful, life is wasteful, and death most wasteful of all. In an evolutionary sense a vast expenditure of living tissue is required for very little result and indeed in the end for no result at all if the Second Law of Thermo-dynamics is accepted as applying to organisms as well as to inanimate matter.

It all has a depressing air of futility about it unless we are prepared to conceive that the meaning of life is not strictly, or firstly, evolution, but *freedom*. If freedom is of value, and if the gift of life is the gift of freedom, then the beings who enjoy it must be really free—they must be free to fail and to die as the condition of not-failing and not-dying, as the condition of possessing lives of significance and responsibility whether at the biological or the spiritual level.

At the culmination of this argument we move out of the realm of biology into that of the human spirit. If we look for it we observe not only biological failure, but human evil. Animals fail but suffer no remorse, only the physical consequences. Man can fail, and suffer all the distress of failure, though it brings him no harm. On the other hand man can succeed physically yet suffer in success all the grief and guilt of spiritual failure. In the sphere of human activities there is evil. Men sin, even in succeeding: men succeed in sinning.

What is the meaning of sin and evil? If God created man free to sin and not to sin, did not thereby God also create sin and evil? One has to ask these questions for it is precisely those who would find a world of organisms in which it was possible neither to succeed nor to fail, or of human affairs in which it was possible neither to make errors nor to correct them, neither to make false judgements nor to learn how to make true ones as fantastic as a Utopia inhabited by wooden dolls, who are most indignant (ironically most *morally* indignant) at the conception of a God-given world in which men commit evil, and God lets them.

III

Animals fail, man also sins. Living things are biologically free, man is also spiritually free. Animals do terrible deeds—they will wantonly maim and destroy. The tiger, the jackal, the vulture stand for acts so alien that they afflict us with horror. But animals are not conscious of the frightfulness of their acts: the tiger is more innocent than any savage, even than any child. It seeks its prey and it wills survival and moves only within the orbit of this animal will. Resistance within that orbit calls forth answering resistance, but it does not, unlike man, seek to swing beyond its orbit. It is not conscious of sin, only of frustration of its appetites or of fear of others. It lives continually in the cruel and burning innocence of Blake's poem and in this, if in little else, is at one with the lamb He also made.

Man *sins*. Man *wills* to sin. In this he is cut off immediately and by the enormity of his consciousness from the innocence of animal creation. Man is aware of acting, even when he does not call it sin, and wills to act in ways which are horrible to him. He is capable of seeking to compel others to do for him that which he fears to do for himself because it is so evil. Man will act at one hour in a manner which he knows in a later hour will cause him remorse and anguish, yet still choose so to act. Man is guilty of bestial sins, as animals do bestial deeds, but unlike animals he wills and succeeds in being bestial out of his nature. He also has within him the power to commit sins which transcend the sins of his animal self, because they are sins of the spirit. They can be pursued and gratified in the secrecy of spirit while in all else, in all that pertains to the body or to society, there is the appearance of right and propriety. Man is guilty of pride, of envy, and of the will to power. He can pursue ambition at the expense of others, hatch and conspire long-sought revenge, enjoy in silence and secrecy the infliction of cruelty upon others. He can hate in his inwardness, prove more fanatical in the pursuit of evil than devoted in the pursuit of good, give himself over to the luxury of his private sins until like drugs they destroy him. The consequences to him of the sins of his spirit are far worse in the end than the consequences of the sins of the flesh which he may immediately recognize and repent, the more easily because his flesh may protest at excesses, while the sins of the spirit he may represent to himself as righteousness and duty both to himself and to others. Yet the sins of the flesh and the spirit mingle, and are not to be separated into categories without thought. Pique, curiosity, boredom, a spirit of perversity, a wish to corrupt others because oneself is corrupted, enter into the supposed simple vices of the body as into the wilfulness of the mind.

> The expense of spirit in a waste of shame
> Is lust in action, and till action, lust
> Is perjur'd, murderous, bloody, full of blame,
> Savage, extreme, rude, cruel, not to trust;
> Enjoy'd no sooner but despised straight;
> Past reason hunted; and no sooner had,
> Past reason hated, as a swallowed bait,
> On purpose laid to make the taker mad.

There is in man, it must be said, a will to do evil, because he knows it is evil and decides to choose evil, because it is argued that this or that experience is necessary to him, and that just because it is sinful and forbidden therefore it is the more attractive and the more essential that he should not be denied it. It is the choice of evil when the good is known and even honoured which creates for man his constant spiritual crisis, his sickness unto death.

Yet here we must pause. Have we any right to talk of sin and evil? When one speaks of sin and evil, is this not hyperbole, a way of saying that there is a common morality to be found among men, that each social grouping has an ethical code and that those acts are approved which support the code and others disapproved because they offend it? Necessarily these will change with changing circumstances and so all one is saying by *sin* is that which, at a particular time, society does not approve. And to translate so simple and ordinary a social process into terms of Divine wrath and judgement on the side of God, and repentance and redemption on the side of man, is to dramatize the process unnecessarily. Indeed, may one not do a disservice to the religious impulse by popularizing the misconception that religion is simply morality—and that therefore you do not need to worship God, you only need to know how to be 'good' in order to be religious?

Though this is once more—in part—the argument of relativism, it is necessary to say something about it.

IV

The common, accumulated morality is not to be despised. It is the consequence of the successive judgements of generations of men as to truth, probity, honour, goodness, and the rest, and it finds expression and means of enforcement in the objectifications of which we had occasion to speak, in the written and unwritten laws of society.

When one examines societies, whether contemporary or following one another in time, one finds that one kind of society favours one kind of law, another an opposite, and that all laws and codes are subject to change or development. This leads to two conclusions, one—that all moral judgements are *relative*, they change from generation to generation and society to society to suit the circumstances; two—that morality is *objective*, it does not belong 'within' man, but to society, it is a social process external to man, decided out in the open beyond him, and 'written in the sky'. Now if the second conclusion were true we should know (even though the first conclusion were also true) exactly where we stood at any given moment of history, because a moral pattern would stand over us, backed by the instruments of society to compel us to be good. When we sinned we should be sinning, strictly, against society in the same way that when we break a law we are defying society. The code of society would be the clear, the exact thing, and man would be the fallible instrument of its execution, the poor scholar before the learned exemplar. But indeed exactly the reverse takes place. Society does not in truth stand in judgement over man, but man stands in judgement over society. It is not really so, that man measures his goodness by the morality of society, but that he constantly measures the morality of society by his own conception of goodness. The laws and codes of society are blunt generalizations of truths inwardly perceived and they seek to impose a common pattern according to those truths, and they constantly fail to do so because they cannot in their very nature be anything but lowest common denominators. They are not clear and exact as man's inner judgement is clear and exact though they are impersonal where man's private judgement is not. This is not to say that man's inner judgement is always perfect while the judgement of society is always imperfect. It is a more complex relationship than that, which is a simple protestantism. Indeed the judgement of society is often more wise because more worldly: it knows the practicable and the possible as against the ideal. It is schooled in limitations. It is keeled and anchored against the instability of private judgement. Moreover as it is an average judgement it is quite true that it will be a better judgement than the private judgement of many. It is a school in which the private judgement becomes tutored, because through the objectifications of society contemporary man extends his knowledge of the judgements and the values of other generations and of the greatest men, and so enriches the material from which a judgement can be made. Nevertheless in the end it is against the conclusions of a man's inwardness that the laws and codes of society are measured and are found to fail. To fail if only in the failure of laws to comprehend the individual and his uniqueness.

With absolute impartiality, Anatole France remarked, the law forbids the rich man as well as the poor man to sleep out at night under the bridges. With the same impartiality the law condemns all men who kill as murderers, all men who steal as thieves. This impartiality is demanded of it because for the most part it must take toll for deeds, it cannot make allowance for all private variations of storm, stress, and temptation. It punishes rather than reforms, which means that it exacts the revenge of society. It punishes breaches of the law, whether in fact such breaches are offences against the morality or not, and by unjust laws it may make the best of deeds punishable offences. It allows, on the other hand, offences against morality which are not breaches of the law to go unpunished. It lags constantly behind the private judgement of its rectitude and is therefore subject to constant pressure demanding its amendment. And law is in the end only upheld by *people*. The degree to which it is maintained will depend therefore upon the inner rectitude of the officers of the law and of the general public. Only their moral *will* upholds it.

With Berdyaev[1] we may go further and accept that ethics is a moral and spiritual *activity*, it arises not simply out of laws and systems, or ideas in the head of man, but out of his moral experiences. His ethical values are formed and grow in continuous living personal experience. Man, therefore, is continually leaping ahead of law.

It is necessary to point, however, to the existence of a *science* of ethics. A science of ethics differs from a system of ethics. A system simply records and explains the values arrived at in independence of it. It codifies, clarifies, and expounds. But a science of ethics seeks to explain the origin of ethics, it must seek to say why men decided that slavery was evil or that serfdom should be abolished having once thought both these institutions defensible, even admirable. A science of ethics may take an historical or a sociological approach or it may seek to evaluate ethical 'phenomena' psychologically. The historical approach discovers the emergence of moral values in the expediencies of societies and therefore removes the moral judgement from the moral consciousness of the individual man: morality becomes strictly empirical or experimental—what works, what is most useful, that is *right*. The psychological approach may—but need not necessarily—discover morality to be simply a neuro-pyhsiological conditioning, or, in the case of the introspective psychologies, the consequences of events in the infantile unconscious.

Strictly speaking, the historical and sociological approaches dismiss morality because they deny the validity or independence of moral judgements, and make morality a function of something else, the rationalization of an unconscious experience, the moral cloak of an appetite, or a prop to power. In this event the doctrine of Thrasymachus is all and justice is what is useful to the powerful and, applied to science or any study, truth is what it is convenient or useful for one to believe. Morality is simply what succeeds.

Enough has already been said about the unfruitfulness of those scientific approaches which come to deny the existence of the field they are examining, and the possibility of any valid judgement upon it, to make it unnecessary to pursue this point

[1] In connection with the arguments in this chapter see *The Destiny of Man*.

THE SIGNIFICANCE OF FAILURE

—of the absurdity of a science of ethics, or a scientific ethic—
any farther. There can only be a science of ethics if there is
first of all a science subject to ethics, or, simply, an ethic which
casts judgement in the first place on science.

The argument of expediency omits altogether to tell us why
a man should ever do what is wrong, if what is wrong is no more
than what is inexpedient personally, or if what is wrong is what
is socially inexpedient why societies themselves should be found
to engineer their own harm. It omits to tell us why a man
should lie sleepless saying to himself that what he is doing is to
his own destruction, yet nevertheless wake in the morning and
rise and despairingly do it. Nor can it tell us why teachers and
prophets should arise in society to challenge the judgements and
performances of society even to the point that they are done to
death for what they believe, if what they believe is only what
society has taught them to revere and admits of no higher tribunal than the judgement of society.

The truth is that the individual is a higher tribunal than
society. 'The individual is higher than the universal . . . the
individual determines his relation to the universal by his relation to the absolute, not his relation to the absolute by his
relation to the universal.' It is because of his relation to God
that man is able to judge of the performances of society. When
that relation goes and he can no longer judge society then he
falls into a frenzy or despair.

It has already been said that the inwardness of man is his
own to mask or to reveal. He alone knows whether what he
desires is lawful before God. He alone knows how much his
life, though he never so much as transgress one commandment
of society, is contaminated with sin. He alone knows how often
in maintaining the letter of the law he sins in spirit. He alone
is capable of judging his own purity of motive, his cleanliness
of heart. And it is precisely against those whose lives are full of
pious practices, who are skilled in scriptures, and honour
scrupulously all that the law asks of them, that some of the
bitterest sayings of Jesus are directed. Not because of these
things, but because of what these things may all too easily hide
—the inner darkness and sterility—are they damned.

If *man alone*, the individual man alone, is capable of the final
earthly judgement about the complex interior strands of his own

behaviour, then there is not to be found strictly speaking on earth a higher tribunal than his own consciousness, or conscience[1] as to his own moral standing. The crowd is a lie, Kierkegaard said. Whence comes that profound power of self-judgement which makes it possible for man to do what no other part of creation can do—to know whether and how *he sins*? It is this which sheds blinding illumination upon the presence and purpose of God, for within man is a God-given power, that through his moral experiences and moral journey in life he may come to apprehend some (though he may fail to adhere to them) of the purposes of God. The meaning of sin and conscience is that there is within us a light which comes from God by which our own promises and performances may be judged by ourselves. Christ calls men to make this judgement and to live continually in the light of this judgement. And when men have truly sought to live by it we witness in their deeds and renunciations how indeed they condemned themselves and set to the remaking of their lives, no matter what the cost.

The existence of inner judgement, of the conception of values by which our lives ought to be lived even against continual failure, demands intellectually the presence of a transcendent judgement. As an intellectual conception it is completed by the acknowledgement that on the other side of fallible man is infallible and omnipotent God from whom judgements spring. It is (to my mind) of the same order of intellectual necessity

[1] This immediately raises the question as to whether the Church is not just such an authority standing over and above man, and around this issue much history has revolved. It is not a question to be answered in a footnote. The position of the Church is unique in relation to man. It does not occupy the same position as any other social institution. Social institutions reveal the working of the minds of other men, the Church is the bearer of God's revelation both through the Scriptures and through its corporate body. It may command, therefore, but not judge, it may awaken, but not compel. In the degree that it is of fallible man it is inferior to man's inwardness—but it is not only of fallible man, but of God too, and in that degree stands above the decisions of man's inwardness. The State stands in relation to man in all earthly matters: there is no loss of power but a gain of it when it resorts to force. It is obliged to use compulsion. But the Church stands in relation to man's spiritual needs and its authority immediately declines if it uses temporal power or other compulsions to enforce belief, even if it uses the compulsion of a social conformity (against belief as a mere social conformism Kierkegaard fought) to maintain its power. The perpetual crisis for the Church is that any institution tends to lay hold of some temporal power. The fact that the Church is discredited by the suspicion of compulsion is, however, the most telling tribute to the ultimate spiritual reality—that there is no spirit unless the spirit is free.

as that which arises when one argues that time is finite and that therefore movement through time is creative and individual lives in time both unique and responsible. One is compelled to go on to ask—creative for whom, responsible to whom? for creativeness and responsibility are personal concepts and the responsibility cannot simply be to oneself alone. There is no answer but God.

We must recognize a paradox. Man possesses or has awakened in him by his moral experiences a conscience, a capacity for clear moral judgements. He possesses also and cultivates with zeal the ability to deceive and to corrupt himself in order that he may hide from himself or throw off altogether the burden of his conscience. He possesses both the light and the bushel to obscure it and the cunning to encourage others to obscure their light so that he may not be guilty in isolation. And with this disastrous quality we return again to the disharmony, the disfunction of man's nature which constitutes his special tragedy and which fills Christianity almost unbearably full with the sadness and longing of mankind.

Yet the tragedy of man's duplicity and corruption arises irreparably out of the freedom we have discovered. Just as there can be no failure in organisms without freedom to fail or not to fail, so there can be no spiritual tragedy in man without this freedom of man's spirit. It is not God who is responsible for evil, though He is responsible for creation. For He has made man free, and it is within man's power whether he chooses the purposes of God or falls away from them and defies God and even seeks to wrench creation altogether from the Creator. Yes, this is man's dream too. That God may judge, that God may end, that God may foresee, that He may recall, does not alter the fact that He has created man free, and in His image. Only omnipotence can make things absolutely and unconditionally free; only omnipotence can withdraw Himself from His gifts so that an unfree debtor-creditor relationship is not automatically established. In this too we may follow Berdyaev—if man is free and his existence is creative, then he may join with God in the tasks of creation, or he may reject them. The threefold attitude, outward to nature, inward to his own being, and upward to God, which constitutes the tragedy of man, constitutes also his especial greatness and power. In such a unique relation to nature and to God he may continually serve as the vehicle of God's creation in His universe and in the minds of men. This throws new emphasis upon that pregnant phrase of Berdyaev's —God is the meaning of human existence.

Chapter Nine

SUFFERING AND GRACE

I

Christianity is *first of all* pessimism. Nothing is more necessary than that this should be said to-day when men ask only short cuts to happiness, and it must be said and repeated that Christianity is first of all pessimism and so must be sharply distinguished from all those assumptions which cling to it, as that it is an escape, or a pipe-dream, or a sentimentality about the world. It must be just as sharply distinguished from the heresies of the modern world, of which one has for a long time been that optimism is in itself moral and proper and pessimism in itself bad whatever the objective circumstances one is talking about. Above all Christianity has to deny the shallow assumption of the innate goodness and perfectibility of man and that most preposterous assumption of all—that there is nothing in man to change, nothing that is unworthy fundamentally, and that all will be made well by reconstructing the institutions and systems of society by which man lives. It is most necessary to say this for organized Christianity itself is inclined to accept from time to time the view that its role is a strictly earthly revolutionary one, or that its primary purpose is to reform or control or speak through the institutions of men rather than into their hearts—and so suffers the Kingdom of Heaven to be placed on the earthly horizon. Pessimism can be evil: it can persuade men to passive despair when action and devotion can save them. But optimism at this moment—in the light of Buchenwald, Auschwitz, and Hiroshima—optimism in the inevitable progress of humanity is treachery. It is doubtful if a greater moral degradation has descended on Europe since the Thirty Years War. It is optimism in the light of this stark truth which conduces to passivity, and pessimism of the Christian sort which predisposes men to heroic remedies. Nevertheless pessimism is not necessarily the same thing as moroseness. 'Certains aiment caractériser l'attitude du chrétien comme un *pessimisme actif*. C'est là en effet notre philosophie des mauvais jours. Mais je crois le christianisme mieux défini par un *optimisme tragique*. Il exclut le prophétisme morose autant que la bonne humeur de sacristie.'[1] Tragic optimism or active pessimism—the kernel of both is the recognition of the torn and divided nature of man beyond any total earthly healing. It is in the light of this, in the same brilliant essay, that Emmanuel Mounier speaks of the difficulty of Christian life— 'la vie de l'homme qui se veut chrétien sera contradiction et lutte, qu'à aucun moment elle ne peut s'établir dans une harmonie durable'.

Optimism in our day does not necessarily take a simple political form. It may do no more than assert, in general terms, that happiness is at once the goal and the right of man. Yes, this is the great utilitarian delusion, that one seeks happiness, and that if only we all seek happiness all will be well. And to deny this is not to assert that man should not be happy. He is robustly able to achieve this in the most desperate of times. No, the error is the assumption that happiness is the end of man's efforts, for if this is so happiness becomes the supreme value and unhappiness the loss, the evil. Unhappiness cannot be understood. We do not know why there should be any unhappiness: we cannot believe that it exists to any purpose and turn from it. Why should we allow it to possess our lives?

If happiness is the goal, how are we best able to get it and in the shortest possible time? We are able to argue that what gives us happiness is what gives us pleasure and as pleasure is more visible and tangible than happiness, to pleasure we devote ourselves. But some things give us immediate pleasure only shortly to make us more miserable. Other things give us immediate pain as the price of a quite problematic future happiness. What seems to have been won in both events is unhappiness, the more especially if some brief experience in this kind of hunt has revealed to us how baffling and elusive is the quarry. Then we cannot enjoy even present happiness for fear of future misery.

[1] Emmanuel Mounier, 'Pour un Temps d'Apocalypse', *Esprit*, January 1947.

Perhaps it simply is, not that what we pursue is happiness, but that when we have decided upon certain ends and pursue them self-forgetfully we are happy in the pursuit—then indeed happiness is something we may deserve but never win by pursuing.

The common denominator of pleasure is sensual enjoyment, it is the fullest enjoyment of our physical senses and our aesthetic and intellectual selves. If pleasure is the way to happiness, the simplest route to pleasure is hedonism. Therefore one may preach a 'democracy' of the senses or of self-expression. Let all be enfranchised. Something on the surface quite simple is indeed commonly asked, simply the uninhibited exercise of our powers. If it is for this purpose that God gave them to us, it is plain good sense to utilize them. Psychologies, educational theories, philosophies, *Weltanschauungen* are built upon this simple premiss, that unhappiness results from the failure to develop oneself to the full.

Alas, the acceptance of so logical and irrefutable a hypothesis constitutes yet another load of unhappiness for man, for the reason that life never grants the full and uninhibited play of all our powers. Life consists not so much of fulfilment as of self-discovery, and there could be no self-discovery save in conditions of denial, restriction, sacrifice, surrender, and—yes, for we have to be honest—mutilation.

The pessimism of Christianity—*pessimisme actif* or *optimisme tragique*—is not an enmity to life but a recognition of its stern and uncompromising nature. It does not seek an inverted pleasure in suffering, for that is also an indulgence. The recognition of the inescapable nature of the experienced here and now transcends the word pessimism. It is more properly, as Mounier sees, described as the tragic view. Christianity believes in the *necessary* tragedy of man's life on earth. The Passion is a symbol for men of the cruel and relentless nature of earthly life.

Tragedy is man's shadow. It is not simply that men's plans go astray, but that the very nature of man's own life, whether successful or unsuccessful from a worldly angle, is inherently tragic. Man is born in another's pain as well as in his own. He begins very early a struggle against his hard material environment. Too early to understand, he is yet entangled inescapably in emotional relations with those of his own blood. He discovers his own powers in the measure that he finds powers as great opposing him. He discovers his own powers in the measure also that he is forbidden to use them. He learns to keep silent. And, after all, his earthly life ends, despite suffering and effort, in the annihilation of the unique and irreplaceable mortal individual in death. Not death out of a clear sky always but after the gradual and inescapable intimations he receives of the fallibility and corruptibility of his body. Man sees death approaching afar off, cutting off his escape, foreclosing on his achievements. 'Man has created death.'

Inherently tragic too is the realization which sooner or later comes to him that in man's greatest and most fulfilling experiences, in his supreme love for another being, in the most creative acts of his hands and spirit, in the most humble and continual search for truth or for understanding of the word of God is failure. Death is discovered there too. The love dies, the creative act fails to answer the inspiration, the search for truth ends in doubts, the struggle to seek union with God is haunted by incompleteness. All this dying is a preparation for the final moment of dying to the world. We die continually to the world and in the words of Péguy, 'quand un homme se meurt, il ne meurt pas seulement de la maladie qu'il a. Il meurt de toute sa vie.'[1] He dies of his whole life.

Man rebels against this destiny: this is in one aspect the meaning of the Renaissance. Death cannot be the answer and another earthly answer is sought. If medicine and science have however failed to find an antidote to death, surely, as compensation for death, life on the planet must yield abundance, happiness, satisfaction for his needs, his body, his loves, and his mind? However—'Is it not for us to confess that in our civilized attitude towards death we are once more living psychologically beyond our means, and must reform and give truth its due? Would it not be better to give death the place in actuality and in our thoughts which properly belong to it, and to yield a little more prominence to that unconscious attitude towards death which we have hitherto so carefully suppressed? This hardly seems indeed a great achievement, but rather a backward step in more than one direction, a regression; but it has

[1] Charles Péguy: 'When a man lies dying, he does not die from disease but from his whole life' (*Basic Verities* (1943)).

the merit of taking somewhat more into account the true state of affairs, and of making life again endurable to us. To endure life remains, when all is said, the first duty of all living things. Illusions can have no value if it makes this more difficult for us . . . *si vis vitam, para mortem.* If you would endure life, be prepared for death.'[1] So Freud, to whom Christianity was anathema, rebuking his age. His consolation has nevertheless a biblical, even a Christian ring, for Christianity announces and faces suffering and is a preparation for death. This tremendous honesty is the mark of the historical greatness of Christianity. It is a measure of its realism.

It is almost beyond irony that so much tragedy belongs to man's refusal to accept as his destiny that the world can never be all for him, for he will be wiped from its face. History in modern times has been shaken by the most tremendous movements which claim that the world is all and has been marked by the bloodiest of strife to secure the success of doctrines whose essence is that human strife is unnecessary and that a world without suffering is possible. The most fratricidal struggles have occurred between those who had opposing views about the proper means to usher in the brotherhood of man. One has seen men compelled to be brothers at pistol point. Yes, and not to exempt Christians, they too have sent men to the Mass at bayonet point and preached the Saviour on the Cross by *auto-da-fé.* Could human frustration go deeper?

How tragic it is that we stand at the termination of more than two centuries of belief in human progress, in its rightness and inevitability, a period unmatched in history for the effort to perfect human societies and to extend human power and human reason. And the outcome? The outcome, just at the moment when the ideals of so many of the idealists appear to be capable of realization, is the most deep and dreadful disillusion. Two suicidal wars, Fascist revolutions against reason and light, police terrors, secret and servile justice, the massacres and exterminations of nations and peoples—not willed consequences, but by-products of those technical skills and advanced theories which sought human liberation by lifting man from the night and superstition of the past into the order and reason of the just society. Only the greatest despair is produced by measur-

[1] *Civilization, War, and Death* (1939).

ing the aspirations of the progressives against the fatal, the tragic realities around us, the problems and hostilities immune to arguments of reason, impermeable to commonsense, indifferent to enlightenment, but full of passion and greed and sustained by human stupidity. Full, in other words, of those human frailties and evils it was hoped to abolish. And so far are we indeed from any perfection of society or of man that we catch a glimpse of an endless vista of human history and human suffering with no perfect society in sight. Here indeed is the true *Martyrdom of Man* of which Winwood Reade wrote (believing in his unhappiness that the religion which was its accompaniment was also its cause).

Because of the imperfection of his very nature, of the very situation of the created and struggling and changing being, all man's decisions and choices are tainted. He seldom has a simple choice between good and evil in any prolonged course of action, but must choose between the lesser good and the greater good, the greater or the lesser evil. It is easy for the Christian who is struck to submit and turn the other cheek. But what if it is not he who is struck, but another? What if he must submit to violence and evil being done upon another or, as the price of ending it, resist in a manner which is also inherently evil? The dilemma of man is that he must ride these moral antinomies. Not the absolute good or the absolute evil face him, but the evil mixed with his own good, the good mixed with his own evil—and they demand decision and action from him, for he must live and act in the world and is not permitted only to moralize about it.[1] For the Christian then, aware of this, there can only be struggle and crisis, though not necessarily always with the tension of these abnormal and aberrant times.

If one ponders the brevity of man's life and the troubles his body must endure and the anguish of spirit for which, often enough, he can find no remedy, and then goes on to think of this misery in terms of all the human beings that have ever lived, and of each individual yet to be borne, indeed this also

---

[1] The moral dilemma of the Christian man in relation to war is most powerfully revealed by the Report of a Commission appointed by the British Council of Churches entitled *The Era of Atomic Power* (1946). This is compelled to admit the impossibility of saying that under *no* circumstances would one resist, or resort to war.

becomes a matter, in that terrible phrase of Kierkegaard's, against which reason beats the brow until the blood comes.

If one cannot dismiss the evil of man's lot as illusion, or at worst nothing more than the temporary discomfort caused by failure to adjust society, one is compelled to ask why. *Why?* In answer there is absolute silence. There is no conceivable *human* reply. There is only an answer if one turns to God, and if man's life is conceived in relation to His existence and purpose. Not simply in resignation, as that earthly life is a trial and a purification and is best endured uncomplainingly. That is a passive doctrine which places man in the position of a *victim*, which is not to be borne. Men will always turn from a Christianity which is possessed of a victim-psychology. Nor in the Barthian sense of man's perfidy and helplessness without the grace of God. No, only if one turns to God with the idea of life as a necessary service to God *in the process of creation* and for which man must be free *above all to suffer*—for creation is out of suffering as much as it is out of love—if he is also freely called to partnership.

It is the superb majesty of this destiny which makes it possible to speak of an *optimisme tragique*. For tragedy cannot belong to automatons, to those who have no responsibility for their acts. Nor can it belong simply to victims. The meaning of tragedy is the acceptance of destiny, and by that act rising above it. It is the human spectacle of man not only sinful but noble too, struck down in his greatness and promise, yet triumphing spiritually in the struggle. We witness not only human evil and misery, but the rising above it. We are ourselves the audience of human courage and grandeur under God.

II

Man is divided in himself. 'Morality in our world implies the dualism of good and evil', Berdyaev has said.[1] Division and disharmony are the signs of man's spiritual stature. For he is not only divided, he is aware of being divided against himself, for his sense of sins is moral *consciousness* which 'presupposes

[1] *The Destiny of Man.*

dualism and opposition between the moral personality and the evil world both around it and within it'.[1] And by this dialectical movement between good and evil, this constant passing over from evil to good, good to evil, man plumbs the bitter depths of himself and his world and by spiritual experience is compelled to grow.

Yet it is painful even to write this down, for if this is indeed the fundamental polarity of our nature and experience, it is impossible to see how the torn human nature is ever going to be knitted together again, for the good exists in relation to the evil, the evil in relation to the good, and the triumph of one or the other is no more to be conceived than the triumph of black over white or white over black. In truth, triumph has no meaning, since evil is no more to be dispensed with by this reckoning than good.

The Christian conceives not only good and evil, but *innocence*. That sin is by man's will presupposes an innocence from which his will must tear him, presupposes that there is defiance or disobedience of the voice which speaks in him from God. This makes imperative something more than an initial state of obedience—it demands a state of innocence of good or evil which is beyond or prior to obedience and disobedience.

It is impossible for man to ponder over the dichotomy of his being without demanding what is the nature of its *wholeness* and how it is to be got. What is the state that God demands of me? every man must cry. To the state of good/or evil man opposes in his heart *innocence*—that which he meets in the young animal, or in the blithe child before the world has fully stained it. Indeed, innocence carries a most profound implication, not to be formulated easily in words but present in the myths of many societies, the implication that the struggle between good and evil promises emancipation from both. In its deepest human significance this is the longing of creation to return to the Creator. And such is the meaning of the Fall. Christianity speaks of the fall of man, of man as existing by his own will in a state of knowledge which is yet a state of alienation from God. And yet not alone by his will in this plight, for the will belongs to the original act and once that has been brought to pass then man lives under its shadow (as every individual man lives

[1] *The Destiny of Man.*

always under the shadow of his own committed evil) and the wounded, the mutilated, the clouded nature of man's being inhibits or prevents those untainted decisions of his will so necessary for his restitution. In this state he is not to be redeemed by himself alone. He cannot lift himself by his own bootstraps. Redemption is by faith and the grace of God. The message of Christianity resides in the forgiveness of sins, in the redemption of man, in the promise to man that he shall rise above the mortal lot of good and evil. The grace of God is the word of God saying that man, no' matter how fallen, is not abandoned. This is the word in the world man most needs to hear.

III

The Old Testament is heavy with the perplexity of man's redemption. The Old Testament Jews believed that the answer to the Fall was to be found in the compact with Jehovah, though they were not always certain what that compact implied. By it they had espoused and acknowledged God to be their God and they to be His people. It was an act of dedication with explosive consequences for history. They witnessed to this compact in the Ark of the Covenant. They were assured that God would lift them up and protect them, fulfilling their imperial destiny by shattering their enemies and giving to them Canaan's land to hold as their own possession for evermore. Intense consciousness of the might of implacable Jehovah haunts all their actions. In the irresistibility, intellectually, and emotionally, of their granite monotheism they know, with the utter certainty that one knows right hand and left hand, that their God is the Eternal, a God above all other Gods, and that in this knowledge they are blest above all other peoples.

The temporal and planetary vindication of the alliance with God was constantly in their thoughts, and as constantly renewed as it was betrayed. Upon earth and in time all things would be made right for the Jews. They were the swords and sickles of God sharpened for the harvest of His wrath and terrible it will be in the day of His triumph. It was in this way that they conceived their role, imposing upon God a tribal function which

conflicted with their most profound consciousness of His transcendence and eternality.

The Jews continued to suffer, the more desperately because
of their fanaticism in the cause of God, all those political and
military disasters which corresponded so ill with the notion of
a God-directed imperial role. The captivity and exodus from
Egypt was followed by the captivity and exodus from Babylon.
All the great empires of this much-disputed corner of the world
overran them. The Davidic kingdom was destroyed and the
temple of Solomon broken to pieces and carted away. Even to
observe the rites of the compact became difficult and the chosen
people degenerated themselves into worshippers of Tammuz
and Baal and practised the living sacrifice of their own children.
The contrast between the God-consciousness of the Jews and
their actual political plight produced that tension which became incarnate in the prophetic stream. The faith that through
the Jews the purposes of God would, despite all, be made mani-
fest gave birth to the Messianic tradition. A king will come, a
great event in the future will complete the Redemption of the
Jews and prove a demonstration of the reality of the covenant.
The intense longing of this great people to be made whole in
the sight of God will be answered. 'Lo, I send my Envoy to
clear the way for Me; and the Lord for whom you long will
come suddenly to His temple.' The apocalypse is foreseen. And
then, 'as for all the nations that made war upon Jerusalem,
this is the plague with which the Eternal will strike them; He
will make their flesh to rot away while they are standing on their
feet, their eyes shall rot in their sockets, and their tongues shall
rot within their mouths'. Not solely to God, but against their
enemies shall the Chosen People be redeemed, the savage old
prophets proclaimed.

In this national exaltation there was little room either for the
personal approach to God or the perception of the spiritual
nature of His ends. Nor indeed could Gentiles be embraced by
any mercy of God. Loyalty to God had to be expressed as
loyalty to the Jewish nation through all its vicissitudes, and the
more zealously one adhered to the Jewish destiny, the greater
the barrier between Judaism and the Gentile world.

Yet within the prophetic tradition another reading of the
compact appears and expresses itself, though always with

difficulty. It is something more than a vision of might and transcendence:

> Can you not understand, cannot you see?
> Were you not told this from the first,
> have you not grasped this, since the world began?—
> that He sits over the round earth, so high
> that its inhabitants look like grasshoppers;
> he spreads out the skies like a curtain,
> and stretches them like a tent

.   .   .   .   .

> Come now! Do you not understand,
> have you not heard,
> that the Eternal is an everlasting God,
> the maker of the world from end to end?
>
> (Isaiah xl.)

God is really God, really the Creator of all, not simply the champion of the Jews. And that God is this kind of God imposes special obligations upon the Jews who realize it, rather than responsibilities upon God to act as policeman for the Jews.

The real compact with God is that His laws shall be written upon their hearts, not upon tablets of stone. God was sick of the slaughtered rams, of the fat from fatted beasts, and of the smell of burnt offerings and asked from men not the external observance of the law, or not that alone, but the movement of the whole heart to Him for only so could He bless them with the spirit.

> Come heart-broken, not with garments torn,
> and turn to the Eternal One your God,
> for He is gracious and compassionate,
> slow to be angry, rich in love,
> and ready to relent.   (Joel ii.)

The turning of men *in their hearts* gave new meaning to the spirit, to the privacy and loneliness of man before God, the imperative need for an inner honesty, which no one save oneself or God could judge. A man is to stand before God as a person, not sheltered by his nation from scrutiny, or buying off His wrath by propitiatory sacrifices. A man is responsible

225

for his own sins—that is the revolutionary idea which emerges —but he who repents shall have his sins forgiven him.

'The person who sins shall die. A son is not to suffer for his father's iniquity, nor a father for his son's iniquity; the good man shall be credited with his own goodness, and the wicked man with his own wickedness.' (Ezekiel xviii.)

Thus the narrow, ingrown racialism of the Jews is gradually denied. God cannot possess the attributes which the Jews have discovered in Him and still be their special property. The role of Jewry becomes itself Messianic for humanity, not temporal and imperial for Jewry. Jewry itself is the necessary sacrifice, it has to suffer that the *others* might not perish. And this is what happens to it, for it is smashed and scattered and carries Christianity along with it in the dispersal. And by the same token how can it be denied that God cares for other men, as well as Jews? Is Jerusalem only in His care that He is 'not to be sorry for that great city, Nineveh, with over a hundred and twenty thousand infants in it who know not their right hand from their left, and with all its cattle?' (Jonah iv.)

The covenant with God ceases to be temporal and becomes spiritual and so man's redemption cannot be sought upon earth but only through man's share in that ultimate realm of God beyond the troubled world.

To the Old Testament the New appears as the perfect historical answer. The Old Testament is completed and rounded off in the New and the unanswerable demands of Job and the false consolations of his comforters are answered. Yet they are answered not simply by fulfilment, but by *denial*. The day has come, the good news is here, the promise of the prophets is being fulfilled, but not by an earthly bliss or universal harmony, but by the call to a new kind of struggle, a different type of sacrifice. The redemption of the Jews is to be secured by the redemption of all peoples—do you think that God could not raise up the stones to be the sons of Abraham? The answer to the hatreds of the years, to all the laments of persecution, is given in the commandment that you shall love your enemies as yourself.

Yet more occurs than the preaching of texts. What happens troubles the world to its roots, and is still troubling it. It is the most complete, and sudden, and appalling intervention of God in the person of His Son Jesus. Now indeed it is made plain that

SUFFERING AND GRACE

God is love by this descent into finite events and persons. Man's deep and destructive sense of sin is by no means the last word about the meaning of life. God Himself is a sacrifice for the redemption of man and no matter how far fallen man may be he can be lifted by the grace of God. The world is not the end: there is the resurrection: the end, the apocalypse, is the coming Kingdom of God.

In the life of the spirit beyond the grave is its vindication—that nothing is wasted, no experience irrelevant, that all acts count and find their justification or their judgement in the life which transcends death. Yet the incarnation is not a message only of joy and a symbol of the eternal incarnation of God in the world; it is a warning that if our lives are as full of meaning and responsibility as this implies, then we cannot escape the judgement of God over the spending of them. 'Whatsoever a man soweth that shall he reap.' The Incarnation placed a solemn charge upon man. Man is sinful, but he is *also* a spiritual being, sharing in the spirituality of the Father, and the Kingdom of Heaven is within Him. The necessary pessimism which belongs to man's fallen state is balanced by the promise of glory.

How great is the necessity that the spiritual agonies of the Old Testament shall receive their consummation! Yet how unexpected is the consummation which comes, when the suffering of man is answered by *the revelation of the still greater suffering of God.*

IV

The notion of a suffering God is an incomprehensible one and intellectually it is without warrant. How can God be perfect and whole and yet suffer? Suffering implies those antinomies of being from which, indeed, we have just expressly derived it. Are we to argue that God, too, is divided against Himself and changing, as man is divided against himself and changing? Does God travail, and not merely in His creation? The movement and pain of creation invoke time, that in which creation exists—but does God exist in time, or on the other side of time, in eternity? In what sense can there be movement, change, and suffering in eternity?

If God is within His creation, in that immanence which entails pantheism, and so bears in His nature its incompletion and imperfection, then of course He must move with it in time and experience its change. But if this is true, then we have to ask all over again how He transcends His creation and can judge it. If, however, He does transcend it, and is truly apart from it, does He then only suffer *for* His creation, identified with it in the love and compassion which a mother bears to a child, a father to a son?

On the other side of the whole paradox, to say that a suffering God is incomprehensible, that no intellect can encompass this proposition, is to imply once more that that is untrue which cannot be rationally grasped and formulated. It is to say that the relation of man to God is one of cognition. The paradox is indeed that God does suffer and that the suffering is not to be understood; as an intellectual proposition it does not exist. For the intellectualization of this matter belongs to the idea of God in an objective sense—to the notion that there He is, laid out in His creation for our inspection, and that the more rigorously we scrutinize it, so exposed to our gaze, the more completely we may formulate His nature and powers in terms to which the intellect consents. Whereas He is indeed the *mysterium tremendum*, and it is in the nature of a *person* that He is revealed to us. It is through His person that we experience His suffering. Only the concept of person, of God as Person, is able to light up the thought of God's suffering. For indeed in my own person I suffer for the sufferings of others without experiencing the experiences which provoked the suffering. This is the spiritual gift of man to live in the being of another without becoming that being. It is incomprehensible without a conception of the person as a spiritual being transcending time and space. If so extraordinary a power belongs to my puny and brief self what power may not be credited to the person of God?

God suffers, God reveals. God reveals His suffering. His relation to man, as Supreme Person standing over my person, cannot be other than one of revelation, no other relation is possible. And the revelation, because of the relation of dependence, is one of love.

We might consider this through a parable. There is a dog possessed of exceptional reasoning powers. Shortly after birth he is taken, because his master fears a plague, and kept in a confined room where he sees no one, but at regular times a hatch opens and his food drops in. He thinks incessantly about this process and formulates it intellectually as a natural law by which, under a compulsion it is impossible to break, his food is thrust into his dark kennel. By this he will measure his days: the noise of approaching food will cause his salivary glands to function in a manner which would delight Pavlov: wakefulness will precede food and sleep will follow it. The known universe exterior to the dog, mostly a matter of inference, is conceived as a mechanism to feed and to house him. Now suppose that the meals grow later and later, that the dog is able to measure this by independent means: he will note the lengthening intervals and assume that the universe is running down. Its energy is being dissipated. Presently, he will be inclined to argue, it will fail altogether and he will die. The animal will not like this prospect, but will not find it against reason.

Suppose on the other hand that there was to be no gradual interruption of the regularity of the meals, but that one day they were to stop (perhaps because the dog's master was ill or absent). Would that not to the dog appear an absolutely unaccountable event, something utterly beyond reason? Would he not examine all his instruments, supposing him to possess them, to see whether they might not be faulty—or even conclude that he himself was under some kind of illusion, in order to avoid the idea of an absolute break in the proved and tested order of the known universe?

Now suppose on the contrary that one day a door which had never before been opened, and was not conceived even to be a door since the idea of an exit was not to be understood, stood open and there stood his master, in full light, bearing food. The animal would be terrified. He would know not simply that something unaccountable had happened, but that what had happened changed the whole of his understanding of life. He would refuse food. The unpredictable presence of another being whose existence had never been suspected and in command of the food would be beyond bearing. But the food is left. The door shuts. There is complete silence and the dog can eat. But henceforth everything is changed. There is no longer an unbreakable universal law with which he has relation, but another *being*. A different being, yet not so different from the dog that he is unable to recognize across the gap a nature compounded like his own. It is by this person, not natural law, that he is nourished. It is to this person that he owes his being. Now he will begin to understand events in the light of this person. He will interpret the movements which precede the dropping of food through the hatch in personal terms. Noises will be interpreted as footsteps, or the action of hands, and voices will belong to persons. Though the dog will make some mistakes, this interpretation of life in personal terms will be correct in the main. If food is late, then perhaps the person who is his master is tired or busy. If it stops altogether, perhaps he is ill and will on the morrow restart. Nothing is unreasonable in all this, though nothing is orderly or predictable. And even though he does not know and cannot suspect the whole of his master's interests and preoccupations he has been aware from the moment the door opened of a circumstance which has transformed his life, lifting it above four walls and food—*that he stood perpetually in relation to another being.* And that nothing—not even the fact that he could not understand this being, or that this being refused to come and see him, could ever alter the fact of this relation. Would he not when this strange and intoxicating idea had taken possession of him, long for and yet be terrified of the reappearance of the master, and cherish the delirious hope that one day he would leave his dark cell and be perpetually united with him?

How better can one express the difference between the relationship of a person to God and a person to an objective order? This above all it has been the task of this book to express. Consider how utterly different in character such experiences are—in the objective world I am free to come and go and my understanding can follow my instruments as far as both will permit me. I formulate the laws of behaviour of something which is ultimately absolute mystery because I can never approach it and get to know it in my own terms. With another, I can know his person in the degree that we both will to make ourselves known, to *reveal* ourselves. I cannot decide that I will know all about X without in the process X learning much about me. The *I* and *Thou* relation is just this meeting or exchange between persons. It is within the power of X to reveal himself, or to veil himself from me: it is a power he possesses so absolutely that nothing I can do will ever break this down while he is a whole and conscious being.

If this is true of X, who is no more and no less than myself, how much more true must it be of God? It is the mystery of God's *person* that is His mystery and it is the kind of mystery which does not lie at all within the terms of the debate existence or non-existence, but in terms wholly of revelation. No doubt we should like to know all, intellectually, and we are not forbidden to seek to know intellectually, but it is within the choice of God, and not within our choice, what of the nature and purpose of God shall be revealed.

There is no person without suffering. Objective laws and processes do not suffer, they occur. Love is suffering, and the salve and resolution of suffering is also love. Wordly pains are lightened because they are shared by others who understand our personal cares. If in the Person of God we find love, it is because we also find suffering. The grace of God is the act of a loving God. It is the most supreme expression of love, the movement of love towards the loved one *despite all*.

The loving and suffering person is able to love acutely and to suffer acutely that which is 'not-I' and is not suffered by the 'I'. It is in the nature of real love that one loves another being. One is ungrown or ingrown until the love of another being has been experienced. To rise to the full stature of love the spirit must find that which is not itself to love. That is the meaning of man's life—both to be a person and to transcend his person in love of others and sacrifice for others. The creation of God is the work of the love of God, that upon which God can expend His love, and draw love out of it. That is the meaning of a worshipping creation. But there could be no love were it compelled. Love is either the free movement of the spirit or there is no love. Therefore God seeks the love of a free creation.

Man suffers in and for his own life. But he suffers, too, that which is most illogical and incomprehensible; as we have seen, he suffers in and for the lives of others. He suffers not because things have been done to him, or one hair of his head has been harmed, but because things have been done to other people, or by them, and the deeper his understanding of these things, the greater his anguish for other men. The suffering of God comes from the perfection of the understanding of God. Suffering and love are the same movement of God. Let us be quite explicit, for the paradox is resolved in this: the suffering and love of God come out of the perfection of God. Farther into this mystery man cannot pierce.

One more thing needs to be said—if we speak of God as a Person, or even, in the mystery of the Trinity, as three Persons, do we not raise against belief still another barrier, the notion of a finite God? Are we not speaking of a God bound by all the restrictions of personality?

'Acceptance of the finitude of God', Dean Inge has written,[1] 'is closely connected with the volitive psychology, and with the rigorous moralism which we have seen is frequently joined with it. It is the conscience in her struggle that demands a God seriously engaged in the same conflict. Perhaps we may say that the notion of a finite God is one that the moralist can never afford to forget, nor the metaphysician to remember.' And he raises this paradox in connection with a statement of Tyrell's which he quotes: 'The fiction of God's finitude and relativity is a necessity of man's religious life, but [that] the interests both of intellectual truth and of religion require us to recognize this fiction as such, under pain of mental incoherence on one side and superstition and idolatry on the other'.

Is God the Person, or triune Person, *finite* in this sense? We know personality only in the darkness of our own mortal existence. We perceive that it is committed irreparably to division, conflict, and finitude. We cannot in any sense understand it apart from the conditions of earthly existence. Yet even as we frame this concept of the limited, finite human personality we recognize how also it transcends or seeks to transcend space and time. It does not simply dwell in the flesh: it is imaginatively and intellectually free of its own flesh: it is able to range space and time and to enclose them within its comprehension: it is able to meet and to merge with other beings, to experience and exchange with them without loss of identity: it shows a continual will to break down the universal isolation of separate and incommunicable objects. This tendency must be counted as opposing also the world of iron and ingrowing egos.

[1] *Personal Idealism and Mysticism.*

In the measure that man achieves all these things we are able to consider the existential person as endowed with fractional attributes of infinitude. How unwise then to assume that the acknowledgement of the Trinity of God is a process of imprisoning God in the limitations of human personality. As our person constantly strives to rise above itself and is never coterminous with its bodily limitations, so God, without body, transcends even the totality of what we in our greatest experiences understand as the person. For God is the perfect Person, and we bear all the marks of our creaturely imperfection.

Chapter Ten

THE PASSION

I

In the Gospels we meet the Son of God not simply as Person but as Presence, not as Word but as Flesh, not as Idea but as Man. This is the final mystery of existence which faces us and it is this with which we have to grapple if the story of the Gospels is true. The spiritual invisibility of God is clothed in flesh and walks abroad and faces man. The God of the Old Testament is remote from humanity: His tenement is the heavens. He is the Eternal and Awful One who covers the sky, who removes mountains, who wipes away man without a trace and causes Job to ask what share man has in His power and glory. How shall He be known and loved of man, and His message heard? The whole of creation groans and travails for this Word of God, for the sign of deliverance. And the saving Word which comes is precisely that God reveals Himself, that He enters into the human scene so that He may be known and loved in this Divine Man. Dr. William Temple wrote, 'What is offered to man's apprehension in any specific Revelation is not truth concerning God, but the living God Himself'.[1] The living, living God! This is the historic fact to which Christianity is indeed in servitude and from which it can never be liberated.[2] If Christ was not indeed the Son of God then all that is left is a handful of moral precepts advanced by a man who had messianic delusions. One can no more separate Jesus from Divinity than Christianity from Christ.

[1] *Nature, Man, and God.*

[2] Aldous Huxley, *The Perennial Philosophy* (1946), advances the view that 'the mystics went some way towards liberating Christianity from its unfortunate servitude to historic fact'. What this liberation means is revealed by Eckehardt, who speaks in this fashion: 'Thou must love God as not-God, not-spirit, not-person, not-image, but as He is, a sheer, pure, absolute One, sundered from all two-ness, and in whom we must eternally sink from nothingness to nothingness'.

Yet what we are faced with in the Gospel story is much more than the Incarnation. God did not just 'appear' as a spirit in the fashion of a man, and speak to men out of the visible form to which they are accustomed so that they might not be too astonished or frightened. No, the Son of God *became* a man. He took on the burdens and cares of human existence. He became a party to human limitations. He suffered in Himself what it was to be creaturely man. Yes, and much, much more. He endured His human limitations in the greatest pain and loneliness and encountered human company at its most vile, tasting the spittle of the rabble on His lips. For the truths that He spoke, the sick that He healed, and for His very Divinity itself He was taken and done to death. We do not face only the simple, radiant, joyous revelation of God to man—would to heaven that we did! We have to reckon also with the most bitter humiliation, the very deepest human tragedy—that the Son of God was nailed on a cross by the men He had come to meet and to save.

Even if one were to call it all a myth born in the unconscious, and breathe again with relief that man had only imagined this dreadful deed, and that it had not occurred under the floodlights of day after all—one would still not be exonerated. For that man should invent this, out of nowhere—or out of nowhere in his outer world—out of, only, his deep, inner torment would itself be a cry almost too fearful to bear from man's soul, a cry telling of man's agonizing need to be redeemed from himself and to find God.

If one doubts that all this is historically so (either that the Son of God was crucified or that a man calling himself the Son of God was crucified) one is not released. The alternative to these possibilities is not a bright, rational world freed from superstition and doubt, with the path of man made clear and shining. No, the alternative is only the quite insoluble enigma of man, the churning, thickening mystery of the protrusion of man's existence out of the void in which it was once hidden, the mystery of man surrounded still by the void, of man conscious in anguish that around him is nothing but the void. That is the alternative—not the abstractions of man presented by sociology or psychology, but despair that man's most profound emotions and hopes have no meaning.

In whatever form one looks at this story, man and God are still to be found imaged in it—the love of God and the hatred of man are both there. Yes, even as poetry and as nothing else, one discovers stamped right through it the tragic pattern of man's life—that God comes and walks abroad and breathes His spirit into man and that man, most wanting God's most love, does God to death.

It was not poetry, and it was not myth, except in the sense that 'the poetry is in the pity'. What happened, happened under the common day to a man who said he was the Son of God. And men were stirred and shaken by this act as by no other deed in history. No subtleties disguised for them the meaning of the sorrowful truth, that God experienced in His Son what it was to be born of woman and to be rejected of men. God sent His Son 'to suffer death upon the Cross for our redemption; who made there (by His one oblation of Himself once offered) a full, perfect, and sufficient sacrifice, oblation and satisfaction, for the sins of the whole world'. That is the Christian rock, and offence, and stumbling-block.

II

The Gospel story—like a coin which, minted long ago and much handled, has become rubbed and smoothed—still glows indeed, but has lost all sharpness. It is surrounded by doctrine, and set in a stony expanse of theology in an acceptable pattern, and has in the course of time become aesthetically decorated for us. In the process all its values have become subtly altered. For the first naked truth about it is that a man in the prime of life was struck down. A man was murdered. And not indeed an ordinary man—though had He been all that His enemies said He was, it would still have been judicial murder at the pressure of the mob—but one who announced that He was the Son of God and was believed to be so by thousands of His contemporaries and by generations of men since.[1]

There appeared in Galilee, that tainted northern extremity

[1] 'People become objective, they insist upon regarding objectively the fact . . . that God was crucified.' Kierkegaard, *Postscript*, transl. by Walter Lowrie.

of Palestine, nearly two thousand years ago, one called Jesus. Flavius Josephus wrote of Him that He was 'a wise man, if it be lawful to call Him a wise man, for He was a doer of wonderful works, a teacher of such men as receive truth with pleasure.' Saint Mark places Him by referring to the annunciative mission of John the Baptist, the prophet contemporary with Jesus, who appeared from the wilderness to draw crowds and to stir men's minds. Saint Mark writes of this as of something about which everyone likely to read his gospel must have heard.

We know little of the boyhood of Jesus among the steep lanes and olive-crowned hills and terraced vineyards of Nazareth. We can only imagine what it must have been like to grow up in that rocky, sun-drenched land, with its stormy winters and stormier politics. We surmise that the young Jesus lived as a working carpenter—not as landowner, or tax-gatherer, or farmer, not even as scribe or scholar or official of the synagogue —but as a simple and skilful worker with His hands, who was devout in His life, who listened to His elders, who steadily regarded men, and spoke enigmatically of the future already at work in Him. Indeed, we can imagine that He lived so long and so quietly among Nazareth folk that they were outraged by His presumption in taking upon Himself a mission. They could not imagine that He had a right to a mission—that it was not all the conceit and vainglory of a young man whose head had been turned by the politics and the prophecies of John. If not that, then worse, He had gone mad. So deeply offended were His own family that this was the most charitable assumption they could make, and they sought to lay hands on Him and put Him under restraint. Perhaps there was the shadow of illegitimacy on His life. We cannot be certain. It is not Gospel talk. We can be sure, however, that He was a member of a small community, that He had a recognized place in it, and that He affronted His fellows by vacating it. There He was, a man with a job, a home, and a family, and He abandons them all at the command of the spirit.

In His thirtieth year Jesus begins to preach, 'Repent, for the Kingdom is at hand', and to minister to men by healing their spiritual and physical ills. He preaches with the kind of authority which dumbfounds and disturbs His hearers. He does not say,

'It is the Eternal speaking', or 'Hear, O Israel, what the Eternal has said', but with the greatest of simplicity, '*I* say unto you' —'*I* tell you'—'*I* command you'. 'Courage, my son, your sins *are* forgiven you', He says. The absolute title to power which is implicit in this kind of statement is followed by the imperative command to the paralytic youth, which brooks no argument or denial, 'Get up, lift your pallet, and go home'. The confidence of Jesus grows rather than diminishes under criticism. He does not admonish His listeners to keep the laws of their fathers, He revises them. Adultery is not simply the act which men had supposed it to be. Adultery begins in the heart, it is first of all the lusting after women *in the heart*. Forget also what you have been told about divorce. There can be no divorce. No certificate can untie those whom God has joined together. Do you follow Mosaic law? 'You have heard the saying, An eye for an eye and a tooth for a tooth? But I tell you, you are not to resist an injury.' Does your neighbour force you to go one mile with him? Then go two. Are you told to love your neighbours? There is no merit in that—anyone can love those who love Him. But love your *enemies*, do good to those who harm you, and pray for those who persecute you, that is the test, that is what you must do. You are commanded to rise above human hatreds and malice. You must seek to be perfect as your father in heaven is perfect.

His preaching challenges men to make a decision. Either they are for Him or they are against Him. For those who are convinced, it is a most joyous revelation. The spirit of God is among them. They follow Jesus to the hills, they crowd upon Him at the lakeside, they bring to Him their sick and dying children imploring Him to heal them, they press close to Him that they might touch the hem of His garment or kiss His feet. His love and compassion call forth their love and worship. He can speak happily of Himself as the Bridegroom, as one who comes in love and calls forth love and for whom there are dancing and feasting. In the bright surge of joy and conviction which follows Him wherever He goes in the first days there is no premonition of the dark end. He commands His disciples and sends them on missions with power to preach and to heal in gift from Him. He performs miracles, raising even the dead. But if rapturous crowds gather round Him, seeking His blessing and hanging on His words, if awe and astonishment accompany Him, we see clouds of fear and anger gather too. Even to people reared in the prophetic tradition there is a new and uncomfortable authority about this man Jesus who possesses a habit of command utterly at odds with His origin. On the one side men are captivated by His brilliant poems and aphorisms and parables; on the other they fear His denunciations, which grow in force and meaning. He uses irony like a rapier. Even at His trial, when all is lost, His attitude is one of irony. His silence under cross-examination, His whole bearing contains an irony which enrages His persecutors because it sees through them, exposes their motives, and dismisses them.

He speaks of Himself as the Son of Man, and as prophets had done no less it was a phrase which could be held to dismiss claims of divinity. But He speaks also of His Father in heaven, with whom He enjoys a special relation, and with whom He can intercede for those who believe in Him. What does He mean? That they should believe the Law, or honour the obligations which arise from the compact with the Eternal, or simply that they should believe in the Eternal? No, He means none of these things, for these they do already. No, He will intercede for those who acknowledge *Him*, who testify for *Him*, who believe in *Him*. It is faith in Himself that He asks. 'Everyone who will acknowledge Me before men, I will acknowledge before My Father in heaven; and whoever will disown Me before men, I will disown before My Father in heaven.' He demands from His followers that faith which the prophets have always sought for God. It is talk which sounds perilously like blasphemy.

If it is not blasphemy, if it is even, on the other hand, a kind of blasphemy to suggest that this ministering, healing, preaching man could be guilty of blasphemy, then there is no middle path. The other question presses irresistibly upon a crowd familiar with the Messianic tradition—'Can this be the Son of David?' John has spoken of the Coming One, and summoned people to repentance and baptism as a preparation for Him. Is it possible that the Messiah is here in the flesh, preaching to us? It was a question which had to be answered.

Even to John himself comes the disturbing thought, and he sends to Jesus and asks, 'Are you the Coming One? Or are we to look for someone else?' The reply that Jesus sends is unequi-

vocal in its irony. Tell John the blind see, the lame walk,
lepers are cleansed, the deaf hear, and the dead are raised.
Tell John to think over this and to use his own judgement.
'Blessed is he who is repelled by nothing in Me.'

Why does not Jesus say simply 'Of course I am!' For the
reason that recognition is of no value unless it is an inward
recognition which is called up in a man. For the reason too that
He knows who He is, and irony is His only reply to those who
do not. Nothing is more revealing than this irony, for it witnesses to an absolute inner certainty. Jesus knows that the mere
assertion of one's importance proves nothing. A man is not a
king because he says so, but because he is born a king, because
in his life he lives the life of a king. He does not enter a town
and say—'Look here, I am your king you know'. That is for
others to say. He enters a town and sits on the throne and commands that those who are to be judged shall appear before Him.

Jesus has no doubts as to whose Son He is. His sole fear is
whether He can sustain in His body the burden of that office.
For He knows that the mere assertion of Sonship is incomparably less important than behaving as the Son of the Father
throughout His whole life. Therefore He does not rebuke His
disciples because they do not recognize Him, but He blesses
Peter for his gift of recognition. He rebukes those who go about
crying out who Jesus is and announcing the wonders that He
has performed as if He were a travelling theatre in need of a
loudspeaker, but it is with sorrow only. His anger is for none
of these, but for the Pharisees who say that His power is from
the prince of devils.

It can be forgiven a man that he does not know who Jesus
is. It can be forgiven a man who, when he knows, vulgarly pro-
claims it. What cannot be forgiven a man is the sin against the
spirit—that he shall see performed under his very nose an act
of healing and grace which is a manifestation of the spirit of
God and slander and deny it. That is the real evil, Christ pro-
claims, to be hostile to grace and holiness, to hate the spirit of
God where it is unmistakably shown *because* it is the spirit of
God unmistakably shown.

In the end Jesus makes it known to His followers that He is
the Son of God in the parable of the son of the owner of the
vineyard who was murdered and thrown out by the vine-

dressers when he went to claim his father's vines. He makes it as plain as a pikestaff that this is what his enemies will do to him, because he is the Son sent to claim His Father's kingdom. From the hour of this momentous utterance His enemies seek His life, and the story moves on to its dread and grievous end.

Jesus walks the Via Dolorosa of His life with the utter fidelity of one who is never in doubt as to who He is or what He should do, yet with the humanity of one who finds the going so hard that He would like to lay aside His burden. He does not, in Jerusalem, issue a politico-ecclesiastical manifesto, or draw up a programme, or lay down minimum demands, or suggest upon what terms He shall take or be allowed to share power. He brushes aside the power that might have been His for the asking. He is quite careless of His safety, though He knows that Jerusalem will put Him to death. These are the truths you must hear, and I am the Son sent to tell them to you—He has grown tired of repeating it, one can see, but He is also a man under the command of God to go on saying it. He does not say to His disciples, 'Come, share my death with Me'. He tells them that they cannot go with Him. He will carry His burden alone. His cup, not theirs, is running over. Their impending desertion and dispersal and denials are foreseen and accepted with a grieving calmness. He knows that they will do what they have to do because they are, though His disciples, fallible men. There are limits to what they can understand and what they can bear. Even with Judas, in whose eyes He reads His coming betrayal, He uses the tender irony one uses to children when they lie, because one knows that they are lying, and why they have to lie, and forgives them as they lie. And so, with the glowing stillness which is never shaken, until out of His humanity He cries to His Father from the garden and from the cross, He moves to His final passion.

One's heart begins to beat painfully as, all these centuries afterwards, one approaches again in the imagination His last moments. We have to recall—and if we cannot Kierkegaard will compel us—that the resurrection could not be foreseen. The resurrection belongs to those who follow after. It does not belong to the moment when Christ faces His accusers and the mob turns on Him. The scattering disciples have not understood, or at the most only half-believed, the dark strange prophecies of Christ. The thoughts His obscure sayings evoked when they were made have been blown away in the gale of terrible events. The whole career of Christ seems at this moment destroyed, His teaching and ministry drowned in hatred and obloquy, His divinely-lit body itself under whip and scourge. No triumph comes at this moment to cover with glory the horrifying deeds which press upon the eyeballs of Peter and are burning up his spirit in despair. For here is Jesus now, the humble joiner who claimed that He was Christ, stripped before His judges. He who had said so much and prophesied so much is silent at last before His betters—silent except for the one crucial admission without which they could not so easily destroy Him.

The priests spit upon Him and strike Him. If you are indeed the Son of God, they exclaim, tell us who struck you! Go on, prophesy! In this way they taunt Him, with the sadism of persecuting schoolboys. One would not have treated a slave so, not even a dog. Pilate is mystified. He can do nothing with Christ and he can find no wrong in Him. He would release Him and the more readily because he is bored and baffled by the internecine quarrels of the Jews which, in this fanatical mountain city, boil over into violence over matters beyond his comprehension. He offers to release Barabbas or this man Jesus to the crowd. It was equivalent to saying to the Jews—If you want a blood sacrifice, who shall it be? Who shall be crucified? There was never any doubt as to what the answer would be. 'Upon our heads be His blood.'

Jesus is scourged. He is dressed up, like a figure in a booth at a circus, in a scarlet gown and a crown of thorns, a figure to jeer at, a scapegoat and a cockshy. Then He is stripped of clothes of mockery and taken through the town and crucified among thieves with the inscription over Him, 'King of the Jews'. So!—'The King of the Jews' is hung upon a cross, is humiliated by an outlaw death! Though the spectacle should have rent the heart of a nail, the citizens of Jerusalem parade before Him and shout insults at Him, at a man dying in agony, in torment, in loneliness on a cross. They come out of the town to gloat over Him and to watch Him die. It causes them intense satisfaction, this dreary, sadistic execution of a man who had preached among them, and of whom, I daresay, they said that

He wanted taking down a peg because He had got too big for His boots.

You there, Jesus, they cried, if you're God—why don't you come down off your cross? If you're the son of God, why don't you save yourself? If there had been a modern reporter present he would have put (laughter) and (more laughter) after each of these taunts. Look at Him! this is the fellow who was going to destroy the temple and rebuild it after three days (loud laughter). Come down from the cross, King of the Jews, and then we will believe in you. Look, He's speaking! What's He talking about? Elijah? Calling for Elijah? Better save His breath. That would be a good joke, to stay here and watch Elijah try to get Him down. Perhaps silence then at last, perhaps the crowd cannot bear the taste of its hatreds upon its lips any more. Or from Jesus comes a loud cry as He gives up the ghost, and just for that they are silenced, startled, that this man is really dead, and that they have killed Him, and that it was all much less trouble than they had expected it to be. Perhaps they think, even, that it was a pity they let Him die so easily. They feel cheated that He has wriggled out of their clutches. It is the Roman army captain, the gentile, alone, who is moved. This man was indeed God, he says, heavy of heart.

It was not all over. The disciples, disappointed of the immediate coming of glory they had hoped for, disperse, but trooping back to Galilee by the stony roads to their old jobs and their half-forgotten families they are caught by an extraordinary rumour. People are saying that *He is risen*. He has appeared to Mary. He met Thomas on the road and showed His wounds. He ate broiled fish with Peter at the lakeside. Of course. He always said He would—He spoke mysteriously many times of rising again and of what He would then do, which was incomprehensible, for after your death you can do nothing. And so the talk goes. There are many who doubt. Even if it should happen to be true, it is difficult to attach a meaning to it. What occurs now—do we begin all over again? It is far from a mass ecstasy or a hysterical delusion, but rather is the slow realization of a certainty which on the face of it looks impossible.

There is the kind of relief which comes to soldiers when their position is broken and they are forced to run for it. As they run

it is incredible to them that all is not absolutely lost. Then someone reaches them and says—No, the battle is going well after
all, you can stop and re-form. The general himself appeared at
the moment of danger and the troops rallied and reserves
recaptured the position you lost. They cannot believe it—they
saw the disaster—how can the tables have been turned so
soon? And the communicant shrugs his shoulders and says
simply—Follow me and see for yourself. They see, doubting,
and are convinced.

What convinces the disciples of Christ's presence is not simply
that the risen Christ stands before them, but that the risen
Christ behaves quite naturally among them, just as if He had
not died on the cross. He has hands and feet they can touch
and a wound in His side from the spear thrust. They recognize
Him when He breaks the loaf. And now He says—as if to say,
stop arguing whether or not I am really among you, I'm
hungry, I've been through more than I can bear, give me some
of that broiled fish to eat. When I've eaten I'll go on talking if
you like. In silence they watch Him eat, the reluctant, the
swooning conviction that here is the Son of God come back
from the dead gaining each moment upon them, and fearful
and joyful by turns as to what this portends in their lives.

That is the earth-shaking story and it has never been better
told than in the Gospels themselves. And whatever our griefs
now over the intolerable evil that men do, we have to ask
ourselves, as Kierkegaard bids us, on whose side we should
have been when no one, not even the disciples, behaved well.
The disciples ran away while the mob tormented Christ and
the respectable, no doubt, stayed at home and discreetly pulled
down blinds and closed shutters. Where should we have been?
It is precisely the offence of the coming of Christ that He comes
in such lowliness and dies in such indignity that one cannot say
of Him alive, that His state, or dead, that His end, pronounce
Him Messiah, but only by the faith in which one met His
Person and looked into His eyes.

We cannot even begin to consider what role we might have
played without being humiliated in advance by the knowledge
that it would probably have been an evil one. We should not
have recognized Him, or we should have persuaded our hearts

that we did not recognize Him, or we should have convinced ourselves that it was expedient 'for the moment' to deny Him in order to help Him in some other way later on. When we condemn the crucifiers, we condemn ourselves. It is humiliation to admit this, but admit it we must. The really faced inward nature of any one of us must indeed humiliate us, no matter by what pride or arrogance we disguise it to others. And it is just that Christ speaks to the real inward nature of man, and about that nature, that rouses so much passion against Him. We prefer the disguise to the self it disguises. We do not seek to be inwardly known. Well, at least that is a tribute to goodness, even if a hypocritical one. But all reformations, all new beginnings in man and in society depend upon the honesty of this inward attitude of man. Christ speaks to this inward man in the real terms of its existence, that is in terms of suffering, not simply of precepts.

The Father might have chosen other means to send His Son or to announce His purposes; means that would have been so irrefutable that hereafter human beings would have nothing to do but to obey, however unwillingly. Why then this role of Jesus, this particular intervention? Not the least reason is just this, that Jesus seeks above all to end the external conformity which hides an inner disbelief. God sends His Son in that form which invites inward assent, in which the hypocritical outward declaration would be worse than useless. God is concerned to make known to man the light of his own soul, not the badges in the buttonhole. It is the purpose of Jesus to say—*Turn of your own will* to the Father. In this alone is the creative religious act, and nothing else matters if this is not present.

Now if God is to enter history, then He has to enter historically. If God is to become incarnate through His Son—if this particular act has been decided upon—then He has to enter historically. If God is to become incarnate through His Son, then it has to be in an historical man, at a particular point of time, yes, and in one given house or hut, in the cry of a newborn babe delivered in the birth pangs of its mother. This is the way of the Son, whatever may be the way of the Holy Ghost.

It often seems as if the entry of God into history would be more acceptable were it vague, diffuse, and ethereal and not so warmly human, so full of blood and tears. But this is wrong.

The God who is diffuse and ethereal is indeed to be found—the universal spirit of light and reason. He has been met at every turn in this book, in the abstract and absolute who is beyond human suffering and human creation. Such a spirit is indeed vague and diffuse enough never to have been soiled in history. But if there is really God in the sense of a Being with whom the human person can have communion, and with whom a relation of love is possible, there is one *necessary* point at which such a Being must reveal himself to man, and that is where the suffering is greatest and the reality is most complete. If the blood and tears of men are unknown to God, man is unknown to God.

III

More is involved, we have said, than that the Son of God becomes man. The death of Jesus is the sacrifice by which man is redeemed; the Son of God dies for man. And here is a further offence, for *how* is it a sacrifice, and in what sense is man redeemed by it? How can it help the desperately sinful world to have upon its shoulders also the burden of having killed the Son of God? Were not things bad enough without it? Does not this deed make man appear beyond the redemption even of God?

These are not objections to be answered easily, but with searching of the heart. A sacrifice any man can understand. A sacrifice is the surrender of that which is most precious, a surrender not without meaning, but a gift given so that that might be done which would not otherwise be done, as when a man lays down, not his pipe or his shilling, but his life for his friend. Now the meaning of the life and Passion of Christ is that *Christ dies* and that it is the will of His Father that He shall die. It is the condition of His earthly existence that He shall be prepared for such an end. Pheidippides, at the end of his sacrificial run from Marathon, fell dead before the Athenians, gasping with his last breath, 'Rejoice, we conquer'. Suppose other circumstances had surrounded his heroism, suppose there had been no way of bringing either good or bad news except in face of the risk that one will be killed by those to whom the message is being brought—would that have been a reason for standing back? Many a man has had to make just this decision and to take the risk of his own destruction in order to communicate with his fellows. In a not so dissimilar sense, genius has sometimes to take this decision. Sometimes a man has taken such a risk knowing that if he died he could not communicate, and yet at other times he has taken this risk knowing that his death would *better* communicate his message than his life, that there is often a situation in which his message or his decision can be communicated in this way and no other.

If it is the decision of God that the revelation shall be made by the Incarnation, then the risk of the Passion has to be added to the certainty of death. If one may reduce this great drama to a bourgeois accounting, a thing one is loath to do, one can say it is a question only as to whether the occasion justifies it. In the fallen state of man there seem to be two necessities. The first is that God shall speak a word to man: the second is that man shall speak to God. Between a transcendent God and torn and divided man a bridge is lacking. This is the situation which Job saw and lamented. The more great and glorious God is proved to be the more miserable and worthless by contrast His creatures become. What is the significance *for man* of his own divided nature? What is the meaning of incompletion if he is never to be complete? And he is more acutely aware of the paradox of his own incompletion the more clearly he perceives God, and the gulf which separates him from God. Is man therefore simply tormented by his Tantalus-like state, by the differences which he can never resolve between what he is and what he might be, what he does and what he ought to do? Is there no way of overcoming the disparity between the known failure and the perceived possible wholeness of life? Is the only consequence of his knowledge of God to be—*despair*?

This is the situation which God has to answer. God has to speak across the gulf that man is not forgotten, or doomed, or simply mocked. This is the occasion which demands and justifies the Incarnation and the Passion. God has to speak his word to fallen man. And God speaks it in the revelation. He speaks it in those words of Jesus Christ which tell men how God is to be sought and how men are to live. It is spoken again and more strongly still in the ministry of Christ, which says to men—Look upon a life lived upon earth, a life full of love, a life without stain, and discover through it what man might be and hope again that you may live as you will to live. He speaks it in the Passion itself, speaks the word that a man may live without rancour and hatred even to the most complete sacrifice, not resisting evil with evil, but overcoming it by His example. The resurrection is the final message of all, giving men the good news of the triumph of men over death as well as sin, or as one might better phrase it, over the death which is the logic of sin.

Yet one must say of the Passion that God not only speaks in it, but *through* it. There is a meaning to its totality as well as to its separate parts. It is not simply that Jesus stands forth as an exemplar to men, to show them how they might strive with God's grace to live their lives upon earth, but that God speaks through Christ of the eternal relationship between men and God.

Men do not only want to know how they might live upon earth; that has no value unless they also learn: *What is the meaning of the life they live in its ultimate sense?* Towards what end outside the world is human existence directed? Or is the earthly life of man all, is his spirit extinguished at death? For what role has God cast him? These are the words which God must also speak. Not how I should live only, but *why* I live, has to be answered. God speaks in Christ's life and ministry of man's life upon earth, but He speaks through the death and resurrection of Christ of the final significance of human life. And the Word is that man's spirit triumphs, that man does not die, that the curve of his life passes beyond the grave, that man is so loved by God that he was made in the image of God and that God destines him for glory. It is the assertion that every human life has significance in an infinite sense, that man belongs also to eternity.

But then not only is God to speak, but *man* is to speak. If God is to speak across the gulf, man is to speak too. What has man to learn to speak? He has to learn to speak the word of *faith*,[1] to answer that he gives himself to God and the Word of

---

[1] 'That is to say, when all confidence in yourself or in human support, and also in the immediacy of faith in God, when every probability is excluded, when it is dark as in the dark night—it is indeed death we are describing—then comes the life-giving Spirit and brings faith. This faith which is stronger than the whole world has the power of eternity, it is the Spirit's gift from God, it is your victory over the world, in which you are more than conquerors.' Kierkegaard (from Lowrie).

God in faith. How is man to learn to speak? It is the message of God through Christ that man shall speak with his heart, shall turn to God in his heart, shall seek and petition God through the deep inward motion of his being. It is the plea that man shall turn in love to God as God turns in love to man. It is the message that since the very existence of man springs from the being of God, man need not feel himself abandoned if he will turn to that from which he has sprung, turn in that love which is itself the most gracious inward revelation of God.

What God does then in this strange and necessary act, this violent intervention in history we call the Life and Passion of Jesus Christ, is to show His love. He enters the sinful world, He crosses the gulf that separates us from Him, He comes in the person which is most dear to Him, His beloved Son, and says, 'I send you My Son to tell you of My love, and of the deliverance which men may ask of Me.'

But then God sends His Son *knowing* that men will put Him to death. God is saying in this deed of such terrible consequences to Jesus but of such hope to man, 'Look, I send you My Son to tell you of My love, knowing that you will do that which is beyond all forgiveness and put Him to death. *Nevertheless* I send you My Son that you may know that no matter how far fallen man may be, even so far that he commits that which is apparently beyond forgiveness, yet he is not so far fallen that I will not redeem him if he turns to Me. In this sacrifice of My Son I show how far forgiven man is, so far forgiven that My Son comes to take upon Himself the burden of the sins of others.'

In the most supreme tragedy of Christ, the most supreme grace of God. No deed could show greater enmity to God than the putting to death of His Son, and no act of grace and of love is sweeter than the self-offered life of Christ. That which happens is that which it is most terribly necessary shall happen, that the love and mercy of God are revealed in the very depths of human tragedy and wickedness, rather than in intellectual pleasure, for it is the *life* of man which stands in need of redemption. That God's love shines *even in Golgotha* is the message which man most needs to hear. It is the merciful immensity of the love of God which alone gives hope and joy to man. There can never be a higher revelation of the nature of God than the love of God.

This is the message and meaning of Christ to the world—
'That God is here, and through the most desperate and dark
moments of man's earthly life, He remains, unchanging, full
of love and that I, the Son, am here, mediator and redeemer.'
To God man is joined in love and creation and suffering, and
through God all things will be made entire and whole for him.

Yes, God is the meaning of human existence, but love is the
meaning of God.

INDEX

INDEX

Dilthey, Wilhelm, 79, 83, 84, 96, 109, 132–5, 136, 139, 140, 141, 142, 143, 148, 151, 166, 178 sq., 184, 192, 203
Divination, 24
Doctrine, Christian, 14 [*see also* Christianity]
Dostoievsky, 147, 177
Driesch, Hans, 54, 68, 69, 70, 84, 96, 123, 135
Dualism, 106, 190

Ebbinghaus, 83
Eckehardt, Meister, 193, 234
Eddington, Sir Arthur, 35, 36, 37, 40, 97
Education for the People, 139
Ego, 86
Ehrenfels, 83
Einleitung in die Geisteswissenschaften, 131
Einstein, Prof. Albert, 31, 32, 37, 99
Either/Or, 166, 170
Electromagnetic field, 34
Elijah, 243
Eliot, T. S., 60
Embryo, experiments with, 68–9
Emergence, theory of, 61 sq., 101, 155
Empiricism, 114 sq.
Empson, William, 60
Energy Threshold, 49
Entelechy, 54
Enthusiasm, 146
Entropy, 40 sq., 61, 74, 75, 101, 203
Era of Atomic Power, The, 220
Erlebnis und die Dichtung, Das, 131
Esprit, 216
Essence, contrasted with existence, 164 sq.
Ethics, and science, 210 sq.
Evidences (of Paley), 37
Evil, problem of, 205 sq., 216, 220, 222
Evolution, 51, 57, 72, 99, 155–8, 180 204
Existence, as paradox, 175; meaning of, 17, 21; and essence, 166 sq.

Existentialism, Christian and atheistic, 163 sq.; demoniacal, 176; Christian, 192
Existentialism (of de Ruggiero), 165, 177
Existentialisme Chrétien, 165
Expressions, significance of, 133 sq.
Euclid, 31–5
Eye, evolution of, 50
Ezekiel, 226

Fall of Man, the, 222
Fascism, 14
Fascist Revolutions, 219
Ferrovius, 171
Feuerbach, 148
Fixation, 92
Foulquié, Paul, 165
France, Anatole, 209
Freudian myth, 88, 93
Freudian theory, 86 sq., 137
Freud, Sigmund, 83, 85, 87, 89, 90, 94, 95, 96, 202
Frog, embryo of, experiments with, 68

Galilee, 236
Gene, the, 39, 47, 49, 57
George I, 138
George, Stefan, 119
Gesell, Arnold, 138
Gesammelte Schriften (Dilthey), 131
Gestalt Psychology, 80 sq.
Gestalt Psychology, 81
Gestalt Probleme und die Anfange der Gestalt Theorie, 82
Gestapo, 200
God, and worldliness, 14; man forsaken by, 16; death of, 16, 21; existence of, 21, 97; ground for actuality, 22; as Presence, 22, 193, 234; three approaches to, 22 sq. idea of, 25; as subject, 25, 152, 166; proofs concerning, 26; in nature, 27, 28, 128, 194; will of God, 29; of the physicists, 36–7; Pythagorean, 36; intervention of, 36, 159; forgiveness of, 52; provi-

INDEX

INDEX

Itard, M., 138
I-Thou relationship, 91, 130, 139, 148 sq., 165, 230

James, William, 79, 171
Jarrold, Dr. Thomas, 139
Jaspers, 165
Jeans, Sir James, 101
Jefferies, Richard, 147
Jehovah, 223
Jennings, Prof., 64, 69
Jerusalem, 241
Jesus, 211, 226; His life and Passion, 234 to the end
Jews, the, 223 sq.
Job, 127, 128, 234
Jocasta, 89–90
Joel, 225
John the Baptist, 237
Jonah, 226
Josephus, Flavius, 237
Journal (of Kierkegaard), 25, 168, 174, 175
Judah, 23
Judaism, 224
Jung, Karl Gustav, 85, 86, 96, 182, 183

Kafka, 165
Kamala, 137 sq., 192
Kant, 37, 105
Kantian school, 79
Katabolism, 46
Kelvin, Lord, 40
Kierkegaard, 24, 25, 98, 156, 161, 163, 165–79, 181, 185 sq., 212, 221, 236, 244, 248
Kierkegaard (Lowrie), 25, 52, 53, 174, 166
Kierkegaard: His Life and Writings, 27
King of the Jews, 242
Kluver, Heinrich, 82, 84
'Knowing and Understanding', 131 sq., 142
Koffka, 83, 96
Kohler, 80, 81, 82, 83, 96
Krafft-Ebing, 92

Laius, 89
Lamarck, 71
Law: in the universe, 29; of averages, 30; of the mass of a body, 32; of dynamics, 40, 205; of chance, 51; of permutations, 51; of destiny, 172
Laws, undiscovered, in physics, 46
Leblanc, Mademoiselle, 139, 140
L'Etre et le Néant, 165
Letter (William Empson), 60
L'Existentialisme, 165
L'Existentialisme est un Humanisme, 165, 176 sq.
Libido, 86, 94, 138
'Life Force', 100
Life, Mind, and Spirit, 61
Life of Richard Weaver, The, 171
Light, velocity of, 33
Liver fluke, 66
Lloyd Morgan, Prof. C., 61, 83
Lorentz, 37
Lowrie, Dr. Walter, 25, 166, 174, 175, 179
Luce, Prof. A. A., 105, 106, 110, 112
Luther, 24

Macbeth, Lady, 140
Mackintosh, Dr. Hugh Ross, 129, 163, 164
Man: his image of himself, 15; atheistic idea of, 16; humanist, 16; existential idea of, 16, 164 sq.; materialist, 16; reason and, 27; Western, 28–9; and an observer from Neptune, 35; and the evolutionary scale, 40; as vehicle of universal mind, 56–7; and evolutionary theory, 57; and cosmic main road, 58–60; and appetite and impulse, 95; demolition of, 115 sq.; as sign-maker, 118 sq.; as anti-evolutionist, 157; transcends world order, 160; a product of the social order, 191 sq.; his forms of existence, 194; his threefold relation, 197–8; and suffering, 198; as fallible being, 198 sq.; and sin

INDEX

INDEX

INDEX

Science and Philosophy of Organism, The, 70
Science and the Modern World, 22, 29
Scum, planetary, 56
Sea-urchin, embryo, experiment with, 68
Self, the, 104 sq.; repudiated, 114 sq.; the whole, 141
Sensations, visual and aural, 109–10
Shakespeare, 51, 140
Shaw, G. B., 23, 100, 171
Sin, 205 sq.
Singh, Rev., 138
Slavery and Freedom, 166
Socrates, 140
Solomon, 224
Son of David, 239 [see also Jesus and Christ]
Son of God, 235 sq. [see also Jesus and Christ]
Son of Man, 194, 239 sq. [see also Jesus and Christ]
Sophocles, 90
Soren Kierkegaard, 161, 162, 167
Sorel, 144
Soul, the, 123
Space-time, 31 sq., 51, 99
Space and time, 105 sq.
Space finite, 32
Spengler, 59
Spinoza, 113
Spinozian ground, 114
Spirit, the, 123; called into existence, 137; free realm of, 170; opposed to nature, 190; the human, 193, 205, 227, 248
Stalin, 181
Stentor, the, 64, 69
Stern, 84, 96
Stephen of Kapuar, 138
'Stimulus into Response' (S→R), 77 sq., 180, 204
Struggle for existence, the, 63, 73 sq., 180, 204
'Subjective madness', 121
Substance, nature of, 113 sq.
Substantiality, 116 sq.

Super-ego, 86, 87
Sullivan, J. W. N., 30, 33, 35

Teleology, 70, 76
Temple, Dr. William, 153, 169, 234
Teresa, Saint, 193
Thermo-dynamics, Second Law of, 40, 205
'Thing in itself', 105
Thirty Years War, The, 215
Thomas 243,
Time, and space, 31; an entropy, 42; irreversibility of, 43; creative nature of, 51, 203; tragic for us, 52; and Christianity, 52; personal track of, 53; and direction, 99
Times, The, 74
Time Machine, The, 51
Training in Christianity, 156, 186, 187
Trinity, the, 197, 232
True Humanism, 98
Types of Modern Theology, 129, 164
Typen der Weltanschauung, Die, 131

Underhill, Miss Evelyn, 193
Universe, belief in an intelligible, 28–9; Euclidean, 30; Newtonian, 30; finiteness of, 32; run-down, 41 sq.; cyclic, 41 sq., 51; indeterminate, 51; understanding of its parts, 57; compared with organisms, 56; discontinuity in, 60; physical weight of, 129; and geometry, 105
Universal Mind, 54
Universe in the Light of Modern Physics, The, 49
Unconscious, 122, 142, 235; Collective, 85; Freudian, 86
Understanding of Other Persons and their Expressions, The, 134, 141
Understanding, the, 131 sq.; theory of, 141 sq.
'Unknowability of Things', 113, 114
Urspruenge (Stefan George), 119

INDEX